THE FALLEN SOVEREIGN
A Story of Revolution and Betrayal

"In the name of the people, for the people, by the people." The slogan that encapsulates the fundamental promise of democracy across the globe.

Mamadou A Wury

GILDED LEAF™ PUBLISHING

The Fallen Sovereign
A Story of Revolution and Betrayal
Copyright © 2026 by Mamadou A Wury

For any information, contact Gilded Leaf Publishing at:
info@gildedleafpublishing.com

Publisher's Cataloguing-in-Publication data

FIRST EDITION
Library of Congress Control Number: 2026902740

First Edition

Wury, Mamadou A

ISBN 979-8-9946694-0-2 (Paperback)
ISBN 979-8-9946694-1-9 (ePub e-book)
ISBN 979-8-9946694-2-6 (Hardback)

Prologue

True freedom is indeed a phantom that has never been pursued throughout the ages of history. No nation upon this green earth has ever existed truly free. All nations are colonized one way or another; it's just a matter of perspective. There are only varying states of colonization, sometimes by the bayonet and the flag; more often, and more insidiously, by ideology and fear. A nation is either conquered by another's doctrine or paralyzed by the terror of being rendered irrelevant, weak, or obsolete. The perpetual invisible chain that binds the world, truth that Salim could never comprehend.

Imperialistic acts are not always born of malice; they are something quite darkly called calculus of survival. For instance, look at France, it might have stretched its hand across the Mediterranean to West Africa just for glory. Or might have been a fear of being overtaken, "not enough" of resources for its people, a fear, potent enough to dent morality to become a weapon. They came first with an ideology of civilization, a pretext so feeble it would snap when met by resistance, exposing the steel underneath.

Great Britain developed an imperial power only to see a single miscalculation in the Americas yield an insurrection to wipe from the map its dominion. Then after the world wars came a new fear, the Red Scare. Born from revolutionary struggle, the United States found itself colonized by a great fear of Soviet communism washing in from the ocean. Today, Russia takes the price for the same fear as well, with its actors demonized over the slight threat of Western ideals bleeding across its borders.

Even the ancient and once isolated, fluffy panda of the East with its thousands of years of history, could not remain hidden forever. After its unpleasant occupation by the Japanese, it rose to become the very thing its neighbor feared, the panda morphed into a dragon. The world now bows before America's mighty power, yet the bald eagle itself fears the bear and the dragon's influence over the rest of the world. This is that tireless, echoing cavity of global fear. No one is free, not even the ones seen as masters.

But the fervent 1950s gave Salim and his minions the notion that tyrants were simple men and liberation a simple act. He had no idea that his colonial masters were prisoners of their own fears. Arrogantly, he assumed he would cut the chains and bestow on his people a purity of freedom not yet known to them, freedom he believed, more than perhaps they even deserved. And they, in dire need of a hero, believed him.

After the French had finally left, Salim and his brethren were left in a vacuum, but they had broken away from the cycle of the old controlling entity to usher a new dawn. Or have they? To the tired masses, Salim was the prophet of their freedom, their strong man who was going to finally heed their prayers. But his rise bore not the messiah, but a man propelled by a petty, almost moronic need to set a point across. His deep-seated imbalance spawned through his bashing of European imperialism subconsciously blocked him from seeing one harsh truth: That his very young nation was still hanging by a thread, a thread being the charity of the Hexagon. His declaration of independence, in the zenith of humiliating a highly esteemed French general in a very calculated manner, was maybe the most beautiful act of defiance; it felt like a victory, but he didn't realize that it was a Pyrrhic one.

Pumped with hope for a prosperous future, there was no thought for the people to brace themselves against impact.
And the plan, which Salim had developed so much in detail, began to come apart without external pressure but from within. His ego, which had once

been his fuel, died out of the creeping paranoia. The very population he had promised to liberate became his next prey. The strong man's word faded away; instead came the starkness of a concentration camp for traitors to the nation. This gulag of terror was not envisaged for those culpable but any mind that dared to stand opposed to the rapid ascendancy of his new dictatorship.

* * * * *

This is the story of the buried face of tyranny. It is not only an account of coups and decrees but the dictatorship that shaped the mentality of generations, a legacy shaped in the tragic inconvenience of freedom for broken promises and a deeper, wretched type of dictatorship.

Chapter 1

Who are we?

The sun hung low over the sprawling plantation of Malakai Entoc, its golden glare sharpening the angles of his gaunt features slicked with sweat. His ashy legs and hands gleamed under the burden of toil, the deep, burnt sienna shade of midnight soil. His big and broad nose blocked his quivering lips, and his two heavy-lidded eyes, rimmed with crimson from sleepless nights and dust, glaring like embers. Around him, soldiers and their kin rose and bent in ragged unison with their dabas in hands thick with calluses, the blades biting into the arid earth that cracked to swallow fonio seeds, the ancient grain that had nourished their forebears. The air vibrated with the raw guttural harmonies of a work song, its rhythm as old as Guinea's mountains, with the voices rising like smoke over the fields. *Humbae jeehrae humbae, ooh jehrae, humbae jehrae haa! Humbae, humbae jehrae aahh...*

The song crept on with the wind scampering beneath their tattered cloth, weathered by sun and toil, stained with the brown dust that stuck everywhere, on their skin, on their breath, and on their destiny.

Malakai's daba arced downward, its edge catching light before it plunged into the soil. Thud. Thud. Two deliberate strikes, as if each stroke would dig another foot of dread. Then, the criminal thought was snatched away by another growl: the jeep growled. Through the haze of heat and dust, Lieutenant Mandiu Daff appeared, surrounded by stone-faced guards. The man's boots scuffed the earth like a funeral drumroll. Malakai clenched the fractured handle even harder. For a moment, his brain flickered away, was it the militia? Dissenters? Had the time finally come to take him away? His heart fell as he straightened up, spine stiff as the barrel of a rifle. The colonel overrode the laborer.

"Sir," Mandiu said, voice hard through laces of impatience. "News from the city."

Malakai did not blink despite the concern, but he composed himself. "You can say whatever it is here, it's ok."
The lieutenant's throat bobbed. He stepped closer, the reek of diesel and panic burning into Malakai's nostrils. "He's gone," Mandiu hissed, low and hard as a blade drawn from leather.

"Who is gone?" Malakai smiled nervously, barely able to hold the smile together.

"Him! He is no more!" Mandiu's whisper frayed away.

"What are you talking about?" Malakai asked, perplexed.

"The radio, we ought to be at the radio station before them. There'll be a coup. They'll purge ranks by dawn. We must go now, sir." Urged Mandiu.

The words dangled from the air like a noose. Malakai's red eyes flicked, a fleeting glare of fear, rage, and cold calculation. He understood, oh, yes, he finally understood. He felt the daba slipping out of his fingers; it landed with a muted thud, swallowed by the earth. He fumbled for his cigarette with hands steadied only by force of will, lighting it with a shaky flame before dragging in the smoke until it scorched his lungs. The song was dead. Faces turned silent and suspended. He jerked his chin toward the jeeps; the soldiers threw aside their implements and fell into steps behind him, no questions, no glances, just discipline.

The wheels churned dust into a phantom shroud as they drove toward Conakry with the bruising sky of the twilight above. Malakai stared ahead as cigarette ash crumbled in his palm. The plantation behind them blurred into the horizon, the people were still bent over the soil, and the song lifted again, but this time it's a humming sound, *hummm, hummm, ahumm mae, ahumm mae, ahumm mae humm mae humm mae...* Though, this time the song is far too soft and far too haunted. They did not know of bullet casings promenading the capital's roads, of generals huddling away in shadowed rooms. They only felt it; the night was holding its breath. They just knew that before dawn, Guinea would wake up into a different world, but for now, the fonio seeds were asleep underground, waiting.

Under that bruise-colored horizon, the night folded its chaos. Crack-wires from gunfire. Ministerial buildings were gulped by shadows. By sunrise, the coup was ripe already, like a rotting fruit being brutally smeared across all the radios and bulletins. The Generals called it a *revolution*; a word the people had heard once before, and when they gathered, they called it nothing at all. All they did was walk to the airport, filling the streets to witness the rumors with their own eyes.

Now, the sky already veiled in pale, anemic light, some withered petals clinging to a dead stem cluster had formed on the cracked pavement. Hands were raised with banderoles in an empty charade, the flags fluttering in a hollow rhythm of a clockwork dirge. Behind those grotesquely made-up faces were scenes of primal agony or colds struck with the surgically placed wax of feigned sorrow. "What a day, huh?" sneered the man in his tatters into the wind. His neighbor, a stooped figure with wrinkles seemingly carved by the bitter years of sacrificed truth, parroted, "What a day, indeed!" The word was crumbling away like ash.

Performative death pangs filled the air. A woman cried out in the open, salt-practicing tear trails down the dust-covered cheeks; across from her, a faceless bureaucrat with lips trembling in a show of grief stared with eyes empty as the promises that fell from his lips and into microphones. Terror from the air clung to every moisture, weaving the crowd into a sickly loom of doom. They swayed with it, they chanted it, and waited for what? A corpse locked away in some box! An ultimate laugh?

Whispers slithered through the throng: "Is it true? Could it be?" As if death were a joke, and the tyrant just a vaudevillian who was ready to leap out of the coffin laughing. Well, you cannot blame them: a baby can be born and be gone before his first nap; those leaders, ah, they cling like mold. They outlast revolutions, droughts, and basic common sense. The decent ones die out early, like somebody we all once knew, someone who hailed from Upper Volta; what's his name again… Thomas something… yeah Sankara, yes, Thomas Sankara; may his soul rest in peace, He died too early. The rest continue, fossilizing into hideous monuments to their own myths. Yet there they were, the masses, gnawing on hope and suspicion alike, too scared to acknowledge relief even as it churned in their throats. And even if these leaders die, who should we hear it from first? A liar; an opportunist; somebody like Lord Baelish, perhaps.

Liars! Are you not intrigued by them? Because I am. How could you not be fascinated by those who profit from deceiving others? They hear a minor detail going around and twist it into a headline. They are carnival barkers who would sell you a scandal before breakfast and sell your secrets by lunch. Gossip is their currency; however, when it comes to that subject, they clam up. The president is dead, a phrase that could have a man disappear or corrected, if you know what I mean. Unless it would be from Manera, a deceiving griot as the Guinean would call him *passepartout*. Poor, wretched Manera, the village's human itch. The man is a freaking anomaly known as every regime's mouthpiece, imbued with such falsehood that if truth ever fell from his lips, it would hiss like a serpent and flee. It's been rumored that if you take the lies away from him, he'd crumble like a pile of dust, lighter than a sigh. He was the one who hissed it first, the president is dead. The very sentence even the community of loose lips feared to utter. How fascinating!

Anyway, as the wait persisted, and unbeknownst to many, they would never lay eyes on the remains of their most loved ruler. Rumors had it that he was being transported in a casket from a Cleveland clinic, where one could better be treated for midwestern heartburn rather than keeping the carcass of a demigod. Fitting, perhaps. Cleveland? Really, how ironic! Not ironic for the moderate skyline arguments; it is truly ironic for that great man to be caught dead at such a location, now believe me, that is something. By passing on unintentional farce, the arrival of the casket did nothing to diminish speculations that surrounded the crowd of onlookers. They had expected matters to be clarified, the arrival would be a confirmation of the somber truth, but ominously, one more mystery was cast upon the funeral scene by the closed lid. No one could see what was inside, this denial slapped louder gossip and conjectures than mere curiosity could. Concern changed from the uncertainty of whether he really died, now it was towards the casket itself. People were not pleading for the proof of death but for a look inside, to reveal the truth they so desperately sought. They yearned to see for themselves the figure that lay within, to validate or perhaps debunk their growing doubts.

Rumors began to swell and spread among the populace; whispers of an empty casket circulated with a brazen audacity, you guessed it, freaking Manera. Emboldened by their skepticism, soon the loose lips community started spreading rumors, well another "headline" if you will: "The casket is empty." They said proudly, challenging authorities to reveal what lay beneath the lid, but their demands were met with stoic resistance, and the truth remained obscured.

Why? You wonder, were these people so adamant about refusing the presented truth. The question lingered, unanswered or answered only with more conjecture. Perhaps, with a little bit of faith and an open mind, people will one day understand the mysteries surrounding an entire nation's stubbornness to accept what is presented to them.

Sealed and safe from the human eye, the casket was made not only the agent of loss. It soon became the relentless symbol of humanity in search of truth Amidst both clamor and incomprehension, the nation was scuttling about in an instance of stubbornness, wrestling with the contradiction his death had ushered. One would need to know what he did to really appreciate the depth of the feeling held against him. He had released them from the clutches of...

Well, let's not digress; suffice it to say, he was an unseen but omnipresent force, overriding through their existence like a thread of fate. To many, his death was like an early Christmas, a long-awaited promise fulfilled. To others, he existed as this earthly myth, a hero forged from collective yearning. But this is not just a story, not his story alone, but a story of a generation. So, let us start at the genesis of all histories: the land of yesterday.

Ah, the past, I love the past, I mean not far back into the thunderous period of the dinosaurs, but an age nearer to human pulse, where chariots clattered over cobblestones and mead recipes led to fiery arguments. I'm totally taken up by such epochs, the dust of which was a potent inspiration. But my friend Allocco never subscribed to his. He's more of a live in the now kinda guy, the second skin he wore was called modernity, however, with the exception of that name, taken not from ancestry but from golden slices of fried plantain, a West African delicacy he revered with near-religious fervor. "Allocco" was, thus, no ancestral title; it was a tribute to crispy edges and caramelized sweetness, a belief in the assertion that perfection was not inscribed upon ancient scrolls but lodged in the sound of sizzling in a skillet.

Let me tell you a bit about the guy. We weren't kindred spirits, Allocco and I. If we were to be likened to anything, it should be distant constellations: somewhat together, yet eternally apart. While I followed the threads that wove histories long forgotten, he was measuring the subtleties of oil temperatures, insisting that the faintest whisper of truth lay in the crunch of a well-fried snack. It was a strange zeal he was animated by, but it had its own logic: true mysteries of life could be untangled through the senses, not the cracked pages of old tomes.

And so, we orbited one another in time: him an errant glutton and I, something like a historian if you will. Our discourses instrumented more like an epochal confrontation of tastes. Yet his eccentricity told a secret: history is not just molded by empires and scholars, but also tangibly shaped by people like him, the imperfect dreamers who find inspiration somewhere between the crackle of a pan and the golden arc of a fried plantain. After all, what is history but a meditation on fragile, crisp moments served hot by those who dared to savor them.

Allocco was and has always been somewhat of a curiosity. His height is average; further adding to the effect of his pleasantly plump figure is a misty aura akin to that of a person who must be propitiated. His face is, in fact, round; one might even say it resembles an inflated balloon, and peering from under that truly magnificent face, a wildly bushy mustache. And those eyes, really! Plump and darn large for his face, gleaming. Behind the hideous round spectacles, these nevertheless delightful faculties twinkle with glee at what joy must be occurring in his vivacious mind. When he laughs, it's as if the brightness of the room erupts in great big warm echoes of oh-so-cheerful chuckling. And let me tell you: never mind just that; his hair troubles me, it's a contest by itself. He has been trying to arrest his thinning, unkempt hair, but has dismally failed. It has an affectionate profile that bounces off in every possible, chaotic direction. Comb, gel, nothing seemed to tame its wild spirit.

His clothing, a riot of color and pattern, a master of mismatched socks and Hawaiian shirts. Watching his chaotic and joyful entrance has always brought a familiar frustration. A frustration of shouting into a void. He would not give my thoughts about the past much of a glance. For him, such things are shadows fading away. Life consists of nothing but the present, best enjoyed with a bowl of whatever was crisping in the pan. He couldn't care less about future events to come, nor what has transpired back in the dusty past.

Staring at him, I sometimes feel the desperate need to justify my own life's work. Is there anyone who perceives history not just as a graveyard for lifeless moments but as a breathable monument? For me, it is the battleground of mankind, where every triumph and failure and whisper of hope become its stones. It is not a record dry as a bone, but a foundation alive beneath our feet. A labyrinth of stories, every room booming with the joys, sorrows, and defiant chants of those whose blood still sings in ours.

Out of the past come roots severed. Inside them lie maps drawn by the kings and beggars alike, treaties stained by ink and rebellions soaked by blood, which taught us what being was. A mirror, yes, but a mirror that does not reflect merely us but the translucent faces of others; others who made the world we call ours. Something Orwell knew too well, when he stated in his classic 1984, "He who controls the past controls the future, who controls the present controls the past." He knew that such was a weapon, a compass, a key. Control its narrative and you hold the future at ransom.

But here we stand, some of us, well, such as this darned Allocco shrugging our shoulders at the weight of millennia, oblivious to the irony: the same "irrelevant past" gave birth to the very words we use to condemn it. For every soul who sees one of history as chains, another finds wings in its pages. From artisans in Florence, whose colors still ignite museum halls, to inventors whose failures lit the path all the way to the stars. Their battle is our inheritance, their wisdom a light in the dark.

The past is not to be considered dead because it lives and argues for its place to remain intact. Within its patchwork such as the Aztec codices, the ancient manuscripts of Sankoré in Timbuktu, the traveling ballads of nomadic poets, the quiet breath of enslaved builders, we encounter the raw materials of compassion. The sensation of a medieval midwife's weary hands, the simmering wrath of revolutions in basement meetings, and the soft defiance of a scribe keeping the truth alive amidst tyranny, they are all felt while passing through its hall. These things are not just dusty old artifacts; they are not only warnings but also blueprints and prayers.

But to Allocco, my "blueprints" were meaningless scribbles. What of identity? These are the thousand tributaries that feed the rivers. Our traditions, our art form, the very flow of language we've derived our existence from, something almost chiseled into being long before we saw the light of day. To forget is to drift about loosely in a hollow present, but to remember! To remember is to stand taller, for we are now standing on the shoulders of giants. The past shall be our anchor as well as our sail. It should teach us humility for the follies that litter the shores of history but inspire courage for the bold deeds that illuminated the way. Through its light, we see not only who we were but who we may yet become.

He would simply laugh at that, I knew. He saw no giants, only the next snack. And that, perhaps, was the core of our great, unending argument. But doubtless, nothing could be more straightforward than this. Alas, for the scornful, they all stand on its scaffolding! Every building block of this world was laid, so to speak, by the sawdusted hands of now dead men; every right that we claim today was carved out of the stubborn rock of battles fought through history. The past is full of darkness, cruelty, folly, and the rot of unchecked power, but all that the past describes is that the weapon should not be confused with the wound. There are no binding shackles; instead, they are lessons dripping with blood and fire. Let us not try to wash them off. To kneel and beg forgiveness for the sins of our forefathers in the name of "progress" is totally missing the point. The past should not necessarily be a sin in need of absolution; it is a compass with its needle quivering toward the truth.

What arrogance to think that we may rewrite it! If history is airbrushed into palatable fables, such an act would be an even greater violence than any injustice of history. The past has no regard for our frail modern sensibilities. It is just breathing in the cracks of ancient temples whispering through yellow letters, wails in the silence of unnamed graves. It is not for us to judge it according to the warped lens of today, but rather for it to judge us. We, stripped bare before its mirror, must ask: Have we learned?

Herein lie dangers: In failing to tell our stories and all, unfiltered, throbbing with life sooner rather than later, we will be caught up in the very tragedies we denounce. Memory is not a thing; it's a promise. A father's war journal, a grandmother's lullaby, and rallying cries that rocked cities these are the strongest threads with which tomorrow is knitted. Cut the threads, and the future unravels into a thousand lonely strings that each generation stumbles through unseeing, blindfolded in that same labyrinth. There are no smiling histories that bring forth progress and no ideological fairy tales.

Progress is forged in the white flame of what was. Let us not flinch where the past is ugly. We should let it wound us, let its incongruent truths hit our ears with a bang! Only then may we hear the fragile tune of what still remains possible.

Might seem like a cliché, but clichés ring false, of course, until you have really felt the weight of what they portend: to stare into the very abyss of human incapacity and announce it ours. "Truth will make you free," they say, but first, it pins you to the wall. Forgiveness, divine or otherwise, cannot unmake the act, only the lie. And like rot, lies fester miserably. Bloat under the skin of history until it bursts forth, not as heavenly punishment but as a self-infliction, full of guilt. The devil whispers, but it is we who choose to wield the knife.

What is damnation if not only the echo of our own volitions? It is a soul that hoards secrets that creates its own prison. If eternal happiness were awarded to virtuousness, it would not be a heavenly gift; it would be simply the quiet courage to stand within the wreckage of our deeds and say: This, too, is me. Scar together the wounds of today with the flesh of tomorrow. But here we are, caught in the haunting ghost of eternity. What kind of act is it that we dare try to hold infinity in our carcass? To imagine fire or light as forever, both unbearable in very different ways. "How does one fathom endlessness?" The mind buckles. Not the flame but the unending terrifies. Just one instant stretched over time until it becomes a scream without sound. And still, we ache for it. This paradox of craving permanence in a world built on decay.

Life after death. The words themselves are the koan, a riddle wrapped in the silence of stars. Science scoffs and demands evidence, but what laboratory could possibly measure the soul? Our beliefs bloom wildly like lilies in the cracks of reason: reincarnation's lotus, heaven's gates, the void's chilly embrace. Such things are not answers but lanterns, flickering, fragile, in the dark. We follow their flickering glow, inventing mythologies to cushion the edge of the unknown. Thinking perhaps, the afterlife is not a place but simply a prism. Our consciousness escapes bone and synapse to refract into some new spectrum of being. Energy, memory, a song without a singer. It's the secret that mystics won't admit death's terror is what makes us feel alive. That clawing, desperate need to know to solve the cosmic riddle is the pulse beneath every prayer. We are Sisyphus and the stone rolling the question uphill again and again: What waits beyond? And when the skeptics sneer, "Prove it!" we smile. Because not having proof is what makes us human: the absurdity of hope. To stand on the cliff's edge of mortality and whisper, there must be more, more beyond these boundaries. Well, yes there is, and there is only one way to find out, not inside a laboratory though.

So let the boundaries blur. Let the atheist light a candle for her mother's ghost; let the saint doubt in the dead of night. We are all orphans here, clutching at stories like lifelines. The afterlife is not a destination; it is the shadow we cast as we walk toward the light. And when the final breath comes, perhaps the truth is simpler than we dare admit: to die is to become the question itself. Unanswerable, eternal and free.

Let us not pretend this is complicated. You need no diploma to recognize the sting of a slap or the balm of a kindness. Good and evil are not riddles, they are rhythms, as innate as a heartbeat. A child knows cruelty when she feels it; a thief, however slick his lies, cannot outrun the acid drip of shame in his gut. Relativism is a parlor trick, a hall of mirrors where the corrupt preen and call it philosophy. "Perception!" They cry, waving their loopholes like flags. But ask the mother cradling her starved child if her pain is a "matter of perspective." Ask the village burned to ash whether the smoke smells different to the arsonist.

Yet here we falter: if justice is more than a fairy tale, why do the wicked so often dine on silver while the pure choke on dust? Why must saints drown in silence, their prayers unanswered, while tyrants stride untouched through storms of their own making? Is the universe merely a dice game, all chaos and cold indifference?

Do not mistake these questions for surrender. To ask, "What purpose does life serve?" is not to deny meaning, it is to hunt it, feverishly, like a wolf tracking blood in snow. Yes, the abyss gazes back. Yes, the void whispers that nothing matters. But here's the flaw in nihilism's sleek armor: even the act of doubting meaning presumes a mind that longs for it. A stone does not wonder, and a star does not ache. We do.

And what of the divine? If God is silent, is He absent, or are we simply deaf? Perhaps faith is not a scaffold but a leap, a blindfolded plunge into the dark with arms wide. Or perhaps the "higher power" we seek is the sum of our collective yearning, a cathedral built not by gods but by our stubborn refusal to let cruelty be the final word.

Cynicism is easy because it's lazy. It is the smirk of the coward who mistakes jadedness for wisdom. But to stand in the wreckage, to see the world's rot and still plant seeds in the cracks, that is defiance. That is alive.

So let the slap-chop of suffering leave you reeling. Let it crack your pretty myths like porcelain. But do not confuse the shattering of illusions with truth. Meaning is not handed down; it is clawed upward, brick by freaking brick, from the mud of our failures. It is the widow who forgives. The soldier who drops his gun. The atheist who prays anyway, not to a deity, but to the ghost of hope itself.

The world wants you to believe nothing matters because it is quieter that way, it is safer, but when you look closer: every act of love, every ragged gasp for justice, is a middle finger to the void showing that we are here, and we insist on being here and if that's not a purpose worth serving, what is?

If there is something driving me up the wall more than anything else, it is the symphony of excuses that follow human failing. The chorus of "It wasn't me; it was him, her, them, the devil on my shoulder!" as if we are all marionettes jerked around by invisible strings. As if the blood on our hands could be scrubbed away with the flimsy soap of "I had no choice." But here's the thorn they refuse to grasp: to deny one's own agency is to spit in the face of what makes us human. We are not puppets dangling from heaven's rafters. We are the hands that hold the shears, cutting our own strings or making new ones.

And what of this phantom; called free will? If it's but a mirage, then every cruelty, every betrayal, is written in cosmic ink before we draw breath. Convenient, isn't it? An already made alibi for the worst of us. "The devil made me do it" becomes the ultimate get-out-of-hell-free card, but peel back the theology, and what remains? I'd guess just a terrified child's whisper: "I don't want to be responsible."

And this is, after all, the strange and paradoxical thought: perhaps belief in free will as an illusion is an illusion itself; a psychologizing sleight-of-hand, a throw-off of credit or dues, whereby the sting of our own decisions is softened. Responsibility terrifies us because we have to look into that mirror where the rot is. We drape ourselves in layers of myth, of Satan's whispers, the iron grip of fate, of anything to avoid the harsh truth that evil is no enemy, that it is in fact a tenant, occupying space in every basement of the soul while rattling its chains when we don't care to listen.

Blame Iblis, the devil, and we may confess our cowardice. After all, what might an entity created from smokeless fire do to a free-willed man, truly free? We couldn't admit that, no! Because accepting it would mean that one admits that there is a human WILL in the equation, and that is not exactly the thing we would want, is it? Because that tells us who we are, or rather who we pretend not to be. We make all these efforts to hide that from everyone else. It is in human nature to deny what we actually are, and the first principle of this denial is stopping any attempts made to find out the roots of our behavior. A behavior that attracts prying eyes into the deepest structure of our mind, and that is one of the main reasons we build barriers, hoping to shield ourselves and prevent others from deciphering our innermost thoughts and feelings through our actions. Actions that we are unsure whether society would approve of, since we are prone to believe that life is what society makes it out to be.

Think of our ancestors' societies for instance. They were arid architects of survival. They faced the world with teeth of ice-wind and talons of famine. There were no philosophical affairs within huddled, fire-lit caves and bodies mapped with the battle scars of indifference to nature. Each day, a venture out to renegotiate with extinction. There was no time to blame gods or demons when the storm's breath froze your brother's last gasp in the air. You simply survived or didn't.

Fire was the first confession of vulnerability. It flickered between the two extremes of its defensive reality: against wolves, warding off shelter, and at the same time it bared the amiss as though the confession were amounts: We are small, and the night is great. They conquered flames as beggars bartering, not as victors. And out into the hunger-gray wilderness they went, spears in hand, chasing the ghost of sustenance when dawn broke. Each step was a choice. Each kill, a testament to will. No devil guided their hand, their needs were just primal in shape and sharp. These first, and still tentative, ways, very fragile, of connecting become, in general, an organization of social order under. Not on account of the divine promise, but from the raw logic of survival. Your fire for my meat. Your watchfulness for my shared warmth. What moral codes were they? Mere life rafts. Yet, even then, seeds had sprouted into the delusions. Otherwise, what is civilization if not the world's most elaborate distraction from the animal truths within us?

Nobody would admit this, but we proceeded to erect walls, first with stones, then walls with proprieties, to shield ourselves from the savagery of a life once lived by our ancestors before us. Look at our art, we say. Our laws, our cathedrals, our mosques! But give a little scratch to the gilding, and there is a pulse of old blood. We condemn the murderer but let more subtle forms of hunger take their place: greed in the boardroom, cruelty in whispered words, violence in conspiring silence. The devil did not invent these. We did.

So, let's stop lying to ourselves. Shatter the stained glass of delusion. When the murderer says it "was the voices that made me do it," ask him: Whose voice? When the tyrant screams, "I had no choice," ask him: No choice but what? To cling on to power? To fill the void?

The truth is uglier, simpler, and infinitely liberating: We are architects of our damnation. Each "yes" or "no" has been an application of the chisel upon the stone. It was not the devil that tempered your rage for a weapon; you did! Unless we begin with that self-forge and with unblinking eyes stare into it, we will remain fettered to the oldest illusion: that monsters are born, not made.

Our ancestors knew better. Their lullabies, sung to the rattle of bone flutes, and their ochre-hued cathedral-in-caves, were confessions of that which we have forgotten: To be human means holding the knife and the wound, choosing again and again between the fire and the dark because hardship's shadow followed them everywhere by day and by night, never allowing them that complacency.

They say we have come a long way. What does that mean, though, when the way is paved by paradoxes? Imagine the giraffe galloping in the savanna: majestic, absurd, a long-legged ballet of survival. Do we measure its path in miles, or in the ecstatic joy of its motion?

Our advancement has also been akin to that: We've swapped spears to satellites, primal howls to algorithmic screams, and oh, in the process, we lost the map of our own humanity. Yes, we have tamed fire into fiber-optic light, put equations to work splitting atoms and stitching galaxies, but at what price? Laboratories hum with flowers of restless minds chasing horizons slipping away like mirages. "Just one more breakthrough." The white coats whisper, as if salvation lies inside a petri dish.

Then, revised narratives of tragedies ask how terrible our leaders are! Well, let's see, they brandish verbal torches that launch hellfire with just a tweet, a grin, or a finger perched over a button glowing like the apple of temptation. They barter in menace in marble halls; their shoulders squared against one another. "My missile can erase your history from the map," one hisses, and his frustrated adversary throws a backhanded remark: "Mine can wipe out your future from existence." How horrible, this mockery of destruction played out on the catwalk of the world whose prize shall be total extinction!

Meanwhile, cracks are widening on the face of the world: more chasms between the Michelangelo-praised towers and the crumbling streets, between sounds that ring with clarity and those cloaked in silence for centuries. Patriarchy laboring its pangs inside these fine halls like a stupid ghost, rattle-chained on the path to progress, incisive enough to make some vain threats. The drudgery from these wars, last sworn to be, now enters in pain under the wounds of nations. The lesson imparted by an overtly pompous Nazi-supporting world war etched certain wishes on our palms, how to divide the indivisible, how to weaponize the sunlight, how to shoulder the burden of knowing the odds of extinction lie in the hands of our enemies.

So here we are, utopians that we are, reconstructing the very ruins we cause. We sew with the same hands that have known how to unmake on the street-long rips. The world spins on, indifferent, amid the ebbs and flows of our savagery and brilliance, tenderness and greed. With time onward in its heavy trail, we stay: all imperfect, all unforgiving, all sighing for grace. Still, with the break of dawn, we rise, almost in rebellion for survival itself, for that fragile, furious prayer that one day, this journey might mean more than just distance.

And yes, eventually it meant something more than just a distance. A whole new Moon-thought was fully alive in the 1960s, exposing a vibrantly exciting chapter in man's history. An era illuminated by audacious dreams, colorful revolutions, and a diversified awakening of far-reaching freedom from the past in which it operated. A myriad of parallel countercultures came into being, each shaking the edifice of the socially accepted and challenging the powers that be. The streets sang the songs of dissent, clamors for change, whether uproarious calls from civil rights for equality and justice for all, or the angry torch song of anti-war voices against the enveloping Vietnam conflict. A wave of creative expression across art, music, and literature sparked the cultural revolution. Bob Dylan and the Beatles became the anthems of a generation clamoring for self-expression and social reform, from the poignant words of folk ballads to the rebellious beats of rock 'n' roll. Pop art too, burst upon the scene. It was in this free world that the rebel spirit truly began to blossom. A huge upsurge of experiments and challenges, much more than could be conveyed in words, simply captured the spirit of a generation anxious to find its voice.

While in America, black people fought for civil rights, blacks in the motherland were battling for freedom from the death grips of their European masters. Meanwhile, gender equality and the right to choose reproductive health care would become the new battlegrounds for women activists. The generation gap widened as parting strengthened between traditionalists and those who wanted to see change. The 60s stood in the annals of being a very complex and contradictory set of events that remained a tangential imprint in historical time. An era that covered itself with great optimism; resilience; and strong belief in mankind's prowess to erect a brighter tomorrow. Possibly, this generation has etched an untarnished impression about always valuing the importance of unity and being active in the fight for a more caring and inclusive world.

Even so, with such societal evolution, people did not get rid of their inherent urge to pave a path towards self-destruction. After the Second World War, a peace organization was formed as a result of discussions between world superpowers for not repeating the blunders of the earlier age, and the same organization is, today, the main threat to existence. Instrumentalized for profit of few; a war of doctrines broke out between two strong blocks of divergent beliefs; Conflict that had come dangerously close to turning into a third world war which in seconds could have changed our world into a dark dystopian society; an annihilation of mankind. The catastrophe was narrowly avoided, and life continued on with the ever-repeated cycle of positive and negative aspects of ideological struggles created by the same despotic governments never disappearing. Governments that never legitimize known norms of civilized and democratic societies. While corporations got bigger and greedier, they also found much better ways of being needed. The very idea that banks and businesses are too large to fail became an understatement, they started to define our society, with people living in a world where manipulation and divisions are incumbent for success. Capitalism, our once cherished system, now morphed into a carefully nurtured illusion, as in reality, people are beholden by a far different force based essentially on the tenets of a powerful, unseen entity manipulating the very structures of society. Look at how today's capitalism's supposed moral justification is socialized. Losses are routinely absorbed by taxpayers in the form of corporate bailouts, while profits remain privatized, a dynamic that blurs any meaningful distinction between capitalism and corporatism. Major industries, defense, energy, technology, finance, survive less through open competition than through deep entanglement with state power. The line between public and private therefore becomes porous, if not illusory.

What we call "capitalism" is not a coherent system but a hybrid of corporate hierarchy and government management, one that contradicts the very ethos of merit and self-reliance it claims to embody. Ultimately, capitalism functions as a discursive project: it defines the boundaries of political imagination, presenting itself as natural, eternal, and without alternative. Its greatest illusion is not merely that it exists in pure form, but that its logic is inescapable, a fiction made real through repetition.

It is all an illusion. And don't get me started on socialism, an ideology wearing a mask of benevolence, communications honey-dripping with equity and justice promises. Peel the outer layer and you would find not salvation but a snake coiling around the soul of humanity. It does not seek *upliftment*, no, it is hungry for possession. Underneath, in all its grand illusions of solidarity lies a colder truth: very cleverly engineered machinery of control to breed dependence as deftly as a poisoner cultivates addiction. It whispers of hope while binding its disciples to a wheel of endless wanting desires manufactured, cravings stoked, fulfillment always a phantom dancing just beyond reach. The more they pursue it, the tighter it bonds them. Myth then becomes autonomy, self-actualization a mockery, and the system feeds on their hunger, leaving them empty as they are shackled by dreams it never intended to fulfill.

These are not ideologies; they are alchemy-alchemizing into subjugation from aspiration.

Although, the architects of such systems understood that this could never survive in vacuum. They turned their gaze outward, beyond territorial bounds, where empires screeched at the prospect of liberation. As the dying grip of Europe on Africa began to slacken an intractable nightmare of unweaving dominions, they had forged new fetters. Freedom became a blunder, and independence, the gilded cage. The old colonialism died, but it only rose like the phoenix in tailor-made suits and boardrooms, called neocolonialism. No longer whipping or clanking chains do we find. Instead, silent and suffocating is the arithmetic of debt.

Debts to be contracted with IMF and World Bank, these twin leviathans born in the smoke-filled halls of Bretton Woods, being crafted by economists with Africa's voice erased from the ledger. These were not institutions of help, but instruments of control, a financial colonialism in the guise of "development." Demonic but creative if you ask me! African nations, just newly freed from political bondage, were lured into another labyrinth: loans with teeth, loan contracts with malice, structural adjustments that gutted any type of sovereignty, economies bent to the whims of powerful institutions. Debt became the new plantation, each payment, another ritual of servitude.

Otherwise, what else is debt but a leash? To take control of a nation's coffers is to take control of its politics. Make politics the bedrock of any system, you become the ruler of the people themselves. Dissent does not face muskets but market-economic strangulation, coups dressed in the mellifluous tones of "stability," paradoxical placement of military bases on the graves of independence like flags. African armies, lacking purpose and pride, are morphed into mercenaries of foreign agendas, trading away their conscience for validation: They put in power despotic governments who in turn enforce orders that press their people into dust, then they throw tantrums, convincing the populace to blame foreign countries. "It's them, they don't want your development." They would say. Or "they made me do it." thereby breeding a system in which deliverance is but an illusion, with power forever located elsewhere, conceptualized within the worldview of a select few.

Neocolonialism's cunning cruelty is in making the world believe that subjugation is dead while its roots penetrate further and deeper. The gleaming, invisible, unshackled chains, the masters smile, with bloodless hands, as the wheel turns on. And behind these polished chains of neocolonialism and velvet rod [control] lies an uncomfortable yet liberating truth: the system is not an auto-replicating monster, but a reflection that mirrors the decisions and actions of those who govern it. The rationale, in all its nuances, stands paradoxical, where power molds and is molded by the will of men.

A man is not born to be a dictator, a tyrant, or a savior. These three characters are forged in the shield of ideology, ambition, and the seduction of control. The economist who designs predatory loan terms, the politician who sacrifices sovereignty for validation, the insurgent who burns villages to "liberate" them; all are authors of their own script, protagonists or antagonists shaped by the narratives they cling to.

What of the engineers of neocolonial debt deep in the shadows of Bretton Woods? Were they conceived with the covetous bloodlust to conquer continents? Or were they really condemned as stewards to pursue a system that glorified in cold calculation as virtue, to reroute exploitation as "progress." Now again, the African leader who signs away the nation's future for a fleeting taste of power. Does he wake up as a villain or as a man who believes he is threading the needle of subsistence? This is where the fatal dance of ideology steps in: A theory makes one arrogantly certain. The subject of derision becomes a medal of honor, they say, if you are convinced that your path is righteous.

But the dance brings forth a new theater; Today's world is not divided into the cold language of left-and-right, socialist, communist, capitalist and so on anymore. The arena of combat is blended into two sides of the great existential divide: with one side being the chaotic carnival of libertarianism, while at the other end lies dictatorship strangling the life out of societies under its thumb. Here Libertarianism, an exaltation of freedom in uncensored terms, begins its one-way slide to tyranny, colliding all two with violence: "freedom of speech" hits "censorship." Its circus where those chanting tolerance throw firebrands at dissidents, where "do as you please" strains into "bow to my truth."

Then the authoritarian bloc snickers behind the scenes as the excesses of democracy keep feeding their growth. "Do you see?" they gloat. "Your liberty" is anarchy. "We are the surgeons who amputate chaos." And censorship tightens, dissent vanishes, and armies once meant to protect become enforcers of silence. It is certainly no chance but rather a pendulum's swing: for every libertarian wielding autonomy as a weapon, every institution camouflaging foreign control as "aid", arises a toxic counterbalance yearning for order in that metastasizes into tyranny.

The cycle is ancient, yet freshly vicious: systems create the conditions that birth their own antagonists. Neocolonial debt breeds desperation; desperation births strongmen; strongmen birth revolt. And in the rubble, new ideologies rise, their architects certain this time they'll write a better story. But the question remains, etched in the scars of wars and the whispers of Bretton Woods, will the authors choose to break the wheel, or simply grease its gears?

Well, the point is that these two ideologies have something in common, they both embody the mindset of a world that imposes a rigid ideological binary and seek to crush all opposition to that ideology. They portray ruthless stance on dissent, showing how their vision leaves no space for different viewpoints. They create a system where people are no longer allowed to think for themselves; minds just must be molded, shaped by an all-encompassing ideology that brooked no opposition. That there is only one path forward, one truth to follow, and any deviation from it is not only wrong but treasonous. Democracy and dictatorship, one was the light, the other was the shadow, but now the line looks blurred, and any who dare stand in the middle are enemies of progress. What does that tell us about our progress as humans?

We've always considered ourselves as the most important creatures, but our existence in this world is deteriorating the very essence of our humanity, even mother nature is tired of us. Our society has become a world where people live in constant negativity. A world shrouded in a perpetual cacophony of leaders, aware of their incompetence, and   yet making people believe that they have the key to improving lives. Look at the treacherous arena of politics, where power and influence collide, where leaders weave a web of deception to secure the coveted prize of votes. Their strategies of deception, honed through cunning and manipulation, betray the very trust upon which a democracy is built. With silver tongues, they master the art of hollow promises, crafting a symphony of hope that resonates with the electorate.

Don't get me wrong, lies in politics are nothing new, they've slithered through the halls of power since the dawn of empires. But once, they were crude, jagged things, wielded like blunt axes. A ruler might lie to his enemies, yes, but not to the people, not unless he fancied his head parted from his shoulders, a gory trophy for the mob. Think of Louis XVI or Marie-Antoinette, their reigns severed by the guillotine's kiss. Perhaps the lies of old lacked the velvet finesse of modern deceit. Or maybe fear kept them honest, raw, primal fear of the consequences. But now? Now we dance in an age where words are as slippery as a greased weasel on a banana peel. Words are no longer tools; they're weapons of mass distraction, contorted into euphemistic labyrinths where truth goes to die.

Take the humble spade for example. Why call it what it is when you can rebrand it as a "fertility-enhancing agricultural implement" and charge triple? Honesty is passé. Why risk pesky moral accountability when you can cloak greed in the silken robes of sophistication?

Lobbying, that glittering farce. Bribery? How gauche! No, this is "campaign support," a selfless donation to democracy's altar with no string attach, of course! wink, wink! A pocketbook handshake, if you will. Money doesn't corrupt; it engages. When cash flows like a river through the corridors of power, we call it "citizen participation." How noble and pure! Never mind the stench of rot beneath the perfume.

Mercenaries now also put on their make-up. "Soldiers of fortune"? Forget that! These are freedom fighters of any nation whose check clears first. They don't fight wars; they liberate, one blast at a time. They are heroes, if you think heroism comes with contracts and collateral damage. War is not hell but, rather, a business trip with perks.

What about torture? No, that is too visceral, too honest. Enhanced interrogation: Yes, that will do it. It's so clinical it could easily appear on a dentist's menu. A root canal for the soul? Pain is not cruelty; it's empowerment. Compliance through suffering, another public service! Just another public service! If you object, well, aren't you just the monster for questioning the greater good?

We have built ourselves this world: a carnival of our linguistic sleight, cheap parlor tricks to dazzle and deceive. The truth lies buried underneath a pile of jargon; a corpse hidden under a golden rug. The real crime isn't the lie; it's calling it a lie. And so, we play along, swallowing the euphemism, bartering clarity for comfort. "He got killed" is not the same as "He died." Huge, huge difference. One is a bullet, the other a bedtime story. And in this shadow play, that difference is everything.

All of this conveniently allows them to put forth constructions of their own that will enable hope and dreams to be realized, and problems solved seemingly with ease. All the while such brilliantly expressed façades kamikaze toward a hollow abyss of empty promises. For the masters of deceit, facts become malleable. They twist the truth however it fits their narrative while using carefully cherry-picked data to serve their mighty agenda. Inconvenient truths go silent, and opposing evidence is made to feel nonexistent. Therefore, giving them leave to pursue their agenda and ideology.

Every choice, law, half-hearted affirmation of a lie, and proclamation of some decree has an ideology that runs like a churning hot heart underneath. An unseen quicksand that holds captive our thoughts and sullies our hands, casting our entire world in its ghastly bleached image. We are prisoners of ideas; bound by beliefs we profess to have acquired freely. But what happens when one sees a leader who once, in supposedly happier days, was a beacon of hope, who was himself chanted in these very streets alight with dreams, as one demonic? How does one soul corrode? What darkness sits in the heart of a man to warrant the death of a thousand screams drowned in punishment by his rule? Standing up against a tyrant is bravery; some might argue: what about the tyrant who bloodied his way into power and silenced dissent then in a blissful sleep, rests under silk sheets. Should he be called brave, or has he traded his human image for the devil of ambition?

I mean, greatness is indeed a double-edged sword. Greatness smiles and caresses legends and scars history's skin; but which hands clasp that handle? A hero walks up on wings of justice, and a tyrant walks up on stairs of bones: both are named great. We eulogize one while burning the effigy of the other; blindly failing to see the bleak truth. Greatness is neither black nor white; it is this very fire raging against our blindness. Hypocrisy unabashed grasps the weakest of moralities like charms of protection. We lament the sins of the dictator but secretly nurse our own sins, our turning away from suffering, trading away freedom for false security in self-comfort and self-pity. We see the evil bean as a speck and strike a hundred cheers, completely ignoring the rot in our own soul.

Dictators are not born. They are made. In the same burning atmosphere of sorrow, where the broken and disordered civilization curses a dictator to rise, he believes and urges, "I will save you." Of course, only mayhem could be an alternative; thus, everyone believes. There were any such avarices, only the frail silhouettes of our collective weakness stare back at them. Dissent is swallowed in their prisons, fists clasped tightly, suffocating laws. But even ash in the darkest nights stirs audacity. A mother has her book of defiance kept hidden within layers of petticoat. Some poet still seeps ink on a truly subversive verse, and a child will one day ask the most dangerous question, the "Why?" That is also where the revolution begins.

To judge a dictator is to stand upon the precipice of human possibility, a superlative and perverse entity, indeed. They are not aliens; they are mirrors. Each dictator is merely a price of our silence, a manifestation of our fears, the gamble with wild power. So, when their statues fall, that is not mere stone shattered; it is the cobweb of illusion, whoever put it there. It is our sin; it is yours and mine. For every soul that bends in allegiance to a tyrant, an equal soul retakes another path, suddenly illuminated. Woken up from the silent whispers of history, it thunders: This is what we are capable of. The question is, which parts of ourselves will we dare to confront?

I've always been mesmerized by the juxtaposition of America, richest and proudest among democratic nations, against China, the mighty stronghold of communism and one-party authoritarian dictatorship, the second wealthiest and powerful nation. Wait, is this a joke? Two worlds, two ideologies, democracies draped in the silken rhetoric of freedom, dictatorships snarling through the iron teeth of control, yet both stand at the end of the line with the same conclusion: richest and most powerful.

What are we missing here? I mean, you have African leaders adopting the same ideologies: the one's picking the ideology of the free world violates the rights of the powerless while on the other hand, the dictators take in arrogance and decimate the powerless. Then barge in the Europeans: "Hold my beer, while I talk to my Mayors in Africa." How free! They ask, forgetting their ancestors have walked these ancient lands and desecrated them with blood for their golden treasures; now they preach morality while having their Heel on the necks of the pathetic African rulers, reminding them "dance to our tune or die of hunger."

Which makes one wonder, what is democracy in Africa? Has it been hijacked, or has it never existed? Because if it does exist, then it gives one a choice and then eats one's bread; free elections allow regimes to plunder rivers and mines, meanwhile silencing all dissenting voices. Dictatorship? A noose sold as a necklace. The strongman flourishes under the liberation flag and then enchains the very people he promised to help. Both systems, however, East or West, are believed to be working in their own spheres. However, in Africa they devour their own! They make them kneel, obey, and survive! This is how both systems, through their surrogates and offspring, have left Africa betrayed, either by others or its own children. Over decades, on this "geological scandal" of Africa, vultures circled; people are put down, painted as beggars, and they forget whose wealth was used to build their palaces. People are called corrupt, and yet the banks swell with stolen billions from the same "beggars". They preach human rights by providing weapons to tyrants that silence cries from the people. The irony festers like an open wound: the very people that claim to despise dictatorship are the ones that go on to create the monsters they then mournfully condemn. However, among dust and heat, concrete resilience has bloomed in the baobab for far too long to be ignored, and people realized that no ideology will ever save them. Not when the game is rigged, not when the world still sees them as a carcass worthy only of being picked clean. Their songs and protests cast a flame that can no longer be extinguished by any empire. They "believe" in no longer being pawns, no longer in the shadows, no, the leaders are in the shadows where they will shamelessly remain until the next military coup because there will be one. It is just a matter of time. For instance, just last week Miba got repatriated from Togo to Upper Volta for trying to overthrow Traore. And three weeks prior, the turmoil was in the land of Behanzin, former Kingdom of Dahomey now governed by the man on high heels. Three weeks before that it was Bissau, and maybe two weeks before that, it was Madagascar… should I keep going? We can't keep up anymore. As for the people, their heart is beating for a dying continent amid one of the world's greatest schemes to bury it alive.

Chapter 2

Ideological struggles

The transoceanic slave trade engraved wounds on the canvas of four centuries of history leaving Africans suspended in societies chewing their labor but denying their humanity. Existence in such worlds was a paradox: embodiment present, but personhood erased. Even the dawn of freedom came distorted: law reduced them to fractions; a ghastly arithmetic to relieve the conscience of those profiting from their subjugation. Yet in this crucible of degradation, resilience took roots. Enslaved Africans fought in wars not theirs; they fought under foreign flags and came back home bearing eyes cleared and edged with irony at liberating others while shackled themselves. Silence was a method of survival that began to fail. It came down to a realization in quiet fury the theft of their lands, the plunder of their resources, the vilification of their dignity. All these things coalesced into a quiet fury, a realization that to remain voiceless was to sanction this sacrilege.

By the 1950s, that rage burst forth into a symphony of defiance. The new generation of the African continent did not take this birth as a monolith but as a chorus of vastly differing voices harmonizing toward a singular truth across the cultures and lands that make Africa enough. Farmers, poets, teachers, and dreamers bore the weight of emancipation, their spirits increasingly filled with the flame of those no longer able to bear so much suffering. Kwame Nkrumah put it in a mood electrifying enough: for him, Ghana's independence turned into a beacon for a single Africa. Jomo Kenyatta, once imprisoned as a "terrorist," emerged to dismantle colonial mythologies and liberate Kenya. Emery Lumumba, unflinching to the last even when threatened by looming shadows, conjured in the mind a Congo free of fetters. They infected each other with a contagious courage that inspired protests choking the colonial capitals with dust and determination.

However, some knew too well that speeches alone do not make a revolution. Behind the headlines, pens became weapons. Frantz Fanon dissected the psychic violence of colonialism with surgical precision: Chinua Achebe resurrected in prose that thundered across continents, Africa's stolen narratives. W.E.B. Du Bois connected through intellect and time oceans, and molded Pan-Africanism into a lifeline for linking diaspora struggles to ancestral soil. And in the shadows of these giants did women like Funmilayo Ransome-Kuti, an organizer, agitator, mother of movements, stood, dismantling imperialist tax systems with one hand while fighting the other patriarch scorn. "Education as resistance," said Adelaide Casely-Hayford, and Queen Nzinga's war strategies in earlier centuries attested to the fact that women in Africa were never passive spectators in history.

This was not a simple revolt; it was the sweat of laborers straining under the scorching sun, students chanting until their throats are raw; villagers living without kneeling before foreign gods or governors. It matured in the whispers from elders evoking ancestral wisdom and in the zeal of youth demanding a future unshackled. With troops rampaging through continents, activists from faraway capitals sample-poisoning, dock workers boycotting colonial goods, and artists leaving their marks of the struggle onto verse and paint. Marcus Garvey's call for Black pride echoed from Harlem to Nairobi, while George Padmore transformed political connections into pipelines of solidarity.

Old wounds lasted generations and bequeathed legacy: not mere idle survival into something evil but brave reclamation of one's name, land, and right to breathe unfettered. Each child being taught what is his, every protest that cannot fade, every heartbeat, even now, echoes: *We are here, and we'll completely remain.*

In that mingling tide of the mid-20th century, it now presents a witness to the same inextinguishable display of crumbling empires' power and nations yearning to breathe free. Guinea, the cradle of moats and rivers in West Africa stood as a storm silent, it was a tiny nation but a place where ageless Mandinka drum still beating up times of the empire of Sundiata Keita, where highlands of Fouta Djallon whispered the secrets of Fulani scholar warriors, and where the Susu and Kissi created lives from earth with hands both calloused and reverent. Yet by 1950, the soil of Guinea bore the weight of colonialism so much as the simmering embers of a people that refused to be erased.

Guinea was claimed by France as one of its territories in the late 19th century. From a collective of vibrant kingdoms, it was turned into mere "territories" under a vast imperial spider web. Conakry, its capital and a port-city birthed out of colonial ambition, was permeated with a fractured duality. One side sipped Bordeaux at whitewashed villas reserved for European administrators while Guinean dockworkers toiled to haul coffee, bananas, and diamonds into ships bound for Marseille. Yet outward flowed the wealth of a land, and unbroken remained its soul. It smashed deep within the furthest portions of the village away from the coast to witness some of the most celebrated events. History, as told by elders, entered bitterly concerning that one who lost a contest against France. Farmers tilled ancestral plots with monsoon rain and promise.

In the markets of Kindia, women balanced baskets of fiery *pili-pili* on their heads, with laughter ringing like a currency which no colonizer could ever seize. In the savannas, the cattle herding Fulani people walked with a kind of royal laziness, as their indigo clothes stained the almost horizon like living art. But just before the colonial odds, forced labor camps scarring the countryside, the whip and chain threatened the dissenting Indigénat Code. Still, joy persisted, and that had been rebellion enough for years. Night pulsed with rhythms of *djembé*, storytellers weaving tales of Samori Touré, and Alpha Yaya who'd fought French guns with swords, and young men debated politics in hushed tones, their eyes fixed on a horizon of independence.

They said so many things that one could lose his wits concerning Guinean foreigners. There were the French bureaucratic tallying quotas for exports; a Lebanese merchant traded cloth for gold; the occasional missionary clutching his Bible like a shield. But in this, Guineans navigated these situations with shrewd grace. For instance, A farmer would offer a calabash of palm oil to a colonial officer, a gesture of both generosity and subtly mocking, showing them how hospitality outlived occupation. It is above such practices that secret societies like the *Poro* and *Sande* preserved rituals no European eyes could penetrate, their masked dancers embodying spirits older than the tricolor flag itself.

Colony propaganda bragged about railroads and schools, which were rather degenerative devices instead of uplifting communities. The bane of the Conakry-Niger Railway, built from the blood of peasants, was employed in carting the wealth between destinations and not dreams. Children learned their French numerals in villages, but their multiplication tables whispered in Mandinka or Fulani. Homes were more like mud huts of condescending lore, but complex buildings of clay and wood; cool in the heat; walls embossed with symbols declaring lineage and resistance. The footpaths, smooth from generations carrying yams, kola nuts, and clandestine hopes, were the only ones that thrived after the rains.

But even in this colonial machine, there was space for seething dissent. And there would be those who could rise to challenge the regime of this barbarizing order: sons of local chiefs, trained to bear with hierarchies introduced by the colonial setting but radicalized by the suffering and things they had to see since most of their household members were poor. One among them was Laysouf, who spent his early childhood under his father's shadow, a canton chief under French rule. It made him develop an instinct to observe early differences in privileges by family due to chasm poverty gnawing at his community. The haunting injustice sharpened his mind to reason against the system that enriches the dynasty at the expense of his people.

Then there was Yaryb, a man born of a wealthy chief in Guinea's protectorate; yet his family clung with zeal to the colonial status quo. But the faces he saw in the village's women bending under the scorching sun in the fields, children gaunt with hunger destroyed his complacency and replaced it with smoldering rebellion. Another was Wadu, raised in a neighboring territory under his own chief father's French-aligned rule, whose education became an ambivalent sword. While colonial schools propagated obedience, they also connected him with the ferment of Pan-Africanism and the fiery rhetoric of liberation movements abroad.

Theirs was, each man in his own way, the beginning of what would unravel the lies that had become part of the colonial project and trouble the delicate balance between oppressor and oppressed. Their paths would diverge: Laysouf would organize clandestine meetings in hushed courtyards, Yaryb would document abuses in secret journals, and Wadu would feast on smuggled pamphlets on sovereignty, but their journeys would ultimately lead to one truth: resistance necessitates new footsteps on the path once trodden by their ancestors.

The classrooms that had aimed to colonize their minds instead armed them with rebellion. European ideals of liberty and self-determination which were weaponized to justify empires, now pierced the veil of colonial hypocrisy. Laysouf, Yaryb, and Wadu devoured Rousseau's *social contract* by day and traded dog-eared copies of *Négritude* poetry by night. Their education became a fever, a paradox that seared their souls. They sat in stiff wooden desks, reciting *"Liberté, égalité, fraternité"* while outside, villagers bowed under the weight of forced labor. The dissonance choked them, but it was the whispers in the shadows that ignited their resolve. In backroom meetings thick with cigar smoke and fear, grizzled trade unionists and sharp-tongued poets showed them the map of their future: an Africa unshackled, not a Guinea; but an Africa. Yaryb wept the first time he heard a griot sing of Samori Touré's wars, his voice raw with ancestral defiance. Wadu memorized every arrest, every strike, scribbling names of the disappeared in margins of his textbooks. Laysouf, ever the strategist, traced supply routes for smuggled goods on the back of his father's tax ledgers.

Guilt was their crucible. How could they dismantle a system that had cradled them in privilege? Laysouf's silk *boubous* hung like accusations in his closet; Yaryb tasted bile when his mother praised his "loyalty" to French administrators. Yet most of the time when youngsters died of a fever the colonial clinic dismissed as *"native frailty,"* fathers' hearts shattered in a storm of grief. These men became ghosts in two worlds. By dawn, they negotiated with governors in polished offices, voices honeyed with compliance. By dusk, they funneled francs into whispered networks, their hands trembling not from fear, but fury. Roads they'd ostensibly built for the empire now smuggled contraband pamphlets. Schools meant to breed clerks became cells of dissent. Even their fathers' titles, *chief, mediator, loyal subject*, twisted into blades. But revolutions, like storms leave debris, and these debris would be like no other.

Then, from the alleys of Conakry's slums, a new specter emerged, a man with no library card, no lineage, no guilt, a nobody really, He was just picked up on the street by great men striving for change, akin to Emery's encounter of Sese Seko outside a wooden maquis bar inside a tin rooved shanty town in Léopoldville. They called him *the Syli*, though that wasn't his name. He'd survived not on Rousseau or rifle-smuggling but managed to weasel his way into the circle of noblemen.

The elites mistook him for a pawn. People who knew him praised his "authenticity," his rags, a living indictment of their silken compromises. His laughter at their salons had an edge, too sharp, too hungry. Where they quoted Adam Smith or Thomas Malthus, he spat parables of hyenas who eat their own for profit. His ambition was a live wire, sparking in the vacuum of fledgling independence that surged during a tumultuous post-World War two era: a time of global uncertainty and transformative geopolitical shift. A War that was a watershed moment that signaled the end of an era and had far-reaching effects on the century that followed. It molded the global political, social, and economic order, laying the framework for subsequent wars. Estranged to what the world had in storage for him, he grew up seeing an imperfect world where the sanctity of human life was often tabooed by individuals striving for control. He felt entitled to a heroic adventure of libertarianism and decided to hold the onerous bundle of the African continent into his hands while victimizing its people.

Salim Retu, such was the name that probably could have conjured the image of his presence, deep umber skin, and a smile so radiant that his teeth seemed to have absorbed moonlight. It was not just his physical figure that turned heads. His name itself might have ecstasy-doomed him to a battleground of raised-eyebrowed, aghast children, many of whom would have afterwards stifled bitter adults scrambling for bandages and explanations. But more than that, it had heft too, with a legacy etched in the very marrow of his bones. He belonged to a long line of rebellions; his blood marked with that of warriors who had never knelt before a colonial fist. Six feet tall, he stood impressive with tight coiled hair warmed under the sun to a golden brown and most often than not, had long and elaborate write-ups. Sharp cheekbones and jawline carved from a rock around eyes filled with a simmering, quiet yet relentless flame. His speech was like a river; smooth and deliberate, laced with a charm that questions your reality.

His life began within classrooms whose walls sometimes echoed the steady rhythms of Koranic verses and at other times, the lisping prayers of French primers. By the time he was fifteen, the art of rebellion, the protests of sodden school lunches and suffocating rules had been mastered. Each act had incited fire against the shadow of imperialism, leading him deeper into the iron-fisted tenets of communism. School administrators would hold their clipboards tighter behind him, while the cafeteria staff seemed to mutter around him grumbling about troublemakers. But Salim didn't lean. His ancestors fought for the land; he fought for minds, with faith as sharp as their spears.

Yet all his dreams turned to dust on the day he blew his EPS exam. The doors to William Ponty, the privileged forge of future leaders in Dakar, slammed closed in gossiping shadow beneath the establishments of his successful peers. But, rather, it sucked him into the Georges Poiret vocational school, which seemed like an anchor more than a springboard. He was pierced by every whispered success story by his classmates, those brilliant destinies like thorns. Bitterness festered, that poison which consumed his spirit, till he could no longer take it. He just walked away, defiant. He chose the ragged freedom of self-teaching over the humiliation of a path he despised.

But in the silence of empty classrooms, Salim learned rebellion in the pages of books. Then were the words his refuge, stolen weapons for the battle, and when he turned to Universal Studies, a program fashioned free from traditions, he took it on as refuge and battlefield, completely merging himself in the writings of Marx and Lenin, crackling like a raging fire in the restless mind of a madman with theories. Communism became his guilty thrill, the lens through which to view the world's fractures: exploitation, the laborers' silent screams. It made away with him. By day, hands were rough, bruised from doing menial work that he was destined to do for the rest of his life; at night, they bore voices sharpened in secret meetings as they were rallying the downtrodden.

The road became jagged, with every step taken being one of defiance. There were hunger and fatigue pursuing him, but determination blazed brighter. He spoke not with brilliance or polish, but rather with raw and wild conviction: his words would weave their way through alleys and hamlets, igniting the hearts dimmed by long oppression. Imperialism, that great beast, became his nemesis. He sought friends in the dark while his power grew overhead, like a thundercloud, until his name resounded like a hymn of rebellion.

No diploma graced him, no institution certified him, but in the eyes of the laborers, the forgotten, he was a beacon. A man who chiseled his destiny not with ink of exams, but with the fire of justice, too relentless and unyielding. His adventure began very much in the shadows, in the darkness where the weight of the systemic oppression threatened to crush his spirit before it even took flight.

Consider a young man who has hands calloused from clerical work all day and for the rest, much like a thief in the dead of night, stolen away from such a life by the flicker of lamplight as he pinched himself from cramped classrooms-between survival and dreaming with daring audacity. He etched into destiny by not signing files for students, but by waging lifelong war in paperless courts for people. It was more than just a job change but also the first incision into a wall of fate that would have to be accepted when he left the ink-stained ledgers for the den-like corridors of the Postal Service. Here, under the hum of bureaucracy, he discovered the slowly boiling discontent of workers, the fatigue, and the missing voices. To the promises, he devoured as if a starved man: dignity, weekends freed from toil, retirements free from poverty.

Then the blow that struck him remained etched in his bones when he rallied workers behind him for a strike of seventy-two days. Some starved; some were afraid. Others saw Salim as a flicker in the wind. Days bled into nights-stained with torment and hope. Ultimately, it wasn't just shorter hours or better wages they'd won. It was the revelation that shook him to his core: *power.* The kind of power that could unmake kings, he thought. The vengeful French authorities, boxed in and steaming with rage, relentlessly offered the workers a forty-hour workweek. A taste of victory, he'd later call a revolution, and within him, was this tiny spark. *If this*, he thought, *what else might burn. What else could I accomplish?*

The idea of politic that was once a distant thought, now pulsating through his veins. Guinea had rich communal traditions which must have sung to him that socialism need not be a foreign graft. The pseudo-mystical heartlessness and spirit of "African socialism" gorged itself upon Negritude's concept, one that pretended the cracks widening between the Cockroach class and the starving were nothing. To him, Marxism wasn't dogma, it could never be bound; it had to be a scalpel-thin, precise and ruthless. But he wielded it with caution, cut to accommodate the fresh scars on his homeland. The colonial spies seemed to give him company in the shadows; some branded him a threatening "Marxist agitator." He had, however, slipped this thin ice with an eagle dance, even as he sheltered under the shadows of intellectual allies in Paris. Change danced to his rhythm, and he roused it on platform rallies.

Salim would walk in the icy streets of Berlin, with the hunger for justice in Prague, and all the way to Warsaw absorbing the chill of ideologies forged in foreign strife. Though, much of him remained an enigma. He is a man who'd quote Lenin by morning and share kola nuts with village elders by dusk. Guinea's fight was his compass, while the rest of the world was hell-bent on claiming him. The path he carved was neither pure nor easy; it wasn't a clean road; it was a dirty and winding road; but it was the Road he decided to follow. The road of that boy who once clutched pen and paper in the dark, daring to rewrite his destiny.

The envy within Salim festered like an ugly wound, gnawing at his spirit and twisting it into something essentially calamitous, the bitter determination to annihilate those he coveted. Consequently, Salim rhetoric became quite venomous and his tactics unorthodox; only vengeance could hope to fill in the markings branded onto his ambition by the honor he believed to be his. Salim had a grim supporter in Felix, the stoic head of *Les Éléphants*. Felix carried the ghost of a mentor by the name of Mr. Biaka Boda; an ex-shaman turned senator, whose very vanishing into the gorge of the jungle had become legend-whispered along the trails of Soumahoro Kanté, who was likewise swallowed beneath similar ancient wood in 1235 in the historic battle of Kirina. To Felix, Biaka was more than a memory: He was a creed who stood for a conviction, a pledge to defy empires.

Felix had founded the African Democratic Rally to unite Africa against imperialism after the second world war, then was later joined by Salim. Yet the flagrant ambition of Salim was a sore thumb. His comrade would dismiss him as an opportunist whose revolt against the colonial masters sounded more petulant than principled. A child denied treats splattering out. And Felix had a theory to support such claims.

There were murmurings about a referendum; the air was filled with tension, like a storm approaching. Intrepid young hearts ablaze with the fires set by recklessness, the irrepressible recklessness of those willing to die in defense of a tomorrow of their own making, now lit a fuse too potent for the French to extinguish. Parchment-thin was the French grip upon the colony, and with every flicker of defiance, this loosening of power became visible in shadow and light. Salim, the opportunist, the scavenger, smelled blood on the wind.

He was a fast man, afraid of fading into obscurity. French officials, hounded and hollow-eyed, were being swept along in the tide of change roaring past aided and abetted by the new generation burning instead of bowing. Change whispered through the slums, slithery and seductive. Salim would not let himself be beaten. It was a get free or die trying kind of thing for him.

With a sharp burst of enterprising defiance, he slid into the colonial citadel. The guards were indifferent and bored. The meeting hall looked like a mausoleum of gilded chairs and moth-eaten flags, standing tall in his presence, anticipating the dramatic gameplay of a Jackal allowed to escape and feed on bureaucracy yet again. By that time, murmurs resumed, and he knew it was time: one breath and gamble forward; his voice trembling yet rough-edged.

"An audience, I'd like an audience." he demanded or, perhaps, begged when intercepted by the young clerk sitting at the front desk. The room stilled. His moment had come.

That afternoon, heat and hubris filled the governor's chamber. Salim stood there, upright, before the colonial pantheon, but the opulence of power dwarfed him. His carefully constructed pose fell apart there; beads of sweat pooled under his collar, and the voice in which he had so recently spoken with bravado, now trembled like a plucked wire, exposing a soul laid bare. A lump formed in his throat. He struggled to find the words. The scrutiny of the room fastened upon him; he was now a specimen under glass. "What can I do for you, Salim?" The governor asked with casual indifference.

"Give us independence," Salim pleaded, the words ricocheting through the ottoman-distant chamber, each syllable burdened with the weight of generations of struggle. "We will vote yes to your referendum if you would let us complete our own destiny, chart our own course through historical waters." As he remained seated back in his ornamented chair, the French governor maintained his steely and calculating stance, unmoved.

"Salim, are you alright?" The governor asked, "Your independence threatens the stability of our empire," he continued, carrying his words as sharp as the blade of a conqueror.

"To cede control would be to concede power, a concession we cannot afford to make." And thus, amid the echoes of a silenced plea, a dream of liberation flickered like a flame blown out by the gales of political convenience. Salim felt this heaviness of disappointment drape over him as the hall echoed with the decided words of the French representative. His request, earnestly made, has been conclusively denied. The authoritative tone of the leader allowed no arguments, and Salim understood that further charges would be in vain. And such increased Salim's rancor toward the French. His clear sclera turned red; his nostrils flared. He tried to hide his anger under a gentle smile but his hemifacial spasm wouldn't agree. With a stiff nod and a clenched jaw, Salim rose from his seat, the scrape of the chair against the floor a discordant echo in the solemn hall. His steps were measured but purposeful as he made his way to the exit, eyes fixed straight ahead, betraying none of the turmoil within. The murmurs and whispers of those around him faded into a dull hum as he pushed open the heavy door, the cold breeze outside a stark contrast to the heated exchange inside.

Out, under the gray sky, Salim halted and awaited the settling of thoughts. Anger and disappointment were wrestling in him, but he knew that he must not take heed of either of such emotions. Instead, he sought out his trusted confidant, Yaryb, one endowed with wisdom and whose opinion he took to heart. Yaryb was a man of paradoxes: a prince by blood but a revolutionary by volition. Whispers trailed him like shadows, alleging ties to the *Nyamakala*, a clandestine sect obsessed with arcane knowledge and political dominion. Founder of the Socialist Democracy of Guinea (DSG), he was armored by the attitude that the power was his birthright. Short of stature but volcanic in presence, Yaryb cut a figure well beyond indifference. His tiny frame hummed with restless energy, as if each sinew crackled with the urgency of his ideals. Out in the world, his shoulders squared, and chin tilted upward, for even skeptics fell silent at the mere sight of him. His eyes - sharp, glittering, alive with nearly feral cunning - dared the world to underestimate him.

They called him *Syliyore*: "The little elephant." It was as much a bitter-wit homage to his ideological kinship with Salim Retu, the towering "Elephant" of Guinea's progressive movement, while revealing the deep-seated differences between the two. While Salim wielded pragmatism, Yaryb sold fire. He could burn or beguile with his voice; before his followers, Yaryb was hailed as a prophet of democracy, but terror incarnate to his enemies. His strength was the razor wit he wielded and an ironclad belief in what he considered right. Yaryb reveled in the dichotomy. "If fear is the currency of change," he would say. With relish, he shattered tribal chieftaincies with the enthusiasm of an artist smashing away at marble, dismissing tradition as "the corpse of progress."

Although, for all his ferocity, Yaryb drew lines even his allies feared to cross. Salim once suggested an alliance forged on the edge of a blade: "We must meet violence with violence." Yaryb drew back, as if zipped with an electric shock. "No," he snapped. "Your methods reek of the very tyranny we seek to bury. I will not dance with demons, even to drown them." The rebuke sealed his reputation in marks and grinders, as a person of inconvenient principles thorn in the sides of oppressors and opportunists.

Salim knew that the little elephant was what he needed on his team, but if he could not have him, then he may very well use him, his hatred of imperialism aligning perfectly. The sultry evening enveloped the palace courtyard as Salim appeared. Shadows stretched across the flagstones like huge blotches of ink. A whirling tongue-speaker, he recounted the latest betrayal in the National Assembly, the rejected reforms, the sneering aristocrats, but omitted the festering secret in his chest: his clandestine negotiations with French envoys, a gambit to trade colonial concessions for power. Yaryb listened, perched on a stone bench like a sparrowhawk, his gaze dissecting every word. "Disappointment is the tax on ambition," Yaryb said with almost a wistful edge. "But you've mistaken a battle for the war. The DSG doesn't bow to assemblies. We reshape them." He leaned forward and steepled his fingers. "Plant those seeds in the streets, not the salons. Let the people's voices drown out our ancestors' whispers."

Salim's jaw tightened in contempt. Yaryb's idealism had always been on the verge of naïveté; yet his words seeped into the cracks of Salim's crushing frustration, building upon his resolve. As the conversation ebbed and the pressure in Salim's chest had lifted, his thoughts became clammy with a crystal-clear focus. He rose from his seat, grasped Yaryb's hand, and then started to leave.

"Syliyore," he muttered, half to himself, vanishing into the dusky twilight. Yaryb remained in the courtyard, ironically in the dark about the betrayal taking shape. Syliyore's rebellious spirit had been enough inspiration for Salim at the moment; this defiance was not an ally but a sort of blueprint. A revolution, after all, could always be harnessed if not outmaneuvered.

Chapter 3

The Price of Power

Damp air, laden with the seriousness of future storms, both the first monsoon clouds gathering over the sharp, jagged peaks of Fouta Djallon and the political tempests brewing in men's hearts, among all that makes Guinea feel heavy. The French National Assembly election dangled like a sword, with sharp edge brought on by ambition in three men, namely: Yaryb, his silver tongue and Parisian polish; Salim, the crafty mercantile prince whose alliances slinks like roots beneath the soil; and Wadu, who has an effervescence within his name such as Fula drumming an ancient hum.

Wadu's candidacy was not born from the backroom deals, but in sacred groves where his forefathers had once before bound blood oaths under the shining moon. The coalition that backed him was composed of Fula chiefs cloaked in indigo robes, their faces etched with the authority of generations, clasping hands with the fiery syndicalists of Lower Guinea, their hands still stained with the red earth of rice paddies. Together, they wove a pact as delicate as spider silk: the Fula would claim the Assembly seat, the others the lesser offices.

But it was Wadu who gave the pact its soul. He was a son of Fouta twice over, born to Dabola's Almami, whose prayers could summon rain, and descended through his mother's blood from the *Almamiyyas,* the warrior-kings who had once united the highlands under banners stitched with Qur'anic verse. When the spiritual leader of Fouta Djallon, Almami Ibrahima Sory Dara, pressed the *kaamilu,* the holy book, into Wadu's palm at the Great Mosque of Timbo, the crowd did not cheer. They wept. For in that gesture lay the unspoken truth: this was not an election, but a consecration. Yet Wadu's power was a paradox. He had surrendered his birthright, the Almami's throne, a seat of power older than the French Empire itself, to kneel in the mud of colonial politics. His critics sneered: *A prince playing democrat.* He was a descendent of one of the most powerful dynasties in the Islamic confederation of Fouta after all. But the people saw the scars on his hands from digging wells in drought-stricken villages, the frayed cuffs of his *boubou* from nights spent drafting petitions in lamplit huts. When he spoke, his voice did not rise in the florid cadences of the educated elite, but in the raw, rhythmic Fula of the herders and weavers. "They think chains are only iron," he told a crowd in Kankan, lifting his wrists as if feeling the ghost-weight of manacles. "But their *papers,* their *laws,* their *taxes,* these too are shackles. And I will break them with your hands or die trying."

Gargling with their absinthes, the French district officers laughed off the situation. *"Let the savages fight over their puppet assembly,"* they muttered. But in the shadows, colonial spies hurriedly took notes. Wadu's rallies swelled, not with hired goons of Salim or bourgeois clerks of Yaryb, but with *people*: Fula women ululating as they marched, Susu fishermen carrying him on their shoulders, Dialonké farmers exchanging yams for ink to mark ballots. Not even the griots, those living archives of tradition, remained silent: *Wadu the Unbroken, Wadu Who Walks Toward Bullets.*

Therein lay the haunted one. At night he paced beneath an ink-black sky in his courtyard, over which there hung a shadow cast by smoke from those French rubber factories. "They will rig the vote," he confided to Fodé Retu, his voice fraught with emotion, "or worse." Yazmine would wordlessly lay a bowl of *fouti tàku* (fonio with okra) before him, her eyes reflecting the same terror that clawed away at every throat in Guinea. But dawning days would see him again at the mosque gates, tearing cloth from his own robe to bind the sores of lepers.

When that final rally came, the sea of torches flooding Timbo's ancient stone plazas, Wadu stood barefoot on the steps of the citadel of his forefathers. Behind him, the drummers of Almami pounded out a rhythm older than empires. "They say we are *subjects*," he screamed, the word twisting like a curse. "But I say: We are the fire they tried to drown in their rivers! We are the stones they built their forts upon, now rising to crush them!" The crowd roared, making the baobabs tremble, and fruit bats took off in spirals into the night.

Touching any soul on that moment were even the French flinching because they had seen something: Wadu, then, was no longer just a candidate. He had become the furious heartbeat of the land, the answer to prayers uttered through slave forts and forest shrines. The electors would cast their votes in ink and lies. But the war, the real war, the one that lay simmering since the first colonial boot profaned Guinean soil, had already found its general. And in Paris, the trembling hand of a bureaucrat hovered over that decree.

The election came not with hope, but with the metallic taste of betrayal. In the mist-cloaked Fouta Djallon villages, where the very air thrummed with the *griots* singing the ancestral valor of Wadu arrived voting cards, poisoned gifts. The local chiefs, men whose authority in the past sprang from sacred oaths, now had become enforcers, suited and booted by the French and stiff in their complicit boubous. The cards were handed out in solemnity, like communion, but the cards were already marked with Wadu's name, the ink still wet with collusion. *"Bless them,"* they whispered, sliding them into calloused hands. "A sign from God Himself."

In smoke-filled cafés around Conakry, PDG (Democratic Party of Guinea) activists spat curses into their coffee. The law had promised secrecy, a solemn pact of trust between voter and ballot; colonial logic, though, had the words turned into weapons. French gendarmes leaned on their jeeps at polling stations, rifles casually slung about their shoulders, as Fula chiefs barred the doors. When the PDG observers appeared, clutching their passes as if they were fragile talismans, they were met with merriment. *"No termites allowed here,"* one chief in Dinguiraye jeered as his men dragged the young PDG organizer into an alley. The crack of batons punctuated the morning prayers.

The fraudulence ran amok by noon. Both in Kankan and at least one box literally burst open with votes for Wadu before the village voters could cast theirs. Meanwhile, in Kissi, a PDG scribe dared protest against the cacophonous atrocities by being stripped nearly naked at the waist and whipped with cane rods, while the French district officer smoked a Gauloise, saying: "Barbarians require barbaric remedies." The sun was climbing, relentlessly baking the bloodstains into the earth.

Colonial radios yelled Wadu's victory and that of his coalition by a landslide, splitting Guinea taut as a ripe fruit. In the north, Fula elders slew bulls in gratitude, their drums resounding through the highlands.

Meanwhile, in the coastal slums where the flame of the PDG burned fiercest, the streets broke into a canorous fury. Women beat their mortars like war drums, and their voices became swords: *"Syli, oh Syli! They've buried you in lies!"* The elephant, Salim's emblem, once a lumbering jest, now thundered through chants as a symbol of crushed justice.

The French governor, holed up in his Dakar-style villa, dismissed the outcry as *"native theatrics."* But Paris stirred uneasily. At the July congress of the French Section of the Workers' International, socialist delegates hands still ink-stained from factory pamphlets, condemned the governor's *"shameless mime of neutrality."* A junior delegate from Marseille, voice trembling with indignation, brandished a smuggled ballot from Labe: Wadu's name pre-printed, the paper reeking of palm wine and fear. "This is not democracy," he declared, "it is farce with bullets." Wadu, now sitting in the Assembly, gilded cages and all, wore his victory like a shroud of failure. The colonial press really had painted him as a statesman, naming him *"The Enlightened Primitive"*, but under the flash of cameras his eyes betrayed a hollow rage. They had turned him into a king of ashes. Every telegram redoubled the pain: Hanging of DSG youths from kapok trees, the burning of stalls of Susu traders for singing ballads of Wadu, Salim's own cousin heading armed gangs through Fouta Djallon to "weed out dissent."

Late at night, the quietness would sting the house in Conakry. The laughter of Assemblymen would seep through the floorboards, *"Your savages still eat with hands, eh, Monsieur le Deputy?"*, while Wadu hunched over petitions for electoral review, his fountain pen carving deep into the paper. But Paris had already set its course for the truth.

The protests of the PDG turned more and more murky and dark. There was some young lady, Rama, whose father died, and, in consequence, she attended vigils at midnight outside the prison of Conakry. Her throat is raw from reciting the names of the disappeared. Farmers smuggled their machetes in rice sacks, and in the thickest of forests, where no French patrol dared to tread, griots were singing a fresh refrain: *"The fire they drowned will rise as steam-and scald the hands that held it under."*

The shadow of the election would really continue to hang over; it was a festering wound. But in the markets, fields, and mangrove swamps, sometimes at night fisherman would patch up nets under lantern lights, and there under that heat would coil a reckoners' snake like a viper. The French had taught them all what starving votes cost; now Guinea would teach them the price of stolen ones.

Salim supporters draped thick, oppressive fog-like aftermath around them. Hope wore into disillusionment, lining faces with bitterness and arresting these into heavy whispers dripping with cynicism. Streets flowed with deep discontent as murals of hope cracked under the weight of betrayal. In the very next days, the nation simmered: a pressure cooker of frustration. Then came the spark: Wadu's father, an inspiration wrapped in controversy, landed in Conakry. His arrival was more incendiary than diplomatic; indeed, a lit match into dry tinder tossed about. The capital exploded, as flames licked the sky from burning tires, chants of rebellion contrasting with the metallic tang of tear gas. Daybreak and Boffa inevitably followed, the alleyways resounding with the chaos of shattered glass and rustling shadows. The DSG's denunciations of violence, trumpeted by the state media, fell into that noise like ash in the wind.

The Indomitable Salim had glued the whole country. Internally, even when fiercely inflamed in emotion-rage, it was that stifled coil of deep indignation over the historical injustice of stealing that victory which was a snake coiling within his breast. Yet, there was the cold-light prudence flickering under the fire of the heat where he understood: another wrong step, and his ambition was reduced to ash. Public persona became, like government: speech that was fiery as he promised shook podiums, rallies where he roared indignantly like a caged lion, all these calculated to the very noun every now and then. His drama thrilled his base, yes, attracted crowds, fists pumped, chants rumbled into a crescendo, but little did it do to sew together the nation's torn seams: each dramatic act, he began to realize himself, was less a call to unity than a mirror reflecting back hunger for relevance.

Appearing somewhere between fury and restraint, there lay an unlikely ally. A man walked up to him at a half-empty room, but it was not the unbridled enthusiasm of a disciple; he confronted Salim with the measured intensity of a strategist. He called himself *The Gardener*, but others called him *The Invisible Hand of the Good Samaritan*. No banners plastered with his name whisked through the air; no cameras chased this silhouette. He worked quietly, bending events through a backroom deal here, a midnight call there, allowing his influence to percolate like a slow and deliberate poison into the political groundwater. "You plant the spectacle," he told Salim, igniting his cigarette from the dim light of the backroom lamp; "I'll tend the roots."

Their alliance was more of need than trust: Salim's stagecraft captured the eyes of the crowd, while the Gardener's invisible hands moved to nudge loyalists, neutralize rivals, and rewrite narratives with ink never dry. Despite the deepening years of partnership, Salim seriously began to wonder: Was he exploiting the shadows, or was he an unwillingly captive in them? The answer, much like the Gardener's real intent, would forever dwell just out of reach, a shadow embedded inside another shadow.

The first public appearance of the good Samaritan happened two weeks prior at this conference room hummed with the sluggish heat of an African afternoon; its high wooden shutters half-closed against the glare of the sun. Colonial austerity clung to the space: walls of faded ochre plaster, a cracked ceiling fan groaning as it churned the thick air, and a mahogany table polished to a dull sheen, its surface littered with folders stamped Confidential in crimson ink. Maps of the territory, bordered in sharp angles of European pens, occupied one wall, with the portraits of the long since gone Governor glowering in oil paint. There was a mix of smells in the air: sweat, tobacco, mildew, and the sharp smell of ink from day reports.

He leaned against the doorframe, brushing the jamb, and relaxed looking. The door stood ajar, and a sliver of corridor light cut through the floorboards, the dust motes drifted in its path like idle thoughts. Yet his eyes betrayed no such languor. They swept the whole room with a hunter's precision: the fidgeting junior clerk, the lengthy discourse of the district officer droning about cotton yields, the rustle of starched collars, before they snagged, for a moment, on him.

He sat near the window, with his back very straight, and his fingers were dragging along the edge of a dossier. Sunlight was pooling in that empty space formed in the hollow of his throat, glinting off a pendant of which he could hardly make out the shape. However, his gaze shot up sharply and suddenly, at any rate, too quickly to be casual. But, then again, not quite. Half a smile appeared on his lips and then he turned back toward whoever had been talking, leaving him to try to dispel the awkward silence between the scratch of his pen.

That meeting kept bleeding onward: feet shuffled under tables; papers rustled as cards would if they were ill-played. Eventually, the meeting ended, with the room exhaling in unison through the creaking of chairs and murmuring pleasantries. He stayed, looking interested in a much-water-stained map of the river basin, while others drifted out-administrators to gin and tonic, clerks to their respective typewriters.

Across the room, he lingered too. A deliberate pause as he gathered his notes, the rustle of his trousers louder now in the thinning crowd. When the last bureaucrat vanished into the hallway, he turned, his eyes meeting Salim's; with a clarity that stripped the pretense from the air. He pushed off the doorframe, the wood warm under his palm. The fan's drone filled the space between them as he crossed the room, his boots stumping like a metronome counting down seconds.

The room's chatter faded momentarily as the stranger's voice reached Salim. "Hello," the man said, hand outstretched with the ease of someone used to commanding attention. He stood a head taller than everyone else, his crisp shirt catching the light as he moved. "That took nerve back there," he added, thumb brushing the edge of his jaw. "We should talk when you've stopped playing hero." The wink he threw in felt like a shared secret rather than mockery.

Salim stood rooted to the spot long after the man's retreating footsteps faded. An electric tingling still coursed through his shoulder where the stranger had laid a hand on it, casual as an old friendship, but one to which they both had never actually said a word prior to this night.

Given that kind of presence, anybody would have noticed that new arrival: the nonchalant grace of a leopard among house cats, the kind of man who enters a room sideways so as not to scrape his head against the door frame. But what on earth for, Salim rubbed at his neck, suddenly mindful of the sweat-soaked collar. "That's not how the game was played, was it? Such men as him rarely noticed men like me unless…" Thought the incriminate Salim as he sat in a courtyard peeling oranges.

Laysouf, a scion of an aristocratic family of Diari, heir to a chieftaincy he had openly vomited on last harvest. He spat Nere seeds at a scrawny chicken pecking near his boots as he unfolded his stack of journal, smiling. Unstable, called the French papers. He'd gone native, his former classmates back at William Ponty whispered, whatever that meant. Fact was this: he had a knack for making formidable enemies.

The look was there to be seen: a handsome lanky figure. His long, lean limbs unmatching his large buccal fat pads face, with sharp features and a protruding chin. His eyes were sunken and deep-set, with soft hair, and his posture slightly hunched, like he was always ready to spring into action. all sharp angles that would not soften. He dressed like a clerk yet moved like one expecting, at any moment, a knife between the shoulder blades. Three posts withdrawn this year alone. Last week, some colonial undersecretary had sent him to inspect roads, which Laysouf enjoyed, mapping out every back route from there to Bamako.

In the rebel world, they had begun calling him "The Gardener." He liked the metaphor-planting ideas, pruning collaborators, watching movements thrive. Let the French think him eccentric; let his father rage about abandoned duty. He does not care as long as the marketplace proved the soil was fertile. As long as he gets to witness Salim confronting tax collectors, his day was perfect.

Laysouf was smiling for the first time in weeks as he licked citrus juices from his fingers. Dawn found him drafting letters in three different hands, the scent of rebellion clinging to his ink-stained sleeves like orange blossoms.

The French Civil Service sneered at his cunning tactics, shuffling him between posts like a pawn, yet they dared not extinguish him entirely. Instead, they kept him close,

Kept close, like a hawk in a cage, with clipped wings but still untamed.

He who graduated from the library of the prestigious William Ponty Normal School in Dakar, was turned from scholar to insurgent, dropped into the drudgery of assistant bookkeeping to the very chambers of the French National Assembly in Guinea. Here, he observed Salim from a distance, a tempest whose voice thundered louder than the waves of imperialism. Salim was paradoxical in nature. Born out of the ferment of a people whose forebears had been pulverized by the shortcomings of their own leaders, he carried the historical burden but would not bow. He cursed the colonial greed and spat at their empty titles-they paraded before him *as mayor of Conakry, deputy to the Assembly*, and the likes, but his fire was unquenchable. Where was the unity? He dreamed of it: French West Africa must arise as one. With The Gardener, a mysterious figure, this was the dynamics of their two-man revolution thereafter, the French capitalized on their skills by planting a trap dressed in gold.

One night, the diplomat spoke to him informally: "We can't stop you from running... but we can make sure you lose." The room stank of champagne and lies. Salim clenched his jaw; his eyes could kill, but he swallowed his pride and nodded, "I'll do anything you want." He gritted out. And yes indeed, they won, 56 seats out of 60, an absolute landslide that cracked the colonial mask wide open. But it tasted rust. The price? Well, compromises that fermented in his soul like rot. In the end, he and The Gardener were sitting on thrones of ash bound together by two-legged secrets and backroom wars that both of them would rather conceal. Their children would inherit splintered legacies, and the ghosts of choices soaked in blood and betrayal.

As for Wadu, He had walked once like a king, he clung now to three puny seats like a starving man clutching breadcrumbs. He refused to kneel, and this was his reward. The French had transformed politics into a cage, but Salim's win converted this cage into a stage, a revolution in disguise. Beneath the triumph, decay had set in. The three brothers, Yaryb, Wadu, Laysouf, were splintered. Yaryb and Wadu turned against each other in sheer, ruthless ambition and scavenging for power as jackals would over carrion. The French sat and smirked, watching brothers eating brothers. Even their puppet, Salim, was wearing teeth that they could no longer pull out.

But then came Laysouf, the storm nobody saw coming. The brothers roared, mocking laughter, *The idealist! The fool who picked a peasant over family!"* they jeered but Laysouf wore their ridicule as armor. He was no politician; he was a shepherd. His people, the Fula of Fouta Djallon, as austere as their primitive highlands, stood with him not for fear, but for faith. Their hearts beat for forty percent of Guinea, and Laysouf converted those heartbeats into a cry for battle. Let his brothers fight for power; he would fight on the soil, in the streets, and in the quiet rage of those who had truly had enough.

The French had really not thought about that. They had their minds on greed, on pride, on their tired old scripts of division. But Laysouf? He did not play their games. He attended to his flock. And flocks, when harassed, become armies.

"They have divided us for generations," Laysouf shouted, loud and clear. *"But today we must choose to unite; not for power, nor for glory, but rather for the dignity stolen from us."* The voices of the Fula people roared in unison, their chants reverberating through the red soil. Yet an undertone of distrust prevailed even in that moment of unity. From the sidelines, faces of the elders gained a deeper scowl. *"You back Salim! This loudmouth, this agitator?"* spat one. *"You would trade your own kinsmen's honor for some fanciful idea of his?"*

Actions spoke louder for Laysouf's response: Setting the door open for the freshly forged DPG's cabinet in the depth of Fouta Djallon was a light of grassroots resistance. The pamphlets promised autonomy while underground meetings buzzed with plans to destroy the suzerainty of French puppetry. But every attempt at a step progressed with the land cracking with every footstep beneath him. The same people began turning against him and calling him a turncoat and a fool, siding with these fiery Salim ideals. Not even with praise for his father's name, the revered canton chief could he be saved from the scorn.

Meanwhile, in Conakry, Salim roamed the corridors of power with a rather bitter satisfaction. For though the French had been put on their heels, they still refused to concede. These "conditions" heralding his easy rise to power were being codified into laws now: economic strangulation;

military "advisors" breaching their way sarcastically into his government; and near constant reminders of the knife between his shoulder blades. Yet, the defiant grin of Salim captured the moment, eyes sparkling as a man already claiming victory. *"Let them think they control me,"* he whispered to Laysouf under the foyers of a moonlight canopy. *"We're using their own weapons to bury them."*

Yet the referendum loomed, 1958, the year Guinea would choose: shackle itself to France or leap into the unknown void of freedom. In a panic, the French unleashed their poison. The villages were flooded with propaganda: *"Independence means famine. Independence means economic strangulation."* The elders joined in the campaign against Laysouf, labeling him a silly man who was taking his people to destruction.
Underlying beneath was now a growing resistance. His underground became a network of whispers smuggling truth into the nation's veins. Farmers, merchants, even poets from all corners and camps muttered the same word: *"Enough."* Some of Wadu's own supporters slipped away, heavy at heart by the sight of his defeat.

Laysouf stood a sea of faces in Labe, the very throbbing heart of Fouta Djallon. Torches flickered like some stubborn stars in the dark. "They say that we are not ready," he roared. "They say that we need them to survive. But when have they ever let us be ready? Freedom is never given; instead, it is taken away by the courage of those who have the guts to spill blood for it!" The crowd exploded, a wave of hope and anger swept into the night. The dawn began to creep, and Guinea began to hold its breath. The French had clenched their fists, while Salim kept his words sharpened. And Laysouf silently prayed to those bones of his ancestors. Whatever was to come now, these lines were drawn. This was no longer a fight against empires. This had become a fight for the soul of a nation. And the storm? It was just beginning.

Two years had passed since Salim became mayor of Conakry, but he still felt trapped under the shadows of his masters. Time has come to put in motion a scheme that would sever the connection with their masters. Masters, led by general Charles de Gaulle, a man of iron will and shadowy power, that loomed over every choice he made, pulling strings Salim desperately wanted to cut. To break free, he'd need to take a risk, one that dragged him into Guinea's remote backcountry, where logic twisted and whispers of black magic lingered. This wasn't a normal project. It demanded knowledge that didn't belong in the clean, bright halls of government. So, under cover of darkness, Salim and his most loyal ally, Guivo Liyana, crept into the wild toward his hometown. Their goal? The hideout of Salimny Guarana, a wizard whose name inspired equal parts awe and fear.

He was recommended by Dembay Silas, the wizard's disciple, a man with eyes sharpened by raw ambition, he guided them, marching across bleak, wind-scoured moors until they reached a shack that looked like it'd been slapped together by nightmares. Leaning timbers, jagged stones, a roof slumped like a beaten dog. There's no symmetry or grace in its construction, as if the old man deliberately sought to defy conventional architectural principles. The land itself seemed to reject it, the structure remaining to decay alone in the void, and the outside was nothing compared to the inside. It stank of burnt herbs, rancid potions, and something metallic, like old blood. Shelves were sagging with ancient grimoires whose pages were covered in symbols that appeared to squirm when examined closely. Cobwebs clung to jars filled with unidentifiable sludge, and dust floated in thin beams of light, as if the sun didn't dare stay long. Salim's chest tightened. This wasn't a safe haven; it was a pit where desperate people traded pieces of their souls for power. Dembay's voice cut the quiet, cold and smooth. "He's waiting," he said, nodding from a shadowy corner. There, bent over a cauldron of glowing muck, sat the wizard. His twisted fingers stirred the brew, and Salim couldn't help but wonder if the man's very existence had warped the house into this monstrous shape, a reflection of his dark craft. Guivo's hand brushed his knife. Salim swallowed hard. This is what it costs, he thought. To escape Charles's grip, he'd have to bargain with something worse, a creature of rot and spells, festering in this ruin. The wizard turned, his grin splitting his face like cracked wood. Salim stepped forward. The deal would be struck here, in a place where ambition and ruin met, where power hid in the shadows, in the hands of an old creepy man.

The old man cast a figure shrouded in gloom, a bunch of grayish curls blossoming all over his head with short, coarse hair, his show or visage oftentimes clothed in soiled, wayward robes hanging loosely around him. But there was an air of calm, authoritative stillness in his presence which demanded respect. Many souls testified to the powers of this warlock; a magnificent skill lay deep within him, packed with disturbing arcane knowledge. His long-tortured intuition shot through the ordinary world to the whispers of the unseen, such flickers at the very edge of reality blurring between tangibility and spectrality. Charms and potions, his arsenal of magic, carefully etched secretly into the memory of the mind. Most convinced that such piercing intellect was corrupt due to a rigid moral code and by an unswerving belief in the redemptive force for love and friendship. But he is by no means a saint. Critics termed him as divisive; a man whose past mistakes and quite stubbornly refusing to learn from them advanced beyond mere mistakes.

Now he stands accused of guiding a nation into ruin by hypocrisy and self-serving motives. His secret dealings, his flawed choices, and many other things were leveling further complications into his character, shaping its fortunes that would seal the nation's fate. Once a shining beacon of the light against all the darkness besetting the wizarding world, Salimny now stood over the infamous edge-the last shreds of his reputation as leader and sage crumbling fast. A single, pitiful choice gave birth to what many termed his most terrible offspring. In the dim confines of his small cabin, the master sat on a worn-out mat with a chaplet hanging idle on his lap.

Salim now entered with his lieutenant, Guivo Liyana, and they both settled after exchanging stiff formalities. Salim then revealed his ambition without beating around the bush. He demanded power as part of his birthright, including his role in single-handedly standing up to the colonial European empire. "The whites are on the verge of leaving our country for good," he said, chin lifted. "So, namesake, I seek your help to steer this nation. You know as well as I, we must unite our people against outsiders, against these Fulanis. This country is ours by blood. So, I will kick them out and I will govern." His words were suffused with the cadence of a griot's fervent practiced tales. Guivo looks at him, confused about the Fulanis' remark, knowing that he was just with a Fulani prior to this adventure, and he will be with another one after the ritual. He stares at him for a moment, then lowers his gaze without a word. The old man let the silence ooze before he raised his head. "Anything more?" he murmured, a thread of unease in his tone.

"Everything?" There was an edge of impatience in Salim's retorts. "We need you to help us attain victory. Our foes have assembled, and all would be blown away if they take over." The old sheikh dropped a brief head bow before turning himself eastward on his mat, legs crossed. With one sweeping motion, he lifted his hands and spread them outward. Suddenly, the wall of the cabin undulated to reveal a setting, nagged by some warped shifting panorama, which made the visitors recoil. Indistinct but viscerally repulsive images moved in the development. "This is what will happen," the holy man said softly. The two men bent ahead, looking through the nightmare which was spreading before them, their faces taut with confusion and fear.

The truth engulfed them like that of a failed dream wandering away from whose lurking meaning all the way through, after which ironically it turned into a road where what was physical met with apparitional. They drifted through a succession of unfixed shadows and grille-piercing light, with every footfall being a whisper of secrets greater than empires, with the very air throbbed with prophecies scraping the shell of the mundane. Here, on this blink of existence, in this threshold between worlds, the would-be king was not a mortal claimant, but a living omen whose fate had been scrawled in riddles that mocked logic. Around them, Guinea, ancient, stubborn, unbroken-perhaps was pausing, balanced on the precipice of an eruption that would shatter the basis of their existence. Reality, which once stood resolute, was now trembling like a disturbed pool of water, threatening to suck them into truths too enormous, too horrendous to ever comprehend.

The prophecy unraveled like a serpent stirring from sleep, sinuous, entrancing, and deadly. It spoke of realms forging upon each other, worlds crashing together until the earth drank blood and the skies choked on ash. Salim stood paralyzed, ravished with ferocity glistening in his eyes as the vision wielded him: a river, raging and red, its howls in the grief of a nation not yet hewed from chaos. The marabout's voice quaked with darkness. *"This* is your crown," he intoned with each word as a funeral dirge. "The whites will depart, but you will drag us all down. A curse of violence will sit upon your brow, your hands will be filled with suffering, and death will set its name at your heels like a beggar's curse."

"Okay!" Salim casually concurred: a sharp-edged word, his smile; all teeth with no shade of hesitation. That vision glared behind him somewhere smoke began coiling into wraiths, violently insulting the furious river on behalf of the screams of the lost. Guivo stumbled back, shock overtaking him. *Madness*, he thought. Or *damnation*. But Salim burned hotter with certainty: a fire stoked by vanity and delusion.

The ritual clawed up, and the marabout's knotted and trembling palms were thrust against Salim's skin as if to purge a sickness nestled in his bones. The chanting curled around the room, syllables older than temples, with a taste of metal and scorched moldering on the tongue. The last note exhausted the old man, the sorrow filling him in an emptying power. "You crave no blessing," his voice croaking, unraveling. "By the hour your bloody reign dawns... I'll be bones. Sparing myself the spectacle of my people's end." And as he predicted the following year, all was silent in the marabout's grave.

Guinea tried to snatch freedom, with Salim's shadow swallowing the horizon. Yet a thread of fear squirmed beneath his bravado: what if the prophecy wasn't a warning, but a reflection? Time would tell, this was, after all, an era in which impossibility bled into common sense.

However, Salim couldn't shake the gnawing unease in his chest. Sorcery's whispers, promises of power, he turned from them all for now. Pride hardened his resolve, but he knew better than to let it curdle into arrogance. That very night, after slipping away from the old sage's shadowed hut, he rode for the capital. There waited Wadu, the nemesis who haunted his thoughts.

Wadu could be considered perhaps too tuff in standing up for what is right with far too much integrity to enter politics. Nevertheless, he was a man of deep-rooted patriotism, with regard for willingness to sacrifice his honor, a man whom others respected. He looked ill-fit to thrive in such a system. It was just a few days before the referendum, and Salim made a secret entrance into Wadu's residence. Though he was too proud to be seen in the company of his sworn enemy, this meeting was one of absolute importance.

After the sun had set late that afternoon, long shadows of gold sank across the stately front yard as Salim made his approach. The deep grey walls of the structure were bedecked in dark green ivy, dominating the landscape around it; its gardens were magnificent and exhibited untold wealth and a great sense of tradition, an air too removed to approach. The pedestrian stone path leading to the front door was shaded by tall hedges, which were manicured to perfection, a contrast to the amber glow cast by the setting sun. Salim stepped heavily, with breath in his chest, foot putting one down slow for the other, as if each step was laden with the anguish of his own resolve. He hovered for what must have been a few seconds at the fated entrance: the light of the sun faded from his sight as the polished brass knocker met with decaying brawn. Its clang seemed to solemnly boom away in his chest and out of his mouth.

The oak door he had now knocked on creaked open to reveal a butler donned in formalwear looking like a penguin, tall in stature, with a straight back and even more professional demeanor. For that briefest moment, curiosity had stolen across the man's face, while to Salim it seemed like it had betrayed all but professionalism.

"Mr. Wadu is expecting you," said the leery butler, stepping aside and letting Salim in. His voice was smooth and cultured, a hint of the world into which Salim was about to step foot in.

The faint smell of leather and old books filled the air inside. Starkly lined hallway portraits of stern-looking ancestors seemed to oppose Salim's way toward the study, watching from above. The walls were nicely covered with mahogany and an assortment of antique furniture, which was a reminder of days gone by; days when elegance and decorum meant the world.

The butler led Salim properly into the study; murmured conversation and clinking of a glass could be heard from within. Once the door swung wide open, Salim was then met by Wadu seated behind his desk, sleek hair shining beneath later rays of sunlight penetrating the windows looking down on him. He cut a mustering presence commanding respect and that mingled with great wisdom that felt almost tangible.

Wadu looked away from his paperwork, his eyes narrowing with surprise. "Salim," he said, his voice warm but laced with the gravity of their shared history. "What brings you here?"

Salim stepped forward, his voice faltering slightly as he struggled to find the right words. He swallowed hard, trying to steady his nerves. "Wadu, I," he began, but his voice betrayed him, cracking under the strain of his emotions as he looked at the gentlemen sitting on the sofa. Wadu waves at the elderly man to give him a moment which he agreed to and left in instant. Salim took a deep breath, his gaze locking onto Wadu's. "We need your help. The Guinean people need your help."

"What do you mean?" Wadu asked confusedly.

"The fate of Guinea is in your hands. It all depends on you, whatever you decide now will determine the future of our beloved country." Said Salim with a sign of urgency in his voice.

The room seemed to hold its breath, the opulent surroundings bearing silent witness to Salim's plea. Wadu studied him for a moment, trying to see if this is a serious request, his expression unreadable.

Then, with a slow nod, he proceeded, "If it depends on me, Guinea will achieve independence without bloodshed. We will all unite, say no, and choose independence peacefully. That is what I wish for, for my country, our beloved country," Wadu replied. However, these were times when corridors have colonial powers' ears because it did not take long for the French authorities to pay Wadu a visit. It was not about the French pride anymore; their patriarchal figure will dissipate before they realize it if these band of simpletons were left unchecked. They approached Wadu as this heavy sense of looming treachery permeated the air, its acrid bite lingering at the base of Wadu's throat like a poison he could not swallow. The visitors' offer, cloaked in the silken lies of *aid* and *alliance*, felt like a blade pressed to the spine of his nation. France's shadow loomed still, in the heart of a land straining to breathe free. Some paratroopers, traitorous sons of Guinea who clung to colonial epaulets like lifelines, were a festering wound in his mind. *How easily they kneel,* he thought, *for crumbs from a table they once built.*

"I gave my word to Salim," Wadu said, his voice low but trembling with the weight of centuries. The words were not merely spoken; they were unearthed from the marrow of his bones. "Guinea will *not* be a puppet, its strings tugged by hands that still reek of empire." His gaze swept over the men before him, their polished boots, their practiced neutrality, and he saw the ghost of France grinning behind their eyes. "Independence is not a *compromise*. It is a birthright."

A murmur rippled through the condescending room; one visitor leaned forward, lips curling into a smirk that dripped false pity. "Regret," he warned, "is a cruel teacher. You will learn it soon enough." Wadu's forehead vein popped out as he clenched his fists, knuckles whitening as if crushing the specter of subjugation itself. The anguish of his people echoed relentlessly in his mind, farmers stripped of their crops, mothers clutching children with hollow-eyed hunger, the fading heartbeat of his people's traditions crushed under foreign boots. "Our land," he hissed through gritted teeth, voice sharp and searing as a blade pulled from fire, "is not a *bargain*." Our future is not on your chessboard." His voice suddenly crescendoed, raw and thunderous, "We will *burn* your shadows. We will carve our name into the sky, *free*, or not at all!"

"And you will. Oh yes, you will." Snapped the French envoy, a serpentine calm in his tone. "In time."

"Time?" Wadu's laugh was a whipcrack. He wheeled toward a young Guinean officer lingering in the corner, Bakary Daff, a man with his nation's face but a colonizer's heart. "You," he spat, finger jabbing like a dagger. "Does your uniform feed your pride while your people starve? Where is your honor? Your *soul?*" The room froze. The officer's eyes flickered, a fracture in his facade, before he spun on his heel, boots slamming against the floor like gunshots. "Run!" Wadu roared at him, the fury in his voice scalding. "Because that's all you can do. Let me ask you this, when your children ask what role you played in the history of this nation, will you lie? Will you claim you *fought*, or admit you chickened out when you were needed the most?" The officer halted, shoulders rigid. For a heartbeat, the world seemed to hold its breath. Wadu's stare bore

into him, unyielding as the earth beneath their feet. "Yes," he whispered, cold and final. "Remember this shame. Let it haunt you." Silence swallowed the room.

Outside, the wind carried the distant hum of a nation stirring, awake, alive, aflame. Wadu turned back to the envoys, his silhouette a jagged cut against the fading light. France's puppets could scheme, could threaten, could whisper of regret. But the fire they feared? It was already lit.

Chapter 4

The affront

General Charles, an oxymoron in the flesh in the second postwar France, a man celebrated for rallying resistance against Hitler's advance now paced palace corridors with the restless energy of a predator, his legacy fraying at the edges. Although history books sanctify him as the "Liberator," his sunken eyes-ringed with bruises of sleeplessness, betray a scheming mind beyond Europe's borders. He stood unnervingly tall yet hunched, as if his spine had bent under the ghosts of promises broken. His scanty hair was slicked backward with grease, which made him look duller than he would have otherwise been observed to be. His nose swollen with age and indulgence, jutted from his face like a misplaced monument. The jawline bristled with stubble, a calculated dishevelment disguising the precision of his ambitions.

Charles rarely smiled. Whenever he spoke, behind thin lips, yellowish and dingy teeth seemed to hide, as if he was hoarding his words like one would hoard currency. His uniform strained upon a barrel chest with knuckles perpetually whitened, his hands were curling as if to choke already on the reigns of yet heavenly claim lands. To admirers, he remained the indomitable architect of France's rebirth, a titan whose grit had resurrected national pride. But in the dim glow of his private study, maps of Algeria and Senegal unfurled on a wall, revealing a darker blueprint: debts disguised as aid, resources siphoned under treaties, battalions rebranded as *"advisors."*

The myth of the war hero had curdled into something sharper, hungrier. Where speeches once crackled with defiance against fascism, they now dripped with paternalistic venom about "civilizing missions." His biographers wrote of a patriot; his aides whispered of a man who'd traded jackboots for pinstripes but kept the same ledger of extraction. The colonies, he'd decided, would repay France in blood and ore, this time not as conquest, but as "partnership." History would call it neocolonialism. Charles called it destiny.

When Nazi tanks in 1940 rolled across the borders of France to crush defense in mere weeks and thereby force surrender under the shadow of the Eiffel Tower, the spirit of France cracked. But through the static of clandestine radios came a voice sharp as a bayonet: "France has lost a battle, but not the war." Thus, General Charles, in exile but unbowed, weaponized the airwaves. His broadcasts pulsed with defiance and binded together disparate resistance cells into the Free French Forces a disheveled army of patriots, intellectuals, and farmers-turned-saboteurs. Charles understood symbolism as a strategy. By tearing up the humiliating 1940 armistice, he turned documents of surrender into tinder for rebellion. His infamous speech from London that June didn't just rally troops; it reanimated a collective identity.

"Vive la France, libre dans l'honneur et l'Independence."

Young recruits marched into minefields chanting his words, while occupied villages painted his motto on crumbling walls. Critics called him stubborn; allies called him reckless, but as Nazi flags burned in liberated towns, even skeptics tasted the iron of his resolve.

Victory in 1945 was not a time for Charles to celebrate but rather rebuild. He moved among the splintered political landscape with the same intensity he had at battlefield maps, purging collaborators while drafting constitutional reforms. To him, democracy was a living infrastructure and not a statue restored, schools replacing trenches, labor rights etched into law. Abroad, he leveraged wartime alliances into diplomatic currency, securing France's seat among global powers through sheer force of will.

The general made himself be remembered as both architect and paradox: a man who preached liberty while centralizing power, who denounced empires yet clung to colonial influence. But in those early postwar years, as bakeries reopened using flour instead of sawdust and children relearned laughter instead of cry, even his detractors whispered that France's heartbeat synced with Charles's own. It wasn't a surprise that he wasted no time to turn his gaze towards West Africa.

The atmosphere was pregnant with the pungent smell of inflated unrest, General Charles, like a child refusing to part with an old worn-out blanket, clung to his delusion. He pictured himself, crisscrossing through the fevered landscapes of West African cities simmering, villages humming around with dissent, an unshakable patriarch of a continent whom he refused to see slipping through his fingers. *"They will be begging for my return once the dust settles,"* he told himself, boots crunching over parched earth, as though the very soil owed him one. His referendum tour was reduced to a garish show-all, empty gestures and contrived outrage. podiums erected in town squares where crowds gathered not to cheer, but to glare. The "YES" he barked into microphones echoed back hollow, swallowed by the hungry silence of a people biding their time.

While the operations were being performed by Salim's henchmen under the shadow of Conakry's alleyways, their laughter was ominously soft and underlined by the thrill of pursuit. The General's impudent empire was decaying from within, now to be its heart cut out by these men. The unwinding started in Dakar. There was no trumpeting announcement; no fluttering flags, just a skeletal framework of a government office where a tired secretary named Ndiaye handed Charles a lukewarm cup of coffee while avoiding eye contact. The Empty chair where the president should have been was louder than any insult. Ghoren, the golden envoy of France in Teranga, had fled, his mansion plundered as vengeance. The people found his discarded desk littered with shredded papers with the faintest scent of his former cologne still lingering in the air amidst the banners reading, "INDEPENDENCE OR DEATH" in blood red paint. These once subdued people were now sharpening their anger as if it were a weapon. Charles's referendum was a lethal poison chalice. To vote "YES" was to dissolve all boundaries and have the colonies sucked into France's gaping mouth as the final humiliating erasure; to say "NO" was to wrench the chains loose. Across village squares and port cities, the elders whispered of ancestors who danced under other stars, free. Mothers inked thumbs kissed ballots as signing unspoken covenants with the unborn. The referendum was more than mere politics; this was judgment. To say "YES" would be a kneeling act, an acceptance of others calling them goats led to the slaughter. Their fragile pride would fiercely resist the very thought.

Meanwhile, Salim sat slumping in a creaking chair in a dimly lit office in

Conakry, white boubou flowing around him like molten ivory. Paperwork was scattered across his desk, an actual labyrinth of laws and loopholes. He wasn't a bureaucrat, nor a slick diplomat. He was a soldier of shadows, trembling as he wrote manifestos with his pen. Around him were rows of men in identical robes, their faces low lit by a lone bulb. *How much was sovereignty worth?* The answer filled their bones and echoed through their marrow, *Everything.* Outside, the wind spoke the scent of rain or perhaps ashes.

Charles, ever the imperial comet, finally blazed toward Conakry, unaware that Salim and his acolytes' trap yawned wide. The ground beneath him had already turned to quicksand. In contrast to the show of control displayed by the new and emerging wielders of power, the small, austere office desk had a certain cleanliness, almost an austere orderliness. Papers were arranged with military precision, a glistening carpet of documents that held the promise of power. It was an epitome of preparedness, a place where those new to this life of politics would stage their competence; to prove they were worthy of the mantle hovering just beyond their grasp. Salim's fingers grazed over the surface of the desk nervously. His eyes seemed to be lost somewhere, dragged down by the weight of the moment. He knew this speech, this moment, sounded important. A fear settled into his chest, viscous with dread, wrapping around him in an unyielding grip.

There was something worse than stage fright now, a fear that spoke of worrying for the people he was meant to lead and failing them. His heart hung on this gossamer thread, and life would punish any false step as indifferent as that. He turned his head and looked over at The Gardener, the quiet man whose shadowy influence had shaped their plans and the one who had in his mind convinced him that they could do this.

"What should we say before the general?" His voice barely made it beyond a whisper, the uncertainty in it thinly veiled. The Gardener was leaning against the desk and wore an expression of practiced indifference. Salim met his gaze with a cool smirk. *"What would you want to say?"* His words were sharp, almost mocking, and a dark edge lingered in his voice, like he was already sick of this question, of this moment. Salim felt his stomach churn. He could feel the sweat on the back of his neck, the prickling of nerves that were quickly turning into something more, something like panic. What if I fail them? The thought circled in his mind, growing louder with each passing second. His fidgeting only worsened. He couldn't afford to disappoint his people, not now, not when they were so close to a future that would demand everything from them. He knew that voice; the Gardener's voice spoken low but firm-recalled all too clearly the faith put on Salim, faith he was unsure at this moment of being able to live up to. "Relax, my friend," he said, strangely soothing but with an underlying force. *"I picked you for a reason."* But Salim's unease did not ease. His heart was still pounding, still unsure. "You should be the speaker today," he muttered, almost pleading. There was something in his voice, fear, yes, but also a flicker of surrender, of hoping someone else would take the weight off his shoulders. The Gardener's lips curved upward into a small, knowing smile, his eyes glinting with a mix of calculation and confidence. *"You know our agreement. We find ideas, and you bring them to life. I don't do public talks."* Salim's eyes dropped to the papers in front of him, his fingers playing with the edges as though he could steady his racing thoughts. "I'm just nervous," he admitted, his voice cracking slightly.

The Gardener relented a fraction in his smirk, though the sharpness hadn't left his words. "Well, you'd be a fool not to. But just relax. We're almost there." He widened his knees slightly, half perching on the edge of the desk, looking over Salim's shoulder with the practiced air of someone who had already won the battle before it had begun.

"Now," The Gardener commanded, "let's see this speech." As he reached for it, Salim reluctantly passed it over to him. The crumpled paper felt more like an anchor in his shaky hands.

The Gardener scanned the document rapidly, frowning. He halted midway through the speech, looking suddenly irritated. "Where is it?"

Salim blinked, perplexed. "Where's what?"

"You didn't put it in the speech," The Gardener said, his tone even but with a clear growing impatience. "We have to ask for independence. That's the whole reason for this speech."

Salim's heart sank. The word *independence* weighed in the air like a spell, like a sucker dream. He let escape a comment he hadn't meant to say, "Are you insane?" he exclaimed, his voice rising with panic. "He won't allow us to read that before the people."

The Gardener's smirk widened, a trace of twisted amusement in his eyes. "We won't be giving him the option."

Salim went stiff. Horror creeping up his spine. "He'll review the speech; in case you've forgotten, they always do." He wounded himself with this faint attempt to cling to any solid sound aspect of reality.

"He won't be doing it." This was said by The Gardener with startling firmness. His smirk widened, for the calmness in his voice was now genuinely unsettling. "We will see to it."

Salim's breath stuck in his throat. Just the thought of opposing the general, opposing the very man they had all been humiliated into bowing to, made him tremble. "Pray tell," he said, voice taut with fear. "We're walking a fine line here. Remember the slightest thing you did that sent you to Niger!"

The Gardener's eyes gleamed, cold and calculating. He leaned in just slightly; the weight of his years spent in the shadows of power heavy in the way he moved. "Relax," he said, as if it were that simple. "Having them hover around me like flies has taught me a thing or two. So, trust me on this one, everything will go according to plan." The command was cool and confident, but underneath, Salim felt the quiver of doubt pinching at his gut.

"What about your brothers?" Salim's tone was shaky, desperately wanting reassurance. "Are they in on this?"

The Gardener smiled preposterously slowly. "Well, they're going to have to be. And they'd be fools not to." Then he paused, letting the weight of that remark sink in for a bit before adding, "If it makes you feel better, I'll do the opening."

Salim breathed again, his shoulders falling in relief. For the first time in what felt like an eternity, he allowed himself to give a small, grateful smile. "Thank you for that, my friend." Said Salim.

"You got it."

The Gardener was a man of few words, but the few words he spoke were chosen with care. He would never say anything without intention and would never act without considering the outcome. Manipulation was his art; he was a strategist in a world that allowed no errors. His mind would always be five moves ahead of anybody else, always observing, planning. And he knew the game they were playing.

As a colonial rule, masters have always reviewed the speeches of their subjects before they were transmitted to the public. The speeches were never meant to be anything more than a formality, words meant to placate, to make the people think they had a say, to let them prattle on without ever truly threatening the power structure. But the Gardener knew better. For he knew that to fight the enemy, they must make sure first that people believe in a common enemy. And this had to be something done in an entirely different tone: a speech which said exactly what the masters never wanted to hear: *independence.*

The land had been torn apart for centuries, leaving the seeds of tribalism in the very souls of the people. With the passage of time, the Gardener, a Fulani, and Salim, a Mandinka, understood that unity was not going to be easily achieved. To gird their fragmented nation, they required the awakening of their people to cross that chasm not just to survive but attain freedom from the colonizers.

After Salim's visit to Wadu and Yaryb, the Gardener, for once, swallowed his pride. He approached and persuaded two of the sharpest Foutans in the educated elite, to join the struggle with him. Together, they would stand, together, they would resist. All had known it, but now the hour had come to say it out loud: Independence was the only wonder working advent of all time. The Gardener wanted the declaration spoken publicly; it would be woven into his speech, given before General Charles was to take the stage.

Salim, looking down at the draft, his heart pounding, felt history shudder in his hands. Whether he would be there to see it was another matter. The speech was written, gone through revisions and finally handed to Charles for approval, supposedly running the usual tired script of changes, edits, and politics too old to entertain; yet that old script would... well, it was a ritual about to die. The Gardener had calmed and planned the fall; it was surgical. The carnival, the parade through the street were meant to keep the general distracted from reality. The celebration was awash with distractions: voices chanting from the crowd, flags fluttering, and banners proclaiming the same old slogan, *"Vive la France!"*, meant to cheer colonial pride. An army of fervent subjects had besieged Charles, praising him in a manner that threw him back in oblivion. Every shout, every scrap of ribbon given, was paid for by precious time.

The Gardener hadn't gone to all this trouble without a purpose. He'd convinced the general that the referendum vote for a *yes* was *a fait accompli*, a rubber stamp on a decision already sealed. The speech meant to reshape the nation's destiny, a fiery demand for independence, had been meticulously kept beyond the general's reach. It wasn't the cautious, calculated address the general would have sanctioned. No, this was different: a declaration, raw and unyielding, meant to shake the world. By the time the general uncovered the truth, it was over. The warning came too late. When he finally stared at the unauthorized words, they hit him like a physical blow. His mind rebelled against the words at first. He read them again and again, his face a mask of shock and disbelief. For the first time in his iron-fisted reign over West Africa, General Charles was speechless. So, underneath it all, the control, which he'd only thought was unbreakable, the power he used to clutch almost like a lifeline, was crumbling right then and there, the reality coiled itself cold and nauseating inside him.

Then the Gardener performed the unbelievable feat that no one anticipated; the shadowy strategist, ghost-like pulling all strings unseen, steps into the glaring open lights of the public eye. This part made all the time freeze the moment his foot stepped onto that podium before it all. A prickling sense unease quickened across skins of the general and his inner circle. They knew: The rules had shattered. Their reign was finishing. That man they had underestimated as a pawn, now stood before them. A kingmaker poised for rewriting history. The Gardener smiled, waving to the roaring crowd, his confidence as thick as the sweltering air. It was the grin of a man who'd felt the scales tip, who'd already claimed victory. He didn't glance at the general or his cronies, didn't bow to their hollow titles. Instead, he simply said.

"You come with a lot of hope, but what you are going to hear today, comes from officials just transmitting the people's will."

With no remorse and let the sentence sink in for a moment, then a round of applause and chatter reverberated in the crowded place.

Then he stopped, locking eyes with the crowd, the very people who would bear the weight of this reckoning. His voice sliced through the square's thick silence, a quiet so absolute the hum of distant flies buzzed like alarms. The audience listened keenly, hanging on each syllable.

"Brothers and sisters…" he began. Stone steady, he continued, "The time has come that the truth must be told." A calculated pause let the words sink like anchors. The crowd, reeling from fate's sudden swerve, held its breath. "We no longer bow to those who landed here as conquerors. We no longer kneel to those who call themselves our masters."

For the first time, General Charles felt the acid bite of helplessness. The Gardener's words weren't mere rebellion, they were war, a gutting of the authority he'd thought eternal. The general's face whitened; his trademark arrogance cracked as he stared at the man who'd been a ghost until now.

The Gardener's speech was short but packed with rage of hundreds of years, the fury of a people ever ready to strike. It was no mere plea for independence, but a challenge thrown at those colonizers who had sucked it out of them. A current rushed through the crowd, wild and crackling, a storm in the very nick of time. Stepping aside, The Gardener made way for Salim to take center stage. This was his turn. His time to blow the glowing embers even hotter. Yet as he spoke, the undeniable truth burned in the air: The Gardener had done the impossible. The general, the puppet master of their suffering, had lost his very handhold.

Charles and company stood petrified and crushed under an avalanche of their own making. This was the reckoning of which they had been afraid. They had silenced their people for too long, and now, with The Gardener's shadow growing, the people had risen, aware that the old world was done for. The silent pause after The Gardener's last words was as loud as any cheer.

The ground shook under their feet. There was no going back, hourglass empty. It was no longer something to be politely requested. The General, standing stiff with his hands behind his back, clawed at the wreckage of his shattered control. This was a humiliation in flesh and blood: these were his subjects, whom he had ruled with casual brutality, and they had outmaneuvered him. Power had been his crown, his scepter, his god. Now it was leaking from his hands like ash, and the very emptiness choked him.

What pierced his heart and knotted his stomach with disbelief was Wadu and Yaryb standing alongside Salim. He would have expected it from The Gardener, that shady irritant had always been a menace, but Wadu and Yaryb? Never. Salim's sworn enemies! They were the polished scions of privilege, the young elite who had jeered at his idealism for years. Yet here they stood as defiant allies in this uprising.

The General's lips twitched faintly as the unfolding truth stabbed him. He'd misjudged them. He'd assumed his threats, power, and hollow promises would have them leashed. But he'd given them *oxygen*. Let them breathe in delusion of choice, and it had turned him toxic. Their defiance was now a dagger in his ribs. The truth struck him hard: he could have crushed them. Cantered in the constitution by force, as his predecessors had done over centuries. They were not the Viet Minh; they lacked the grit to defy his strong empire. One lie from him could have broken their spines. Now, that chance had slipped away from him.

The people woke up. His chains did not matter anymore. They had tasted the fire of rebellion and wanted to feel its burn. Now their blood was truly redder than his. Their right to freedom is an unassailable one. That was when the General realized: the tide was set to drown him. Movement fluttered on the edge of his vision. His head jerked toward Salim, rising with a calm that felt like a slap. Salim stood, white robes on full display against the dull podium; a white handkerchief held tightly in his fingers as a banner of pride. His breathing hitched, but it was not that of fear. No. Something hotter coursed through him now: molten, unyielding resolve. For a moment, one heartbeat, one pulse, Salim hesitated, scanning the crowd. His heart hammered, but the deep roar surrounding him of shouts, chants, hope was drowning the ticking of time inside-in-doubt. Pride rose deep and sharp, sweet at the core. This was it. The *moment*, the very one he "bled" for. He was no longer a mere dreamer; he had become the closed fist of the people.

The crowd erupted; the sea voice of the people birded by engorged wings of his spirit. They saw themselves in him a man among them, not above. He was the voice of their heartbeat. He had just handed them back their stolen treasure: the right to dream.

Salim gripped the microphone. Just as his fingertips brushed the cold metal, the world stopped its breath. The General glared, numb, unable to avert his stare. Within minutes, blood had seeped from his grasp. With all might right, power was stolen from him. It was gone; all of it.

Chapter 5

The infamous quote

S alim stood like a caged bird staring at the iron bars. A bead of sweat on his forehead revealed a storm brewing inside. His hands trembled around the microphone as he tightened his grip to conquer the fear raking his throat. Each breath felt like drowning; each exhalation was muffled by the suffocating weight of fear. The General's glare pressed down like a furious foot crushing a cockroach and crushed to that little resolve he'd managed to scrape together until The Gardener's gaze steadied him, an anchor in the storm.

A silent heartbeat. Then:

"Today," his voice cracked through the air, "today!" He scanned, "Today." He looked at the Gardener, who nodded. "Today, we're not here to ask for permission. We don't beg for approval. Today, we are here to take what's ours, our freedom, our right to stand as equals, not as subjects, not as ghosts in the soil we've watered with blood and sweat." And the stadium froze. Every breath remained unbreathed. He felt the sweltering heat of their stares, the tangled knot of hope and terror on their faces. The air had crackled; it was charged like lightning about to tear into the sky. At that moment, Salim knew it was not his alone. It belonged to the silenced; to those who were never allowed to scream their truth.

"There is no dignity without freedom. We prefer living in poverty with our dignity intact, over living in opulence under slavery," he said proudly. An infamous quote that would resonate beyond borders, without any knowledge about the severity of what he just did.

Salim's voice boomed forth from his lips raw and defiant, as if the ghosts of his ancestors seized his voice. The room erupted not in mere applause, but in a primal roar whose vibrations shook the walls. Tears were mingled with cheers, a tempest of hope and rage that swept through the audience like wildfire. Across the podium, the General got frozen, his ashen face telling the reality: his reign was crumbling, reduced into ashes by a man who dared to visit what had been forbidden.

Salim stood undeterred; his eyes fixed on the sea of faces before him. They were not just an audience; they were a network of spirits, whose breath was now one heartbeat. "The oppressor's hour has ended!" he cried, his voice slicing easily through the din. "Our freedom is no longer a plea; it is a birthright!" Every syllable stoked the crowd further, applause falling like drumbeats until his speech became less a declaration than sacrosanct.

Now when the General stood up to respond. *"Then all you have to do is vote*

No. For I pledge myself that nobody will stand in the way of your independence, "he said with frayed composure. Did he really mean it? The General sat back feeling uncomfortable as if he was sitting on a porcupine, he rose and precipitately went bac to his car, forsaking his *hat* on the table, which became the most symbolic defeat borne by a European leader. Salim started waving his white handkerchief to his people, which became a symbol of what he was. A white flag, symbol of "we come in peace." The cheering continued as he continued waving his handkerchief left and right with a wide smile as if mocking the General. This became what we say in Moliere's language, *"L'éffronté l'a affronté et l'a affronté."*

Salim did not have a road paved with cars, but he was always known to be present with his white handkerchief floating through the window of his car. What's a white handkerchief in one's hand on every occasion if not a mask of civility.

Days passed, Guinea's trite "No" echoed from one end of the world to the other, standing alone as the solitary uprising in the French empire. People filled the streets with euphoria, shouting, *"Vive l'indépendance!"* As if the air itself had caught fire. Salim, now a god for the people in their eyes, towered above the General with pride in emulation of the famed resistance of his forebears to colonization. Neighbors hailed him, nations jealously watched. They regarded him as the person who stood up against a colonial empire and became both a symbol and the father of independence in the region. Yet, in the background of all this happiness, there was room for a dark cloud: France, being embarrassed, could not perhaps retreat with dignity. They could not let him influence others to ask for independence. Although, this was more than just "Influence others." No, it was more than that. It was almost that he felt impregnable to the brutal reality of what was to come.

People were dancing; oblivious to the thought that the hard-won dawn might yet drift into darkness. Freedom was only the first battle; just when you start thinking that France would peace out, like a sensible guest after the party's ended! Nope. Think again! Forget about *Au revoir!* It was more of a *Hold my baguette; I'm moving into your backyard.* France had suddenly become that clingy ex lurking in your Instagram DMs, leaving cryptic messages like "You up?" at 3 a.m.

Even after Guinea ghosted the colonial entire relationship, France kept popping up uninvited, like a bad habit or a telemarketer who just won't take no for an answer. Meddling? They had enough unsolicited advice to fill a bakery and about as much self-awareness as a pigeon at a chess match. Naturally, the Powers That Be called an emergency session of the Problem-Solving Committee for Inconvenient Heroes (motto: "Why liberate when you can obliterate?") What a Herculean task there lay before them! Destabilizing some pesky liberator? Please! That's our expertise. The colonizers have had all the time in the world to perfect destabilization ever since they invented "civilization" a word they themselves defined as "the art of politely stealing continents while sipping tea."

Overcharging taxes on that Tea later and thinking things will go well after that. (if you catch my drift)

Anyway, a dastardly plan must be set into motion for the downfall of the hero, and it was just the easiest.

Let's face it: colonizers, they always knew how to stay one step ahead. Why? You ask. Well, because the subjugated were too busy, you know, *existing*! While the oppressors had mastered the ancient art of *"rules for thee, but not for me."* A Masterclass in Hypocrisy, taught in institutions like

Oxford and Yale, and that *Parisian café where coups would be discussed over a double espresso.*

It all began with the "enlightened" crew deciding to revisit their ancestor's homes, carrying the Holy Trinity of Colonial "Innovation": Bureaucracy, Bibles, and Brutality. They called it "progress." But let's get real: What it was, was systemic dehumanization, with a complimentary twenty percent off genocide upgrade! Their "civilizing mission?" A gleaming PR for an empire so ruthless in its efficiency that it managed to rebrand entire cultures as unpaid interns. "You'll earn peanuts," they chirped, "and think of the resume boost! The exposure!"

For all intents and purposes, if one is to understand it, let us set the stage back in the century in which France set eyes on Africa. The thing is that this time it was not for gold or spices; they wanted human lives, slaves. France became the third-largest shipper of enslaved African during the transatlantic slave trade, capturing 1.3 million people in their homes. Nearly hundreds of thousands of souls lost their lives during the torturous sea crossing, their very potential snuffed out by the unforgiving ocean.

The French wanted an outlet on the African coast as the slave trade flourished. They seized Saint Louis in Senegal in 1659, which will be the hub for their hopes. They would cling to the coastline for the next couple of centuries but with little regard for the vast interior regions. The 19th century, however, changed everything; land hunger and fear of rivals lit a fire under Europe's empires.

Two factors fed the frenzy: First, the continent was turned into a chessboard by Europe's imperial powers scrambling for supremacy. Second, the Gold Coast of Africa whispered promises of unimaginable wealth, gold, oil, anything Europe's factories could ever desire. France took Senegal as a stepping-stone. When General Louis Faidherbe became governor in 1854, he rudely thrust French power into Gambia. But the Parisians felt the pinch for money and stopped his grandiose designs to conquer the Niger Delta and Mali in their tracks. Those blueprints would conveniently lie wintering until the drama's next act arrived in the 1880s.

This was the dawn of the Scramble for Africa. European armies no longer marched clandestinely with precision to carve the continent out, but they now proceeded openly with ruthless determination. Thus, between 1884 and 1885, competition became cooperation of sorts at the infamous Berlin Conference, which would forever seal the fate of an entire continent. The conference was requested by the King of Belgium from the German Chancellor Otto von Bismarck to organize the assembly of European powers intent upon carving Africa into separate pieces, as if it was nothing more than a huge wild plantation to be exploited. The men sitting at this table, representing Europe's great colonial empires, did not view Africa as a land with diverse cultures and histories worthy to contemplate, but rather as a territory rich in resources inhabited by "primitive" peoples, in their minds, being less than, who only had any use insofar as the land's wealth could be extracted from them.

The Berlin Act formalized the plunder: Instead of fighting for what they considered finders-keepers, they would simply divide and share it. At the beginning of the 1880s, 80% of the continent was still under indigenous rulers. By 1900, this number had changed; with 90% of the continent under European domination. Guinea was one of those pieces in the imperialistic chess game.

There might have been ways for the natives to resist; but by the time the colonial powers had begun their conference, the continent was already divided. The nature of these divisions made any such likelihood of resistance almost nil. How does a spear duel a cannon? How does courage manage a worthy shout above the roar of a Gatling gun? The answer came in ash and silence.

The Africans tried as much as they could against these indefinable odds. Across all areas of the continent, small resistance pockets emerged, guerrilla fighters and warriors fought the incursion with what little they had, but their victories were short-lived. Over and over again, the efforts were thrown down by superior firepower of the Europeans. In brutal campaigns suppressing rebellion, thousands went down into unmarked graves, and many more bowed down to their conquerors, surrendering their autonomy, their lands and their dignity to fray like old cloth. Some chose to remain hidden, retreating to the forest or the mountains to avoid the imperial gaze, while others resisted in silence, clinging to what little they had left.

After Europeans have finally entered the interior of Africa, the first wave of intrusion was missionaries who came with their knowledge of "gods", languages, and customs. These missionaries told the indigenous peoples that their ways were inferior; African civilization was a myth, and true enlightenment could only come through the adoption of European ideals. With these doctrines, they spread across the continent teaching a few who would become colonial intermediaries, the puppet rulers who'd wield power upon their own people on behalf of their new masters. These colonial agents were usually so selected for their pliability that they were inculcated with this very difference: they began separating themselves from the masses by way of an ever-deepening assertion that they were superior because they had been chosen by their masters.

The new lords of the country, very methodically, studied their new subjects. They observed everything-from skin color, to body shape, elbowing out from hair texture to facial features and so forth well ahead into the putative hierarchy of inferiority. The subordinate division on the basis of the subtlest of facts fueled insecurity and hatred with the instrument of which fear instilled in them the mastery of the new lords; they taught them to see themselves through their eyes and thus to define themselves in terms of what they were not European.

Reeling with heavy walls imposed by capitals far away, the continent lay fractured. Such division could not rise and unite in a common breath to resist. From this fractured land arose a figure carved out of the deepest pits of human ambition: King Leopold II of Belgium, whose name became almost synonymous with cruelty. He did not merely rule; he feasted on them. With his silver tongue, he hoodwinked powers of the world into granting him colonial Congo as his personal trophy. It had the grandiose name *L'État Indépendant du Congo*, a title dripping with irony. Independent, huh! This was just an illusion, a lie. This was no nation, but a slaughterhouse draped in velvet, where rivers ran red, and forests whispered with the ghosts of the stolen.

Leopold's Congo was a fever dream of greed. Millions were chained to his hunger for rubber and ivory: their lives were crushed into profit. Hands were cut off for not meeting quotas; villages were wiped out for opposing him. Even the land seemed to cry out in grief, with its soil and soul plundered for sale. Imperialism cast off any pretense and revealed its true snarling face: a system in which human beings became tally marks and whole ways of life were sold off both in body and in spirit. Africa, having already bled from a thousand wounds, bore this new scar deepest of all.

As human beings we are educated from early childhood in caring for and nurturing things which are ours, will be our families, our communities, our land. It is a natural instinct to protect what we claim and to see it grow in prosperity. But looks like Congo's copy somehow got lost on the way. Believed to have been blessed with all possibilities of a promising destiny, Congo ended up becoming the most wretched land therein today. It was not the land that was protected, nor the people who were cared for, but rather an entire nation that was sacked and browbeaten. What should have been a land of opportunity and flourishing potential instead became one of the most miserable places on Earth.

In today's society, privatization, as it is, is thought of as the badge of honor that is bestowed upon efficiency and control. We are assured that the private sector will do what the public sector cannot, that putting resources or services in the realm of corporations somehow sets them ablaze with innovation and excellence. However, there is a flaw in such a logic: if privatization is really reserved for that which is valuable, then, Congo has just completely shredded that reasoning. With regard to the people, the land, the hidden wealth in its soil, there was nothing considered more precious. Instead, it was stripped away, a stripping of essence and reshaping to cater to the appetites of the powerful. In asserting his dominance, King Leopold turned the narrative of what was supposed to be an independent nation into something unrecognizable, a stage for every nightmare of exploitation so that his legacy could be secured.

Eager to demonstrate his imperial reach, he sent his crew of miscreants to Congo with an unmistakable message. His first speech to his so-called "subjects" would stain history, etching itself into the consciousness of the Congolese, a frigid decree of their fate. His words held no compassion, no trace of shared humanity. His words weren't political; they were a claim of possession, a declaration of absolute rule over a land and people silenced in their own story. Leopold didn't address the Congolese that day. He stood surrounded by soldiers, bureaucrats, and agents, men already sharpening their knives to gut Congo's soul. His voice, steady and cold, cut through the air, but his message wasn't for those who'd bleed for his ambitions. The king was no fool, his speech was a theater for Europe, for kings and rivals who'd either applaud his brutality or hunger to mimic it. That speech became a pivot point, warping Congo's destiny. The memo wasn't lost after all; it was just modified and imposed on the land. And as Leopold's edicts calcified into action, a shadow fell over Congo's history, one that would stretch its fingers across decades. This is how it unfolded:

"Dear Pastors, and fellow countrymen, go to my humble abode Congo-Belgian, you'll be there to look after the disinterest of these savages of their rich lands to avoid confrontation and dislodge us out of the country before we amass enough wealth. What I'd recommend to you pastors and priests, is to evangelize them to the spinal cord so that they would never want to revolt against the injustice you'll make them endure. Make them recite "Happy are those who cry because paradise belongs to them. It is hard for the rich to get to heaven than for a camel to get through the eye of a needle." Do everything in your power to scare them of being rich. Sometimes get violent, convert them through lashes if needed, torture them, keep their women away from them for nine months, make their women work for you, sleep with their women if you want to. Make them pay taxes every week during the Mass and divert those taxes presumably destined to the poor to open your own businesses. Ask them to die of hunger while you fill your bellies with whatever you can get from this wonderful land. Mistreat and indoctrinate them with things that you don't believe in, and if they ask, "why do you preach this and do the absolute opposite?" Tell them! "Follow our lectures and not our actions." And if they insist, display your furiousness, and beat them to their final gasp or lynch them. Always remind them that any venture in a revolt and plans to ask for freedom will result in getting caught and being slaughtered. Tell them that their sculptures in

their homes, all craftmanship are works of the devil, confiscate them, and put them in our museums or in your houses. Make them forget their progenitors, so they adore yours. Make them pray on their knees and force them to recite erroneous verses many times. Never give a chair to a black man, never give them cigarettes, never invite them to eat with you regardless of whether they kill a chicken for you every time you come at their houses. Furthermore, in the wake of achieving all this, then Belgium will be rich, and they will comprehend that these Machiavellian stratagems were concocted for the sole purpose of helping ourselves."

The king's commands were not ink on parchment; they had steel behind them. Leopold II carved genocide into history with these words; fifteen million souls, women and men, children, and aged ones died on his watch, their last breath mingling with the very earth of Congo they had loved. But these were not sufficient to satiate the beasts; rebellion was another commodity. Those who resisted were butchered and their hands and feet collected in baskets to serve as ghastly trophies. The so-called quota of killing was to stand testimony that loyalty was not wiped by honor but by forcing men to slay men, fathers to surrender their sons.

The cruelty of Leopold, however, was something on display. In 1897, in his manicured estate at Tervuren, he opened the doors of a human zoo, an abhorrent drama with Congolese men and women imprisoned like exotic beasts. An invented "African village" sat amid ornamental ponds and sculpted hedges. The victims were not in any ghostly situation but were in the sights of every tourist, who flocked to gawk, tossing coins as at a carnival. Behind a fence hung a peculiar sign: *"Don't Feed the Animals. They Are Fed by the Organizing Committee."* Leopold never stepped foot into the land he looted but instead imported his victims as curiosities, their personhood wiped out to give shape to his colonial dream. The victims shivered in the cold of Belgium, dressed up in farcical "native" costumes, forced to mimic in caricatures what little was left of their stolen lives. Some gave way to starvation, while others were drained by despair.

Did the crowds laugh, just as the Romans cheered when the unfortunate gladiators, enslaved warriors were unleashed in an arena and dueled to the death for entertainment of the so-called civilized public? Leopold's enterprise was not merely evil. It was *profitable*. Even after he sold Congo to the Belgian government, the carnage continued, the machinery of exploitation too lucrative to dismantle.

What haunts most is not the scale of the horror, but its choreography. This was not the chaos of war, but a meticulously engineered hell. A king enthroned in a palace of lies with that single hand turned people into fuel for his greed. The land wept so severely, the rivers choked with bones, and Europe, draped in its delusion of enlightenment, applauded behind it. Of course, the wound of Leopold's Congo was no aberration; it was a cancer that metastasized. Across the continent, colonization unfolded like a plague, its agents cloaked in the righteousness of empire, their boots crushing the throats of ancient civilizations. Entire populations were reshaped into chattel: bodies moved to plantations to bleed sugar from soil to mines where diamonds crusted their lungs, to ships that carried them beyond the horizon of their own histories. The transatlantic slave trade before this had already hewn a highway for suffering across oceans; colonial rule refined the vicious cruelty, institutionalization. Chains became contracts. Lynching became policy. And all of it was baptized in the rhetoric of "progress."

Consider the French for example, in 1899, as Leopold's human zoos still drew gawking crowds, two officers, Captain Paul Voulet and Lieutenant Julien Chanoine, marched into Niger under the tricolor flag. Their mission, they claimed, was to "pacify" the land, to stitch Senegal to Sudan under France's imperial quilt. But Voulet, a man whose name curdled into legend for his butchery in Upper Volta in 1896, carried no map of diplomacy, only a ledger for slaughter. It was a campaign so vicious it earned epithets like *The Killer Trail* and The African Apocalypse. Villages were erased, not with fire alone, but with terror: children speared, women paraded as trophies, men decapitated and stacked like cordwood. Voulet's soldiers, drunk on impunity, turned the Sahel into a macabre theater of cruelty.

This was colonization stripped bare. No fancy exhibitions; no genteel lies about "civilizing missions." Just one raw, screaming truth: empires fed on human flesh. Voulet and Chanoine, like Leopold, knew that showmanship was the very currency of domination. They turned executions into spectacular public teaching moments; all survivors would speak that language. Voulet, tragically underfunded, was consequently savage in his treatment of the opposition. When camp followers would grumble about hunger, he executed them, all men, women, and children, such was his economy of bullets; bayonets were much more efficient. The atrocities so horrified some of Voulet's own men that they deserted him. Then they used enslaved locals to haul their cannons, as the whips cracked skin to the rhythm of marching boots. Those who couldn't move fast enough had their flesh served up for the vultures' dining, while despairing signs were etched in the sun-white bones under stark rays.

The horrific tales reached Paris, so much so that a warrant for Voulet's arrest was issued, not out of moral fervor, but out of sheer ignominy. A detachment of sixteen officers from Mali had been dispatched to intercept him and was confronted with unspeakable carnage: villages razed, corpses further insulted, an entire community wiped out beneath the banner of France!

Completing the descent into madness, Voulet dubbed himself a "black emperor" and vowed to carve a kingdom from the land he soaked in blood. Neither he nor Chanoine, however, had a glamorous ending, nor a heroic last stand. Instead, their very own soldiers turned mutinous, disposing of them in the most sordid manner imaginable. Yet the legacy of carnage survived. The "Heart of Darkness" was no mere metaphor; it was a literal blueprint, replicated on either side of the border. Its architects were decorated and pensioned; their sanguinary mission was uninterrupted, thus laying the cornerstone of French dominion over the Sahara. By then, France's African Empire was a firm notion: a federation of eight territories stretching from Mauritania to Niger, eight times bigger than France itself, with Dakar as its capital.

The iron-governance of colonial rule-of-the-day by the French may have symbolized the very storms in which it hurled these lands. Incipient insurrections such as the Tuaregs' uprising of 1916 were crushed with appalling might, and this resulted in these desert-dwelling Tuaregs to endure summary executions for resisting an unacceptable law. The very grave question then hangs over their heads: How many Congos? How many Nigers? How many millions of screams have disappeared into the silence of history? The conquerors wrote their victories in marble and ink, but the country remembers only through ash and bone. Their so-called "civilization" was simply a bonfire; humanity was left to dig their way through the smoke.

Today, Leopold's Museum still stands tall in Tervuren, whispering in marble halls of unmarked graves. From the ears of the survivors, it is a *monument to forgetting*; but the land still remembers, it always does.

They first stripped away the names, not merely names given at birth, but the names in ancestral tongues, river names, warriors' names, names of their heritage. In their place, entered numbers, cold and clinical, scrawled into the ledgers as though they were so many cattle. Next, they went at the traditions: dances silenced by clanking chains, stories smothered under the heel of scripture. What dignity? For the mere free. They treaded upon lies: *"Adapt,"* they coaxed, *"and freedom will follow."* The rotten promises dangled: *better wages, legal rights, a seat at the table.* But the chains only grew subtler, tightening with each generation. Yet even in darkness, the human spirit flickered. When war engulfed the world, twice, Europe came begging. *Fight for liberty*, they pleaded, as if liberty were a currency they'd ever shared. Millions of Africans marched into Europe's infernos, clad in uniforms stitched with hypocrisy. They charged trenches in World War I, their blood soaking foreign soil. They helped liberate Paris in World War II, only to return to occupied homelands where they couldn't vote, couldn't breathe without permission. Although, amid the chaos of battle, a truth seared into them: *Their masters bled red.* They saw terror in their eyes when mortars screamed. They watched them weep for mothers like any mortal. *Wait a minute,* they whispered, as the myth of invincibility crumbled to dust.

Exhibit A, they were constantly positioned as cannon fodder by their masters, frontline sacrifices to spare their own, yet in the backline when victory was being celebrated. Anyway, the ruse backfired. In the stench of war, the subjects learned to wield new weapons: observation, strategy, the quiet calculus of rebellion. Some of them returned home hollow-eyed, their minds infected with dangerous questions. Others, like Salim, burned with a different fire. A fire that spread.

The French sensed the shift. When veterans dared to ask for rights and promised compensation, they had those who didn't stop insisting disposed of, and for the others, crumbs would be offered: parliamentary seats, hollow titles, the theatrics of so-called "overseas territories."

Guinea fell into the trap in 1946, but men like Salim and Wadu decided otherwise. The drybrush crackle of his voice would ignite the masses: *"They fear us now,"* they'd say *"because we have seen them naked. Their power is a farce."*

On the other hand, the road to liberation had become a minefield. Some leaders sold the revolution for a piece of influence, seduced by the opium of nearness to power. But those who had tasted both battlegrounds and betrayals knew this was not for taking a seat at the master's table but to replace the master altogether.

The French knew very well that their subjects knew what they were afraid of being revealed. The subjects now wanted their masters to know that they knew, but the French, however, acted as if they didn't know to see if their subjects would accept their masters' feigned ignorance. The subjects saw through the charade and refused to bow any longer. They would squint their eyes with each patronizing concession and grind their teeth with every empty reform. The rules of the game had changed. Across the continent, as resistance embers were cranking up, there blossomed a certain hard realization: freedom is not and will never be *given* by empires; it's torn from their grip, tooth and nail, by hands that remember their own strength.

Salim's voice gathered strength, cutting through villages and cities alike like a storm. The colonizers heard it too: The shuffling of pamphlets, the clenching of fists, the rustling of papers during midnight meetings where maps were redrawn by faint candlelight. Africa was not asleep anymore. It was dreaming of fire.

Chapter 6

The betrayal

This zeal of Salim was too great; some might even qualify it as a strong passion akin to that of a fool. To him, the world was indeed a canvas of oppression, and with each brushstroke, so to speak, is a declaration of independence sought to reclaim its colors. He saw himself as a liberation prophet, his voice booming like thunder against the storm of European imperialism. Yet, in his righteous fury, he could not comprehend the snug little fragility that bound those threads of his people's survival to the West.

"I will use my powerful and zealously righteous voice to eradicate all this misfortunate European Imperialism put upon our noble land. For Africa, and for the sake of the world, I will liberate us." He barked, blinded to the delicate balance of power that could change tomorrow. He humiliated General Charles, and this humiliation was not a victory but more like the spark in a powder keg. Salim was standing tall with pride, unaware that the ground beneath him had already begun to crumble. Neither he nor his fellow revolutionaries had so far succeeded in melting the ground underneath the advancing very organized French general's wrath.

The French response was not an answer to scale retaliation; it was a symphony of wrath, no midday or twilight; only one eternal dawn. They descended upon the barren land, much like locusts do. They disassembled telegraph machines and radio transmitters, unscrewed Lightbulbs, with their fragile glasses cradled as if they were stolen jewels, and the telephone cables coiled into serpents slithered back to their ships. What could not be carried was demolished on the spot: plantations were set on fire, schools were turned into a mere skeleton of brick, medicines poured into gutters wherein hope curdled. The nurseries once rejoicing in harmony of laughter were crushed under the deliberate weight of destruction. Horses and cattle were not starved but gunned down, and their bodies together were revered as monuments. They called it *collateral damage*, but the truth would hiss and scream louder for whoever cared to listen. This was a lesson set down in fire and blood. A warning to any who dared dream of defiance. A warning to the Malian people, to the Senegalese people, to Upper Volta and so on…

For the people in Guinea, the victory started tasting bitter. The air was rife with the stinging scent of smoke and rotting fruits; the erstwhile soil underfoot bore scars wrought by the weight of retreating trucks. Children clutched their empty bellies; the mothers' lullabies had now turned into dirges. Salim walked around the wreckage like some man whose unshakable resolve was adrift again in a tempest. What remained behind was more than sufficient to qualify as the memories of a defeated people whom the French crushed: They had fled, yes, but not before choking the very nation for breath. Roads lay gutted, factories fell silent, hospitals became empty shells. The "independence" he had once championed seemed like a golden cage, its bars constructed by his own hand.

Nonetheless, the bitterest draught was sipped by the colonizers themselves. To have to leave the shimmering beauty of a land endowed with gold and iron and resign oneself to Senegal's parched peanuts and salt? The irony gnawed at them, a ghost in the halls of Paris handing them baskets of peanuts instead of Guinean's baskets of gold. Well, at least they knew that Senegal is a no-go zone for peanut allergy homies. The entire country might as well be one giant Legoland, but with *peanuts*. Although, there's still a glimmer of hope! Now, before you go crying into your allergy meds, let's talk about the real national treasure: the men. Apparently, God hit the "create superhero" button here. Like, every dude rolled out of bed looking like he's auditioning for the 300 *Dakar Edition*. Six-packs? More like a *national uniform*. In this place, it's the default dress code of the day. I don't make the rules! Even scientists are baffled. So, ladies, if you're cool with risking anaphylaxis for a chance to swoon over human statues chiseled like a melanated Zeus, I guess... *priorities*, am I right? Just don't forget your EpiPen.

Anyway, people got consumed by fear and this summoned different perspectives among them. they believed the French's departure to be just calculated strategy. *"France will never leave,"* they claimed, and whispers lingered: *What if they return? What if this humiliation festers, breeding a thousand Charles's?* Their exit was a performance of finality, yet their glances backward betrayed an unresolved hunger. True, the land might heal. However, the people might never forget the cost of Salim's dream. A dream people viewed as necessary, but was it necessary though? Because in the quiet hours, when the wind carried the echo of explosions, some wondered, was it freedom that dawned, or merely a different shade of shadow? The French, after all, had a long memory. And empires, like phantoms, seldom rest, they are always concocting new political strategies. And as a poor country just pray to be on their good grace or be prepared to be hypnotized by catchy phrases like *"liberté, égalité, fraternité"* while quietly hissing *"but touch my colonies and I'll burn your croissants."* France, that elegant Hexagon, has always danced through diplomacy like a mime trapped in a bureaucracy, waving a baguette of *realpolitik* while clutching its colonies like a toddler with a contested teddy bear. Quite ingenious I'd say.

Look at the French-Vietnamese War for instance. Post-WWII, the French clothed in the moth-eaten grandeur of empire insisted on Indochina being just an extension of their terroir, while Uncle Sam's FDR chirped about global freedom, real independence, like a peppy scoutmaster. France kept its fingers in ears shouting, its response. A theatrical gasp, they would not stand for it "If you liberate our colonies," they hissed, "we'll join the Soviets!" Oh! Yes, the same France that earlier clutched pearls in horror at the communists, suddenly threatened to elope with them, all in order to retain their petite plantation in Vietnam. The audacity! It's much like threatening to marry your archnemesis because somebody took away your usual café table. Like… what the hell?

However, the poor Viet Minh were not impressed, they were not having it at all, bless their relentless souls. They must have fought with the energy of at least one hundred thousand pho chefs wielding ladles of defiance. France, ever the drama queen, turned to America: *"Support us, help us in erasing these insurgents, or we will defect to the Soviets!"* they sulked again, like com'on, this is getting ridiculous now, but, well, with a cry and knee-deep in its own Red Scare panic, America kept doling out artillery like an indulgent parent bribing a tantruming child with candy. Spoiler alert: France shit the bed big time. It is quite a thing for an empire to beg for armistice, don't you think? In other words, they didn't just lose the war; they somehow tripped over their own épaulets, fell face-first into a bowl of phở, and had to slink out of Vietnam mumbling, *"We never liked noodles anyway."*

The irony is that France received all the help but couldn't cut it, and in the end, left the US in Nam to fend for itself, stop the commies from spreading their ideology. Today, the two Vietnams are united under a communist ideology. Ain't that something!

Anyway, undeterred, the brave French made their way back to West Africa. Ah, Guinea, this needy nation (France's words probably). The Hexagon deployed its UN Security Council veto like a toddler brandishing a "NO" sign. When Guinea dared whisper *"independence,"* France spun into full boulevard théâtre mode. *"If you even look at Guinea,"* General Charles barked at Eisenhower. *"We'll quit NATO and evict your troops! Enjoy explaining that to Kansas!"* The U.S., not keen on a transatlantic game of chicken, side-eyed Guinea until JFK, who; bless his Camelot charm, finally slid into Salim's DMs.
Through it all, France's mantra remained: *"C'est transactionnel, chéri."* These colonies are bargaining chips. And our allies? Just temporary hostages. Principles? Boy please! We have none, it's just a garnish. And yet, for all their savoir-faire, they still couldn't hide the fact that their imperial soufflé had long collapsed. But hey, at least they kept their veto power, the diplomatic equivalent of a participation trophy. Vive la France, indeed.

When France left Guinea in 1958, the new nation quickly shifted its focus eastward and established a close relationship with the Soviet Union. It was Moscow's first substantive success on the African continent, an opportunity it made the most of, with stratospheric zeal. Led by its first president, Guinea pursued a radical socialist path. Partly inspired by the

Marxist-Leninist ideas of the Soviet Union and the practical socialist model established by China, Salim set about transforming his nation's political and economic landscape. His dedication to socialism, which may have raised eyebrows in the West, found a huge audience among the Soviets and the Chinese, twin global powers in the communist universe. To them, Salim was a brave figure, bold enough to defy a colonial regime in the name of a new Africa, an Africa based on the tenets of Marxism.

An energetic overhaul was envisaged for Guinea by the Eastern Bloc, full of pride and resolution for revolution, in paramount importance, of the anti-imperialistic sentiments. Finally, Salim placed supreme importance on Guinea having the same values as the communist powers. For the Chinese and the Soviets, a mere political alliance would not have been sufficient: instead, they looked on the prospect of an African state that could stand as a beacon of anti-colonial struggle and socialist construct. To them, this small country could be the Castro-style exemplar of the socialist future they projected onto the continent. Then soon joined the party, the two Germanies. The Soviet Union aligned socialist, East Germany, GDR (German Democratic Republic) and the democratic capitalist, West Germany, FRG (Federal Republic of Germany). The FRG, under Chancellor Konrad Adenauer, thought it was crucial to preserve its influence in Africa, but was reluctant to the idea of providing too much in the way of support to Salim's regime for fear of antagonizing France. Sheer colonialism.

Anyways, the French had to leave Guinea as the West derided their handiwork across the Third World. However, supporting and allying with a socialist government would have alienated France from the West German government, which quite notoriously sought to curry favor, being that it was all Cold War stuff. The FRG had commercial and strategic interests that made them hesitate to burn their bridges with Guinea and (in theory) dilute the Soviet bloc's monopoly in the region; however, this still gave them foothold in an almost decrepit geopolitical chess space where the aim was to deliver "help" well, I guess as long as the "help" does not let Guineans socially embarrass themselves by allowing another power to surreptitiously penetrate and seek control into their new home, like cluster bombs. Here lies the affair itself, a reminder of how fraught and the choreography of Cold War diplomacy was built, where factions were established not merely on the weight of overlapping ambitions but whether they could traverse the ingress matrix of local and global hostilities. Salim's Guinea was in such a highly charged atmosphere that it would not just be a shining example of African independence; it would also become a pawn caught up in the Sino-Soviet conflict at the same time as the East-West ideological demise of the gravy ideas.

Although, it's rather ironic to note that nothing warms the heart like watching two countries who can't afford lightbulbs cast the world in a lecture on "solidarity." The Soviet Union and China, the intrepid geopolitical underdog with the economic muscle of a soggy turnip are extending their bony bureaucratic fingers to Guinea. *We come in peace!*" they stated, presumably as their own people lined up for bread rations and sanctioned delusions. Who needs bread when there's a heady smell of anti-imperialist rhetoric intoxicating the air?
Let me sketch out some scenery so you can see what I'm talking about. So, the world still coughs out the ashes of WWII, and here comes Guinea, fresh off telling France to take its baguettes and shove them. Along come Moscow and Beijing, stumbling like drunk uncles at a funeral. *We shall help!*" they slurred, though "help" meant, if anything at all, swapping Guinea's colonial chains for a spanking new set of ideological shackles. The Soviet Union, still regaining its balance over Stalingrad-based vodka

flashbacks, and Beijing, where the economy runs solely on chairman Mao and the tears of starving poets, if anywhere in the world, that's the dream team.

Salim, the Guinean's idealistic maestro had a vision: friendship based on "mutual respect," not France's *quid pro "we own you."* How dare he! The French clutched their berets in horror. *"Mon Dieu!"* they gasped. "Next, what will these colonies want? *rights*!" But Salim, ever the optimist, bet the farm that his African brothers would rally to his cause. Spoiler: they did not. Turns out, voting "NO" to colonialism is easy; voting "YES" to sharing your last grain of rice with a broke revolutionary? Less so.

Meanwhile, Moscow and Beijing's "aid" package was a masterpiece of socialist satire. Beijing sent copies of *"how to grow my own crops, for Dummies"* and a lifetime supply of suspiciously glowing tiny elephants. Moscow? A crate of expired vodka and a pamphlet titled *"How to Sanction-Proof Your Economy."* Guinea blinked. "Is… this a joke?" But the Kremlin and Beijing's regime were dead serious. "This is *true* solidarity!" they crowed. "We take *nothing*… except your dignity, your resources, and your future!" The French, meanwhile, sipped Bordeaux and cackled. "Let them eat… whatever China's eating!" they sneered. Because nothing unites former colonizers like *schadenfreude*. As for Guinea's neighbors? They suddenly remembered urgent appointments. "Can't rebel today, got a… thing. With an… elephant. Very important elephant. Oh, no, a Syli we should say."

In the end, Salim stood alone, clutching his "friendship" treaties like expired coupons. The referendum? A landslide "YES" to *"Actually, We Like Electricity."* His allies? Ghosted him faster than a Tinder date after a rant about sacs of millet. And his pseudo-brothers' so called unite to expel imperialism? Collapsed quicker than a pyramid scheme at a socialist convention. They all voted yes with over 95%, even *they* themselves couldn't believe it. *"Bunch of traitors…"* Salim's reaction towards his pseudo-brothers to which they'll only have to respond, *"We got wheat… you got squat…"*

Anyway, I guess the lesson for the Guineans here was pretty clear. When the "anti-imperialist" cavalry arrives on foot, holding IOUs and ideological manifestos, maybe just… keep the colonizers? At least they bring *pastries*. Salim was left alone twirling his tail like Looney Tunes to pay the inevitable price of trusting a pseudo-unity orchestrated by the spurious brothers he believed to have his back. Salim realized the consequences of his frivolous decisions and was not only discontented with the outcome but also could not bear the idea of General Charles having the last giggle. All he knew was that no matter the consequences he stood up for a noble cause, or did he?

Chapter 7

The first presidential act

The downfall of empires often begins not with a roar, but with the quiet, stubborn flicker of a single flame, one that those in power mistake as harmless, until it scorches their thrones. The French withdrawal from Guinea was less a strategic retreat than a hasty, undignified shuffle, as if l'Hexagone had stepped on a hornet's nest and fled, swatting on the horizon. Yet in their wake, curiosity bloomed among the French citizenry like a perverse rose. *Who was this Salim*, they whispered, *this audacious upstart who'd rattled the gates of their vaunted General Charles?* A man who'd never knelt before the glory of French "civilization," who'd spat in the face of a war hero's legacy? They had to see him for themselves.

They came as tourists of condescension, clutching cameras and colonial nostalgia. They expected a caricature: a ranting demagogue, a jungle warlord draped in animal pelts. Instead, they found a man who wore dignity like armor. The only thing he wanted was to be seen as an equal to the white man and not this African man sitting on an intersection corner, or an aisle of a mosque dressed in soiled garments extending his palms for alms. He believed that the society he aspired to have could not exist without the sovereignty of the country. He stood unbent, demanding nothing but acknowledgment. *"Look at me,"* his silence seemed to say, *"not as your subject, but as your equal."*

But to the French, this was heresy. Newspapers harped on him as a madman; diplomats just dismissed him as a "tribal nuisance." Yet back in Guinea, his very name was a drumbeat. Villages burst out in song when he arrived. Farmers came to offer yams at his door. This was a man not speaking of empty words like independence but of sovereignty a world where children would learn the language of their ancestors and not the flat vowels of French verbs. But Europe treated him with a venomous scorn. They froze him out from aiding, laughed, as his nation barely took its first steps. Let him fail; *let his people taste chaos without our steadying hand.* What they missed was Salim's greatest weapon: their own hypocrisy being on show. Every sneer from the French, every loan blocked, every headline dripping with condescension went on to build him in majestic proportions. To his people, he was Prometheus, stealing fire from the gods. To Paris, he was a cracked mirror, reflecting their fading glory. And when they isolated him, they did not realize they had conferred immortality on him.

For the years to come, his Chevalier thought; Guinea's children would be reciting his speeches in the schools that the French had never built or had built and destroyed out of spite. That irony would be rich enough to taste. The empire, which had meant to make an example of that man, had, instead, found itself making him an amphitheater upon which he could strut. For now, however, there is nothing more that the French can do but leave.

The departure of the French left Guinea adrift in uncharted waters, where uncertainty mingled with newfound autonomy. Now, within demanding corridors of power where ambition whispers and democracy roars, nation stands at the brink of a defining chapter. Anticipation coils like a snake around the weight of choice, elections that shall either decide or reconsider the nation's path. The streets pulse with debate; halls resound with seriousness. The very air quivers with urgency. Up from the nomination podium rise candidates carrying stories of promise and visions. However, politics does not offer shadows here: every move, every speech is laid against the relentless scrutiny of the public eye. Beneath the sparkly sheen of campaigns and politics lives the quiet heart of democracy, and the electorate's silent power to carry a future through an uncertain storm.

As Guinea turns the page, history's ink still wet, the dance of democracy unfolds. Meaning, therefore, shall be given to the tale not by victors but by the chorus of dissenting voices rising, insistently. For it is in their echoes, so contested, so weak, that lie the dreams of a nation. Salim, the man forged in the fire of labor unions, his politics rooted in the grit of dockworkers' strikes and the simmering discontent of colonial exploitation. The man who refused to kneel. The man who made The September 1958 referendum Guinea's fulcrum. The man whose PDG mobilized villages, markets, and unions into a roaring chorus of "Non!" to French domination. The man who transformed austerity into allegory after French Administrators fled, taking blueprints, ripping telephones from walls, smashing lightbulbs in government offices in a petty but symbolic unraveling behavior. The man who declared *They left us nothing but our dignity,"* turning scarcity into a rallying cry was now elected as Guinea's first president which was less a contest than a coronation by acclamation.

The Democratic Party of Guinea (PDG), now synonymous with the state, snatched all seats in the National Assembly. Salim's vision seemed to have merged with fragments of Marxist rhetoric and Pan-African zeal, thereby portraying Guinea as the shining star amongst liberation movements throughout Africa. Industries left by the French were nationalized, collaborators of the colonial era expelled, and alliances were sought with the Soviet bloc and allies. At this critical moment of autumn of 1958, as the tricolor flag whipped down and the red-yellow-green standard of Guinea rose, Salim emerged as the embodiment of the boldness of a nation daring to invent itself. The shadow of choice had engendered the president; the future, fractured as it may be, was now untouchably theirs.

What hummed in Conakry at birth-painting independence was not independence as Salim found out, freedom was a labyrinth. It was October 1958, exactly two weeks after the crowd rejoiced over their Declaration, and like vultures the world's evil eyes began to circle not with talons bared, but with briefcases and diplomatic smiles. Walter Reichhold arrived from the West German consulate, braving the fierce sun, his polished shoes brushing the dust of a nation still finding its footing. Bonn had sent him to secure the allegiance of Guinea before the East could sink roots into this fertile soil. However, as Reichhold stepped on the tarmac, there came a shuddering of confidence in his mind. The East Germans, swift and shrewd, were already there. They had come days earlier, Carl Eckloff, Georg Stibi, Paul Markowski, bearing promises sealed by the ink of GDR President Wilhelm Pieck. Their hands clutched recognition treaties, words grudgingly defined by the familiar words. *"Solidarity,"* they murmured, *"brotherhood."*

A German claiming brotherhood with an African darker than Senegalese tirailleur in 1958. What a knee-slapper! To Retu, these were rescuers, their presence was a lifeline. France had retaliated for his defiance by stripping Guinea of everything, bureaucrats, infrastructure, and even typewriters. Isolation loomed like a storm cloud, and the East's offer glimmered like shelter.

Reichhold met Salim, the weight of history pressing between them. After all, they never dealt with each other, so awkwardness lingered for a while. The West German's voice was cordial. Although, beneath the soft voice was hidden the blade's edge: Bonn would recognize Guinea, *but only* if Salim spurned the East. The Hallstein Doctrine hung unspoken, a guillotine poised to sever ties with any nation daring to acknowledge the "Soviet Occupation Zone." Salim listened, his face a mask. He had not expected this chess game so soon. Inside, he seethed. The French had painted him a communist puppet and murmured their very own lies about Moscow's tutelage. He had never knelt before the Kremlin; only once, in 1951, had he wandered those East Berlin streets scarred by the tragedy of war, a delegate at a peace congress. Now, it felt like a shackle to him. *"I am no man's pawn,"* he thought he might roar. But Guinea was vulnerable, like a sapling in a hurricane.

Reichhold stifled his irritation, which was burning, but he saw that Salim was far too painfully naive. The man clung to the conviction that both German states were represented at the United Nations, an alleged assurance for Guinea's own recognition. He did not realize they were nothing but observers, mere shadows sitting in the halls of power. In Salim's mind, ingratiating his government with East Germany was only a practical precaution against Western apathy. But Reichhold could see that, should West Germany dawdle, East Germany would end up stamping its ideology on the very soul of Guinea.

That night, Reichhold hammered out his report, the sharp clatter of his typewriter cutting through the night's silence. *"Delay is fatal."* He jotted down. Guinea was not so much sliding into chaos as it was confronted with that crucial decision. With every hour that passed, those Eastern bloc diplomats squeezed the grip tighter, dangling experts and infrastructure as bait, a distraction from death shackled under colonial chains. Ridden with pride and need, Salim wheeled on the edge of this constricting noose.

The telegram shook the officials in Bonn. The arena of Cold War was shifting to African soil, and Guinea was its testing ground. Let it tilt East, and many would follow, a red tide lifting up to Europe's doorstep. Reichhold's words thundered through the corridors of the government: *Move now, or watch it slip away.*

It was in Conakry that Salim defied the winds of liberty, carrying with him the salt of the sea air and the fever of new freedom. He stood proud beneath the sun, never begging for mercy: not from Paris, not from Bonn, never even from Berlin. Yet as German emissaries approached, their altars gleaming like sharp blades, he was confronted with the bitter irony of independence: independence was a delicate balancing act, and every step held the danger of casting the chosen new master into shadow.

Not only Guinea, but the world held its breath. In Salim's office, there was a clock that ticked. Paris, lurking behind the curtains, watched. The corridors of the Quai d'Orsay, heavy with the musk of an old empire, now thrummed with quiet fury. Such fury! Guinea's "Non!" never stopped ringing in French ears, too deep an insult combined with an ever-growing stain. Yet pragmatism reared its ugly head above that precedent of pride. Diplomatic cables crisscrossed the Seine like a bridge; Bonn's insistence that Guinea snub East Germany carried in itself an insult which Paris rather grudgingly relied upon. *"Let the Germans play the bulldog,"* snorted some officials. Behind closed doors, though, they seethed: Yes, punish Guinea, starve it of legitimacy but not at the cost of handing Moscow a foothold in Africa.

A memorandum dated October 24 slithered very ominously from the French Embassy in Bonn: *"Encourage recognition... but delay formal ties."* Now, that was the height of hypocrisy. Let others prop up Salim's regime, while France clung to the illusion that it had some leverage. However, by then, the Americans and the British were on the move, ever eager to counter Soviet whisperings; by the end of the month, whispers turned into vows: Washington and London would recognize Guinea. The news hit Bonn like an instrument of torture.

As far as West Germany was concerned, vaunted by the Hallstein Doctrine as a solemn vow to isolate the East, it could not sit on its hands any longer. A telegram from Adenauer went crackling through the wires on the 31st of October: immediate recognition, economic promises, an envoy dispatched. None of that pomp and circumstance, the cold reality of need. The British recognized within hours; Americans followed two days later. The dominoes fell, just as Salim had envisaged.

The dense and choking air thickened in Conakry with irony that had become unbearable for the wind to carry. Spurned by the rejected colonial power, the former colonizer could now only witness helplessly as its allies rushed to embrace the nation it had tried to strangle. Salim was always a tactician, and he masked his victory. He thanked the West cautiously while softly shaking hands with the East. Reichhold's economic envoy came loaded with promises of machinery and marks, but the GDR's doctors and engineers were already weaving through the hinterlands of Guinea, a presence full of quiet defiance.

Yet, sovereignty in itself was always a quick-spending currency, Salim mused. Every deutschemark, every dollar, was tied to conditions: the West demanded that he freeze out East Berlin; the East muttered of betrayal should he comply. And France? Paris bode its time like a jilted lover, withholding ambassadorial ties and refusing to dignify what it could not forgive.

As November's rains lashed Conakry, Salim stood at his window, the horizon blurred by storm and smoke. In Moscow, Mrs. Matilda's radio crackled with Khrushchev's latest boast, Eisenhower's reassurances, Charles's icy silence. Salim smiled, thin and weary. At last, Guinea was free, yes, but freedom, he was learning, was simply the right to choose one's chains. Overall, What Reichhold did not know in his first encounter with Salim, was that the considered naivete from the unexperienced Salim was a subtle Marshall swindle of *The Gardener* to emphasize the geopolitical relevance of Guinea to the rest of the world. Otherwise, how else could his tiny country have powerful nations so invested in it. How could such a nation force the world to make its move, because the world did make its move. Now, Salim would make his as Guinea's soil still smelled of burnt colonial files and the sweat of hope.

The nation stood barefoot on cracked earth, clutching its new flag like a child's blanket. Salim, with his silver tongue and tailored suits, carried himself not as a leader but as an aria, a crescendo of promises sung to a people drunk on the wine of liberation. When the general assembly handed him the presidency, the streets erupted not in cheers, but in *sighs*, the sound of a collective inhale, as if the country had been holding its breath for centuries.

They called it democracy. A word too polished for the jagged edges of their reality. The assembly, stacked with Salim's loyalists, anointed him with a swiftness that felt less like ceremony and more like surrender. Beside him stood *The Gardener*, his shadow in a crisp uniform, whose laughter echoed through legislative halls like the click of a rifle's safety being undone. Together, they spun visions of roads paved with gold, schools that would birth philosophers, and rivers dammed to electrify dreams. The people wept, not from joy, but from the raw, animal relief of believing hunger might end.

Then it happened. Cracks went unseen. Though, not when Salim's image blossomed overnight on billboards, those demon eyes tenderly following citizens like a kind god. Not when dissenters started vanishing from the cafés, their empty chairs heavy with unsaid words. The children in their subligariae, on the other hand, felt all of it. In the way their mothers' hands shook while stirring glutinous rice. The sudden hush whenever the radio crackled with Salim's voice, an intoxicating medicine coupled with toxic bile.

As the poet Sitram would later write, *"We built our house on a foundation of hymns, only to discover the bricks were made of our own bones."* By then, it was too late, too late to realize he was nothing but a murderous charlatan. The so-called "prosperous future" revealed itself as a fever dream. Salim's factories stood as skeletal as the men who built them. Agricultural reforms left the fields naked; the earth scorched with greed. And the children, the wide-eyed inheritors of the revolution, became the currency. Boys were delivered into militia trucks; their mothers' wails drowned in state radio anthems. Girls traded textbooks for buckets of well water, shrinking their futures with every mile.

The first president did not lead. He *consumed*. His reign, baptized in the euphoria of freedom, became a slow bleed. The people had mistaken his theatrics for strength, his slogans for salvation. They did not brace for the impact. How could they? To doubt Salim was to doubt the very idea of Guinea, a sin against the holy trinity of flag, fight, and freedom. But the land remembers. It whispers through the baobabs that watched him rise: *You cannot feast on hope and wonder why the bones left behind are your own.*

*** * * * ***

"The future looked gleeful, but the revolutionary regime established was a failure from all domains: political, economic, and social. The promising tomorrow was missing; the revolution ate its children and left a taste of blood and bitterness." **Djibril Tamsir Niane**

March's sun didn't shine on Conakry, it simmered. With a molten eye, lidless and unflinching, it scorched the city into submission. Noon, in the vernacular of the land, was a verdict, a vise of heat squeezing hope and sweat out of the cobblestones. Shadows fled, cringing into crevices, as if even darkness feared what the light might expose. The atmosphere was trembling, taut with unsaid words and undone acts. Salim, sculpted from the very darkness he courted, stood poised on the brink of prophecy. Newly birthed in the land of unchained hope, Guinea barely allowed her fingers to reach Salim before he whipped his demons into existence, their whispers intertwining with that of the saint. The sky softly gelled, charged with a foreboding so sticky it clumsily clung to the skin with every sweaty breath, breath by labored breath.

People felt clustered in a tight room with no oxygen. For instance, before it became a literal fashion crime to outshine His Majesty in North Korea, a dashing duo, Gael and Labadho, had already committed the ultimate offense: looking too good. After a brief and stylish adventure through Dakar, where their razor-sharp outfits and gravity-defying afros were so powerful they practically functioned as public art installations. They were, of course, swiftly apprehended by Salim's militia, not for any actual crime, but because their impeccable threads and celestial hairdos posed a national security threat. turns out, when your fit is that fire, even your wardrobe gets profiled. But fortunately for them, they had the fits but weren't too fit and threatening to be considered capital offenders.

Anyway, on that month of March, a crowd therein roared unrest at the sight of barely more than a boy, Saif being dragged through the square, wrists raw from the ropes. Theft was the charge laid against him. But what those eyes conveyed, bloodshot with terror, was the theft of innocence from a nation still lying in cradle and freedom. Rifle cracks shattered like snapping of bones. Saif's body jerked and fell down as if a marionette whose strings were cut off. There was a touch of silence in that brief moment. Then began the wailing.

Women doubled up and splattered skirts with fresh blood, while some retched into the dust. Their bodies reacted in anger to the show. A pregnant woman dropped on her knees, her dying womb letting out a loud cry of loss. The earth seemed to say no to accepting the sin, a stain of Saif's blood lingering, a scarlet accusation. But Salim looked impassive since his soul was a void where empathy could have been lodged. The people of Conakry staggered home, clutching their children, whispering curses. But the landscape beyond the capital slept in restful ignorance; it had not yet stretched its shadow over the execution.

By year's end, that shadow would deepen. In Guecke, irony pooled with every breath, as thick as the hot tropical air above. Once liberators and soldiers, now they hacked through the crowds marching for basic necessities with their machetes glinting like malevolent stars. They left hundreds of souls: fathers, mothers, children; bodies strewn like shattered pottery. Thousands more were writhed in the mud with their wounds weeping into the soil. Sangaré Toumani, architect of the uprising, fled through back alleys, his breath ragged as his comrade Kalas shoved him into a hidden cellar. *"Stay down!"* Kalas hissed in a tremulous voice. Above them, screams crescendoed.

When the doctors eventually arrived, men from Kankan, Kouroussa, Dabola, their well-known hands had little cause to contain that blood-flowing slaughter. A French doctor commandant, face ashen, staggered back from the corpse of a child. *"This... this is Verdun,"* he choked out, the words a dirge, *"but Verdun had an end."* His gaze swept the ravaged streets where flames licked the sky and rivers ran crimson. He did not know this was merely the prelude.

The head of Kankan's constituency, Lansia Dane, hurried to witness the unnecessary bloodshed, which, like other carnage, becomes one more bitter haunt in a country that had once been so hopeful. He sternly cautioned the rescuers that anyone who dares talk about what occurred here, even to their kith and kin, would be executed. Unfortunately, at that time, such words were not taken lightly. Having loose lips, could have one's whole bloodline executed.

As the wind grew dense, oppressive with unspoken weight in Kankan in those final days of November 1959, heavy not just with the dry Harmattan dust but with a creeping dread that seeped into the marrow. Lansia Dane's orders had come like a venomous whisper, slithering through the corridors of power: *Round them up. All of them.* The albinos, the city's blind, men who navigated markets by the scent of ripe mangoes, women who sang lullabies in braille, children who laughed at shadows were deemed unworthy of the light.

Military trucks, beasts of rust and roar, prowled the streets. They descended on the post office, where the blind once clustered to hear letters read aloud; they raided pharmacies, where hands groped for vials of hope; they stormed the weathered home of the revered Cheik Kaba, its walls still humming with sacred prayers. The soldiers laughed as they worked, their breath reeking of palm wine, their boots kicking up spirals of red earth. When the trucks careened into Bate-Nafadyi, the world seemed to tilt.

What followed was not a massacre but horrific theatrics of efficiency. The blind were hauled like sacks of millet, limbs tangled, faces pressed against the cold metal floors. A grandmother's cane snapped under a soldier's heel; a toddler wailed for a mother already silenced. They were stacked, *one atop the other, like pallets of bread*, alive, breathing, trembling. The pits yawned open and hungry. Some begged, and some prayed. Others simply hummed the songs their ancestors had carried across centuries. The earth swallowed them whole, their final breaths mingling with the soil.

And what rationale could justify such a heinous act; you'd ask? Well, because Salim's idol, Kwame N'Krumah was coming. His divine gaze, so the fevered logic went, must not falter at the sight of Guinea's "shame." Better to bury the evidence of suffering than to confront it. Better to bleach the streets with blood than risk a visitor's fleeting discomfort.

But Kankan's terror was merely the prologue.

In Kissi, weeks later, the flies found the child first. A boy of three and a half, his head severed clean, his tiny hands curled into fists. When the killer was caught, he did not flinch. *"The committee told me to do it,"* he said, eyes glazed with a zealot's certainty. The local commissioner, a man who wore his indifference like a tailored suit, shrugged. Files vanished. Cells stayed empty. The boy's name dissolved into the static of bureaucracy.

This was Salim's new nation, not the work of a lone monster but a rot that festered in the hierarchy. His disciples, from the lowliest clerk to the men who sipped whiskey in ministerial offices, had learned to feed the darkness. They slit throats and severed limbs, with the help of faceless strangers from neighboring countries. The truth was in the soil, in the unmarked graves that dotted the land like open wounds.

Years passed. The bodies piled up, women with their wombs hollowed out, men missing limbs, children whose innocence had been bartered for power. Each crime a sacrament, each lie a brick in the fortress of their rule. And the wind, when it blew through Kankan, still carried the echoes of those buried alive: a muffled chorus of *why, why, why?* A question without an answer, lingering like a curse.

The fear, in Guinea, had a taste, like ash and bile. It clung to the tongue, thickened the air, made every breath a labor. The people knew, *of course, they knew* who lit the fires, who filled the wells with screams. But to speak was to vanish. To point a finger was to lose it. And so, the lie festered: a putrid narrative that painted Salim's enemies, faceless marauders from beyond the borders, as the architects of Guinea's agony. The truth curdled in their throats, unsung.

How does a nation forget? Not through grand brainwashing, but through the slow poison of terror. Salim's Party, the PDG, did not need slogans to hypnotize. It had Momo.

Momo, actually it's Momo Jo Soumah, a name spat like rotten fruit, was Salim's shadow, a man whose soul had long been sold to the delirium of power. Sinewy and serpentine, he slithered through the underbelly of

Kankan, recruiting killers from the fringes of neighboring countries, men with hollow eyes and cheaper morals. They were not mercenaries; they were sacraments. In 1954, when the African Bloc of Guinea (BAG) dared to challenge Salim's ascent, Momo's handpicked ghouls descended like locusts. They wore BAG's colors while they worked, raping women in the name of "unity," slitting throats to "purify" dissent. Mosques burned, their ancient Qurans crackling like kindling. Homes were looted, then torched, families herded into wells, *alive*, their final pleas muffled under tons of earth.

"Join us," Momo would hiss, sweat in his breath being a pungent mixture of a gin and gunpowder, *"or become fertilizer for the revolution."*

The PDG's mantra was a knife pressed to the throat of reason. *Salim, or chaos.* Progress, or pits. Resistance howled out of grief, clutched the party's banner like a shroud. They sang it at rallies, voices neither filled with fervor nor full of resignation for the role of sustenance. Even those merchants and imams who loathed Salim, along with mothers still hearing their children's ghosts wailing from the wells, repeated his lies. To hate him openly was to die. To love him in secret was to rot.

And what of Salim himself? The man who railed against France's "imperialist cancer" even as he siphoned its riches. Who denounced colonial greed while his cronies pocketed bribes extorted from poor laborers. The revolution, he declared, was a "clean break" yet his regime thrived on the very systems he vilified. French engineers built his roads. French banks funded his purges. The hypocrisy was grotesque, and the people were choking on dissonance.

In only one year after independence, the PDG was no longer a party. It had become a cult, with the doctrine literally written in blood. Those who dared whisper, *"This is not what we fought for"* were swiftly gotten rid of, handled in unmarked vans, then herded into rivers swollen with dark secrets. The newspapers, already gagged, were filled with stories of "foreign infiltrators" and "tribal saboteurs." Neighbors distrustfully eyed one another, wondering who might sell a rumor just to save their own skin.

Yet, in the silence, in the darkness, the truth pulsated like a fresh wound: The disappeared, the tortured, the wells echoing script-less tragedies. The people knew. They had always known. But knowledge, when devoid of power, is a dirge humming under every forced smile, every staged parade, and every hollow *"Vive le PDG!"*

And so, Guinea moved forth, a nation of ghosts towards a graveyard future. The promise of the revolution was served to the people as a pot of vomit, the liberator turned jailer, and the savior turned reaper. The shadow of Salim stretched far, and within that darkness, erupted the laughter of Momo a bone-cracking sound, reminding that in this new Guinea, swallowing one's scream was survival.

Chapter 8

The beloved one

It was the beginning of a coalition of imperfect souls, each a mosaic of dreams and flaws, who believed they were carving justice from the rock of history. Wadu, Laysouf, and Yaryb, three names that were going to echo through these valleys and hills of Guinea. They would walk the same path, though never would they see the world through the same lens. Their disagreements were sharp, their visions crashing like the sea against the cliffs on which it spends itself. But amidst all this tumult, there was respect.

It was Wadu, with quiet dignity, who first conferred upon Yaryb and Laysouf the sobriquet "Fathers of Independence," a nomenclature which by itself burned with sincerity. It was Laysouf, bold and unyielding, who called Wadu "the most honorable man he knew," a truth spoken as though etched from his very heart. Ideologically at deluge, they shared but one bright dream-a Guinea free from the imperial chains.

However, let no myth conceal them. Freedom fighters as they were, these men were politicians and humans in the same measure as the rest of us. They wore ambition as armor. They got into conflict with each other while trying to reach that same high objective, they all held secret scruples while sabotaging each other. Such was the irony that made their struggle a dance of unity and discord. Laysouf's fiery conviction turned Guinea's liberation into a people's movement. He was a man of soil and carried the torch of independence into all villages, weaving freedom into both farmers and shepherds. This performance, however, distanced Wadu and Yaryb; not in bad faith but in full allegiance to his vision. Their philosophies were barriers to his goals, distractions that would seclude him fully from the real cause, severing the imperial chains that bound their people.

This story was of fire and shadow, of dreams birthed only to be endlessly betrayed because it asked not anyone's taking sides, but rather for looking at the whole picture, violent and non-violent, triumphant and indifferent. Most importantly, however, people were asked to face the day after the dream was achieved; to weigh whatever followed that should never have been neglected. For history is one of flawed, brilliant human beings who dared change the world, not a tale of saints and sinners.

Among Salim's most cunning gambits was his campaign to seduce the diaspora, those sharp-minded revolutionaries softened by Western libraries and café debates, back to Guinea's red-earth chaos. He wrote to them in ink stained with borrowed urgency: *The soil remembers your footsteps. Come bleed for it again.* It was a masterstroke, this repatriation of half-assimilated minds; their return lent his cause the gloss of intellect while stoking the people's hunger for unity. France, after all, feared nothing more than a fractured colony learning to speak with one tongue.

And Salim? He wielded words like a blacksmith's hammer; each syllable forged in the furnace of his elementary-school French. Who needed Sorbonne degrees when you could unravel a man's doubt with a proverb, or stitch a nation's pride with a folktale? He spun independence not as some fever-dream of radicals, but as algebra, inescapable, and elegant. "A people's worth," he'd declare to rapt crowds, "is measured not by the gold in their earth, but the fire in their throats when they say *enough*." The French scoffed at his "rationale," but even their sneers fed his myth: here was no frothing zealot, but a logician of liberation.

Yet his true genius lay in exploiting the quiet math of human longing. When facts frayed, he let faith take over. *Believe hard enough*, his rhetoric whispered, *and the world bends*. The people did more than believe, they *needed* to. What was colonialism if not a decades-long lesson in swallowing lies? At least Salim's fictions tasted like hope. And when doubt flickered, they remembered the labor strikes of '47: Salim, then a rail-thin union clerk, standing belly-empty before batons, shouting *strike* until his voice splintered. He'd gambled his bones for theirs once. Now they'd gamble their future on his tongue.

* * * * *

In the brave early days of Salim's political journey, during a time when the sun relentlessly baked the streets of Guinea with possibility amidst disillusionment, a man whose very name suggested both promise and peril clutched the Democratic Party of Guinea's nomination letter. Before him dangled the French Assembly seat like a golden key if only fifty French francs could be scrounged together to legalize his party; fifty francs that mocked him like the dust devils swirling at his barefooted feet. Fifty French francs. A pittance for the colonizers. A gaping chasm for a man who had slept on borrowed mats, who had eaten hope for supper. For weeks he haunted the doorways of relatives and comrades, his voice fraying as he spun with those thumbs of liberation visions, only to return empty-handed every night, the silence of his empty pockets screaming louder than his speeches. The time did not only gnaw at him as a mere logistical failure but as a cruel metaphor; Salim, that orphaned son of a blacksmith, had a lucky tongue but left nothing but ashes behind. Promises melted away before him like mirages: unpaid loans; fractured alliances; his own party's trust as brittle as dried cassava.

Yet, when he stood before the masses, it mattered not. The rich, molten timbre of his voice would put strained backs upright. *"They dangle francs before you, like bones to dogs!"* he'd rage, his forehead glistening with sweat as workers leaned in, their calloused hands squeezing into fists. *"You break your backs to line their pockets, our earth, our sweat, our gold! Why settle for crumbs when we can seize the feast?"* He paused deliberately, allowing rebellion to stir with his gaze as it swept over the crowd. "Follow me, and your children will eat from the same table as theirs." A little seduction dressed up as salvation, and the workers swallowed it whole. His genius lay not in the grandeur of his lies but in their simplicity, he conjured their hunger, their rage, their wounded pride.

But it was his raw humility, almost theatrical, nearly sacramental, what etched him into their hearts. In the village squares, he would drop down on his knees before the wizened chiefs, the earth biting through his flesh, his voice cracking like that of a boy. *"By Allah's mercy,"* he would plead, his palms upturned, *"see me not as a politician but as your son. An orphan with nothing but this fire in my chest to give you."* There would be tears in the mothers' eyes, while the men would grunt in approval. Truly, there was no slick opportunist among them but a brother, imperfect and fierce, who wore his desperation with pride. They did not merely vote for him; they claimed him, the guy who kissed their babies and drank bitter tea with them while every syllable spilled with his own hunger.

The rise of Salim was not just against the odds but because of his contradictions. To those who followed him, unpaid debts were less of a failure and more of a forum for kinship; broken vows were cracked armor, shared by the people against an empire which asked so very much of them. He became a mirror for his people: they saw not neat ideals but jagged hopes, and in the fractured glass, they saw not a leader but an awakening. This fiery combination of strength and weakness is what forged his legend and drew Guineans toward him in very thick cords of recognition even thicker than loyalty.

His ruse never failed, and to unravel why, one must retrace to the silence that molded him. A fatherless boy raised in rooms hollowed out by absence by a mother who was burdened with shame, which was almost her second skin. Otherwise, she scarcely spoke of the man whose legacy was nothing more than a disputed name and a little boy seeking to fill the absence. Young Salim learned to map missingness in the pauses between his mother's words and in the way other boys' laughter would turn him sour at the mention of fathers. Each empty boast of paternal pride twisted the knife deeper, until the wound became a compass, teaching him how to weaponize longing. He mastered the language of emptiness, and by adulthood, Salim was giving these empty opportunities back to the whole nation for them to see their own hunger staring back.

Anger became a constant companion that settled upon his chest, conveying forces of sorrow and rage to make his world seem smaller and darker. It was rage that would fester and ferment until the whole man became consumed by it, transforming acute annoyances into opportunities to lash him out and every slight into justification for his rebellion. He was angry at the world for having turned its back on him and his father for leaving him to grow up an unanchored boy without dignity.

One could say that anger sculpted him into something dark and outside the box, to an extent that he could make the world revolve around his will, even if crawling through the muddy roads of iniquities was required. He became very talented at faking and impersonating, almost smiling when that was expected; almost pleading with begging, speaking the language of pity whenever begging was needed. Words grew sharper than knives. Promises were as hollow as the void that should have been filled by his father. He learned that no matter how invincible and self-satisfied a person appeared, they're all just walking around with holes inside them, a buyable hole too, if you have the wit to discover it.

Salim had a face people trusted, and a voice that gave them reason to believe in him, just long enough to get what he wanted. He always knew how to bend the truth, whether consciously or subconsciously to present himself as the protagonist in his own sorry story. It wasn't hard; he had seen it done a hundred times, heard his mother's voice soft on occasion when referring to his dead-beat father, and even the dim glimmer of pity from his friends whenever they asked him about the man. And again, he had learned well, oh, how he had learned! He had learned that the world is full of people who are waiting to be taken advantage of, eager to give what little they have in return for a sense of having done something decent.

By the time he was a man, he had perfected the art of the ruse. There were no lines he wouldn't cross, no shame he wouldn't stoop to. To him, lying wasn't a crime; it was a tool. Begging wasn't weakness; it was leverage. He had become someone willing to use his pain, his past, and his rage as a weapon against everyone else. And when they gave in, when they handed him what he wanted with that satisfied, gullible smile, he would smile back, and for just a moment, he would feel what he had never felt as a boy: in control. Powerful. As though he had finally won the game. And yet, underneath it all, the hole remained, the emptiness left by a father who had never been there, never cared to be. And no matter how many lies he told, how many people he bent to his will, he could never quite fill it. But that didn't stop him from trying.

Anyway, he knew that he was already in the conscience of the poor laborers he started fighting for as he would constantly claim. The people opened what today we would call a GoFundMe page for him to provide the fifty French Franc. People could relate to his struggle. Women were the fiercest combatants for his cause at the point of refusing themselves to their husbands if they would not adhere to the DPG and knowing that he could not have done it without them. So, in gratitude he became the first to "emancipate" women in West Africa. He believed that the emancipation for women was not an act of solidarity but an obligation. Although, emancipation for women is still a controversy in Africa whether it is a reality or an illusion.

As someone who lost two of his grandparents in exile while resisting colonization, Salim got a valuable lesson, he believed that kindness is weakness, and this is the most important ingredient that causes one to be exploited. This belief made him reinvent himself into someone not to be reckoned with, due to the reminders of centuries ago when innocent dark-skinned people welcomed pale skin with colored eyes, people into their homes and fed them. In return they were stripped of their dignity, enslaved, slaughtered, and transported to foreign lands to serve as machines. The hearts and minds of the people of Guinea were in fragile states, they would have trusted anyone who could have given them hope or prevented them from living through the same calvary their parents did. As Bocar Biro had enunciated to his brothers during the invasion of colonial powers,

"Mo yahaali poret daaka o yahay daaka poret." "Whomever does not show up in Poret Daaka for the battle, will show up and set a camp to undergo the wrath of colonial lashes." Salim swayed his "brothers" to do the same when in fact most of them did not need convincing at all.

They were ready to come back home and help. The diaspora was returning to do its part. A bitter change hung heavy across West Africa, stifling and inescapable, a paradox of hope and despair that clung to the throats of those who dared to breathe it. In the cities bordering Guinea, cranes clawed at the sky, stitching steel and glass into the structure of ancient landscapes. The French, in their zeal to humble Salim, had unwittingly seeded a farcical garden of progress. Harbors swelled with foreign ships, railways spiderwebbed into the hinterlands, and boulevards designed in the image of Parisian grandeur gleamed under the sun. Yet these monuments to modernity pulsed with a silent rage. Colonial edicts slithered through government halls, strangling local ambitions even as they fed the illusion of growth. The people watched, their pride curdling into resentment, as the fruits of their labor were plucked by distant hands. Innovation thrived, but it was a borrowed vitality, a heartbeat sustained by the very forces that sought to own it.

Meanwhile, Guinea languished in the shadow of its neighbors' fractured prosperity. People came to the realization that freedom was a thorn, not a torch as the leaders of Guinea made them believe. Not only that but cut off from the chokehold of colonial "guidance," which was seen as the only obstacle to the prosperity of Guinea, the country withered, its soil starved of the institutions that might have nourished it. Schools were crumbling myths. Hospitals existed as rumors. In villages, children's bellies swelled not with food but with emptiness, their eyes hollow mirrors reflecting a future already pilfered. The earth itself seemed to recoil, fields yielded less, rivers soured, and the wind carried whispers of a storm-balls rolling in the next day's horizon. Farmers clutched their hoes like relics of a dying faith, while the young drifted into cities only to find streets of dust and promises as brittle as bone. Guinea's "freedom" had slowly been turned into asphyxiation by the same people who promised positive change.

And France, armed with its smuggler's cunning, sharpened its knives to impose western ideology. The world turned its gaze away as Paris anointed itself *gendarme* of the continent, its mission draped in the velvet lies of "order" and "civilization." In backroom chambers, maps of Africa were carved with invisible blades once again, but this time it is regimes being swayed by Moscow's emancipatory speeches marked for extinction. Guinea was the perfect Guinea pig. Covert operatives, their faces blurred by shadow, wove webs of sabotage.

But in the interlude that was silent amidst the chaos, defiance flickered. In those were impassioned stories by old men about empires that once stretched across the horizon. Mothers sang antiquated songs into their children's hair, melodies laden with the undying spirit of generations. The horizon ahead was indeed gloomy, but darkness could be a womb as well. Beneath the anguish lay a fermenting truth: empires rot from within.

For instance, the ink was barely dry on the armistices of 1945 when France, war-ravaged cities still pockmarked, and pride raw from occupation, began reconstructing its empire through a more silent conquest. The *franc des Colonies Francaises d'Afrique*, the CFA franc, was not just any currency. Well, the one stamped with the serene portrait of

Marianne, the goddess of liberty, was unable to buy this lie of independence; rather, it was the one stamped with emblems peculiar to the African continent, mostly allegorical symbols. Otherwise, how else would the lie of independence be sold to the public. It seeped into the veins of twelve African territories like a narcotic, sweet with promises of stability but laced with chains of subjugation. Not printed in network capitals of Africa like Dakar or Abidjan, but in the limestone guts of France at Chamalières, its very fibers whispered the colonial mantra: *You are ours, even when you think you're free.* After all, control the coins in a man's pocket, and you oversee the bread on his table, the riots in his streets, and even the loyalty in his heart.

It is just that Guinea's revolt in 1958 struck such a blow. While the other colonies knelt at the altar of golden CFA handcuffs, Salim's Non to General Charles resonated far and wide like a cracked bell. By 1960, the rump government of Conakry began to issue its own Guinean franc notes crudely designed with the silhouette of a woman wearing a headscarf, manufactured in socialist factories in Prague. To Paris, this was sheer rebellion beyond forgiveness. The CFA was the last tie of binding France to its *civilisatrice mission,* if you will. Snap it, and the whole edifice of neocolonial control would come crashing down.

Jacques Foccart, the architect of France's shadow empire, understood this like no other as he paced his office like a caged jackal. In his labyrinthine office near the Élysée, under green desk lamps, glowed maps of Africa, pins marking uranium mines in Niger, cocoa plantations in Côte d'Ivoire, and now, down over Conakry, a glaring red pin. Over the years, he had sanctioned coups, bribes, and puppet presidents in Africa with his many mists of intrigue, but Guinea's currency gambit required a subtler venom. Charles's *gray eminence* knew power in its rawest form: currencies as weapons, ink-stained paper mightier than battalions. Sitting on the opposite side of the desk was the SDECE spymaster, Maurice Robert, his fingers steepled. No armies were necessary: a whisper here, a bribe there, and down would roll the presses of Chamalières, not with CFA notes, but so counterfeit Guinean francs that they would put to shame even those of socialist Prague. *"Money,"* he muttered quoting Cicero as if it were scripture, *"is the nerve of war. We will sever theirs."*

The plan was diabolical in its simplicity, but genius, the dollar-for-dollar anarchy kinda way: the Guinean franc was to be counterfeited out of existence. Nothing like the back-alley clumsy forgeries; no, this was true cut-throat economics. French technicians, veterans of the Banque de France's engraving studios, replicated with ghastly precision on designs made in Prague. Indeed, they went a lot further: paper with linen content, capable of resisting Guinea monsoon humidity, inks that would not fade under the equatorial sun. Oh, the irony! Even destruction left with a better panache than the authentic currency they intended to wipe out with their counterfeit bills. Which instead of devaluing the genuine ones, just replaced them, undermining the intended purpose.

Operation Persil, named after the detergent (that cleans without a trace) kicked off in the monsoon season of 1960. Crates labeled "Agricultural Equipment" filled with counterfeit banknotes to the tune of hundreds of millions poured into Conakry's port. SDECE agents posed as Lebanese textile merchants and Soviet aid workers, quietly pouring lots of hot cash into markets. Market women haggling over yams, black-market traders smelling a kill in the water, hoarded rice and salt, placing demands to be paid in French CFA. The Guinean franc wasn't just crumbling, it was evaporating.

In Paris, Jacques was sipping Armagnac, savoring the chaos. *"So, independence, huh?"* He sneered at Maurice, *"Let them eat inflation."* The Nazi playbook had been his muse; Operation Bernhard had almost sunk Churchill's economy with fake British pounds. But this was quite a lot crueler. The British knew the enemy; Guinean peasants clung to francs better than the ones they had yesterday, unaware that these notes were just French lies clad in African symbols. In the smoke-filled parlors of Conakry, Salim's economists whispered a counterstroke. They declared a currency exchange: all existing francs had to be surrendered in exchange for freshly issued banknotes incorporating new features that were harder to reproduce. Through 72 hours, queues snaked through the streets, with people surrendering their life savings, real or counterfeit alike. French forgeries? piled in warehouses and then burned. Flickering flames licked the night with the Persil francs turned to ashes, a bonfire of vanities, where Guinea declared its defiance visibly. Jacques could barely contain his wrath, and Maurice did some fast recalibration. The Spider's web shuddered but remained intact. Guinea survived, hurt, but sovereign. The CFA franc, however, outlived empires, outlived ideologies, outlived even the men who forged it.

Operation Persil had now long-wrapped shadows reaching beyond the frontiers of Guinea, slipping into the jagged cracks of the old French empire. In Conakry, SDECE agents tried funneling rifles into the hands of disgruntled dissidents, erecting a patchwork militia to coax the country toward anarchy. But paranoia, that great unraveller of conspiracies, had set its poisonous seeds already within the wildering web of plots. Whispers slipped through back alleys of Dakar and found their way into the ears of Guinean spies. By the sweltering May morning of 1960, when Senegalese police forced open crates labeled "Agricultural Machinery," the truth lay nakedly present: warehouses of Belgian rifles, German pistols, and French arrogance, all stamped with the invisible fingerprints of Paris. Once a quiet accomplice to colonial machinations, Prime

Minister Mamadou Dia now a fervent nationalist held that very incriminating evidence like a dagger. His protest against France was by far crackling with all the fury of betrayal: a colonized turncoat turning the knife against them. "Senegal is a sovereign country and will not be used as a gateway for clandestine artillery to destabilize our neighbor." He snapped.

Maurice Robert, architect of the crumbling scheme, scribbled away in his memoirs: "We gutted Guinea's economy like a fish. Yet Salim... that street-corner prophet... he *survived*." The counterfeit francs had done their shadowy ballet, torching markets to ash and reducing salaries to jokes. While Guinea's economy was flushed down the drain, Salim managed to foil the plot merely because the whole affair had been discovered and dismantled in time. Being under enormous pressure and fear, however, Salim knew it was one thing to humiliate a superpower with words, quite another to attempt to confront it. He tucked his tail between his legs and tied his tongue to live and fight another day.

France's commitment to maintaining its interests in Africa went far beyond mere diplomatic strategies. So, its gaze shifted to the oil-rich jungles of Cameroon. Here, independence was not a negotiation but a necropolis. The Union of the People of Cameroon (UPC), its ranks swollen with radicals who'd tasted Marx and Mao, dared to dream beyond France's iron nursery. Their leader, Félix Mounié, was no firebrand, he was an inferno. To Maurice Delauney, France's viceroy in all but name, Mounié's sin was not ideology but *audacity*. "A man who refuses to kneel," Delauney muttered to his aides, "is a man who must fall." Maurice Delauney, an official, entrusted with the sensitive task of choosing the country's new leader. The priority was to find a figure who would be presentable, well-trained, and, most importantly, loyal to French interests and he found one. Oh, yes… he did find one. Amadou, a member of the same party, UPC. So, *Mounie has got to go.*

Enters the picture, William Bechtel, a mercenary, charlatan, and ghost. With a press pass and a vial of thallium, he slipped into a hidden safehouse in Geneva to meet Mounié, the room thick with unspoken tension and fogged with a mask of betrayal. They talked weapons, alliances and freedom. Then, over a little coffee with oblivion in it, Bechtel watched the revolutionary's hands begin to shake, and by dawn, a twitching husk was all that was left of Mounié. By week's end, Swiss pathologists traced the poison back to the Parisian puppeteers. Delauney knew better than to admit even a crumb of this. Yet, in the archives rests one single surviving telegram: *"The garden is weeded. Plant the rose."* The "rose" soon blossomed: a puppet president was installed, and UPC bones buried in unmarked graves.

In Libreville, the farce reached its zenith. Gabon's oil flowed like a black Nile into French refineries, and in return, Paris gifted its "ally" a president so pliant he might have been carved from rubber. When Charles visited in 1967, he didn't bother with diplomatic niceties. "Here," he boasted to journalists, "I feel at home." The subtext hung heavier than the equatorial humidity: Gabon was not a nation but a franchise, its leader a district manager in blackface.

They called them *"les gouverneurs noirs"*, the Black Governors. Men like Léon M'ba, who let French paratroopers crush his own coup attempt, or Omar Bongo, who turned his palace into a clearinghouse for Elf Aquitaine's bribes. Their loyalty was measured in crude oil and uranium; their legitimacy laundered through sham elections. To protest was to vanish; to resist was to choke on thallium-laced wine.

Salim survived. Mounié did not and he was just the first of many. Gabon's oil still fuels Parisian winters. The CFA franc lived and remained tethered to French banks. Today, West African nations are still trying to abandon the CFA, but the ghost of Persil lingers, and African leaders always scurries under their mothers' skirts when the populace mention *"We want out of CFA"* a cautionary tale of how currency, that most fragile of papers, can be both a nation's lifeline and its leash.

This shows that decolonization was never about flags lowered or anthems rewritten, it was about who held the scalpel when the body was cut. France, the best surgeon of them all, ensured the scars it left were ones that ached in the rain.

Chapter 9

Meli

As time goes by, the hour of crisis turned toward appeal in Guinea. The nation's plight was rather dreadful by the day, and people flocked to the clarion call of their new leader. Among them, Samba Meli, a man who envisioned that something extraordinary-to-the-point-of-ability could influence him to initiate the process of change. Meli's mind was a strange fusion of charisma and intellect. He saw patterns invisible to others, the hidden logic beneath. Where most saw confusion, he saw maps, routes towards destiny. His rare perception, born of low latent inhibition, allowed him to glimpse connections that eluded even the wisest minds. He did not merely think; he saw. He knew he was destined to go forth and transform the very face of Africa into a continental dream which would nurture and raise her children as her own. Into this tenuous balance stepped in Meli's comrade, Salim. The genius was the fountain of brilliance, Meli; and Salim was the typhoon, a maelstrom of instability and undisciplined madness. With Salim, the border holding sanity and insanity was blurred. His ideas were spontaneous, subversive, and recklessly avant-garde, all of which made the beauty of that vortex of chaos even more enticing. He never recognized boundaries, and whatever he did might have either ushered in transformation or obliteration. The whole world had to be measured against his will, and that unpredictable aura to his character was both charm and terror that attracted the diaspora.

Chaos, as it often does, had summoned equilibrium, and Meli had answered. Where Salim had burned with untamed vision, Meli held a mind like a scalpel, carving raw ambition into plans that could be accomplished. Meli was not just the supporter; he was the rational mind, the strategist, the genius who stood alongside Salim to turn his fevered imaginings into actual possibilities. A strange pairing, perhaps, yet powerful; Salim, the unhinged leader, with Meli as the calculating genius who knew just how to steer that madness into a common cause. Meli would invariably be a member of the inner circle of power, always passive in how he would influence every decision. Like Laysouf before him, Meli served as a distant intellectual architect, yet with a much greater flair. Meli was always quick to smile; his perfect teeth gleamed in every encounter, as if the world was a grand stage and he was the only one that truly understood the script. Behind that ever-present smile, however, was a mind working constantly to see that Salim's recklessness did not spiral into catastrophe but rather emerged as the transformative factor in Africa's destiny.

The origin of Meli meant the origin of loneliness, as an old folk saying goes. The story of Meli started in Poret Daka, victorious lands where the colonialists with boots trampled throats but could not choke the hum of the rebellion. Its soil held within the bones of resistance fighters like Imam Bocar Biro, who raised arms against chains of oppression. Meli was raised by a mother hardened by losses, five children stolen away by fever. She named him after the Meli tree, a venomous paradox of danger and resilience. *"It survives because it warns the world not to touch it,"* she would say, gripping his small shoulders. The name turned into a prophecy. By twelve, he knew every act of rebellion in their history by heart; by twenty, he pledged to write his own. Survival, strategy, and the alchemy of turning poison into power had been Meli's world since long before he crossed path with the chaotic Salim.

At six years old, Meli's world split open like the first light of dawn. While other children chased games in the dust, he stepped into the hallowed silence of the Koranic school and the almost empty corridors of a primary school, his small hands clutching knowledge like a lifeline. His was a mind which devoured the lessons, voraciously. It craved them with an insatiable yearning. When the chief of the canton looked into the eyes of that boy, with brilliance brighter than the sun-scorched savannah, it was indeed as if destiny had whispered into the chief's ear. *This one*, the chief must have thought, *this one must go further*. Against tradition, against expectation, Meli was sent to the city, where Western-style schools stood as gates to a future reserved only for the privileged. But Meli was no ordinary child. He might have been far from the son of a canton chief, but he had something canton chiefs' offspring did not have.

Carried on those narrow shoulders was the weight of all hopes in his village, and he vowed to prove that their faith was not misplaced. Years unfurled like scrolls of triumph. Meli climbed, the way a climber ascends a cliff, the heights of academic achievement to have his name echo in the classrooms as one who determinedly strove to attain what he could. Yet even, standing atop the pinnacle of where his father's education could take him, he felt an ache deep inside his heart. Knowledge, he realized, was an ocean, endless, infinite, and he took only a sip at its shores. Now to the prestigious William Ponty Institute, the hub of the brightest minds in Africa. It was there, amid the ferment of ideas and the hum of youthful ambition, that he met *her*.

Jadika.

Her name drummed in his blood. She was strong-willed: fierce and uncompromising, an unwavering flame to his restless fire. As they say: Behind every great man is a greater woman. But Jadika was no shadow. She stood right beside Meli, boldly calling out to him, her belief in him a fortress barring the inroads of doubt. Yet, for all her strength, she could not shield him from reality's merciless sting. Money, or rather lack thereof, gnawed at his dreams. The once-promising halls of William Ponty had turned into a cage. With a heart weighed down as if by stone, Meli walked away, swapping textbooks for ledgers at the African General Government in Dakar. The colonial mechanisms mauled his days but could not douse the fiery blossom of longing in his chest. Time trudged by. Filing papers was Meli's task, but Parisian lecture halls would be where his mind would wander, straining to hear faint echoes of dearly loved debates. Then came a moment of awakening: The colleague, that one who'd seen him scrawl equations in the margins of reports, grasped his shoulder. "You are meant for more." Those words cracked open the shell of resignation. Meli, now a man hardened by loss but unbroken, seized his chance. He conquered the baccalaureate, once, twice, as if defying time itself. And then, with the recklessness of hope, he boarded a ship to France.

Paris held the tempest at bay. Without doubt, it's the closest thing to city life alive with the pulse of Pan-Africanism. In narrow cafés and smoke-filled rooms, Meli found his tribe: Alioune Diop, a man whose pen challenged empires; Sheikh Anta Diop, who tracked the roots of stolen civilizational history in his groundbreaking thesis, *The African Origin of Civilization*, proving that the pharaohs of Egypt wore skins dark like his. Here, among these thinkers and rebels, Meli's purpose crystallized: law school was not merely a path toward degrees but a weapon, sharpened to knock down the chains of colonialism, just as he would when crowned with that doctorate in 1954, whereupon he accepted the manifesto that it was not just a title.

By 1955, the boy who once stood in awe before chalkboards now occupied the highest post, that of the Office of the High Commissioner of French West Africa (AOF); this was the maximum a native could attain in the colonial upbeat hierarchy. Two years later, he became General secretary, a titan navigating the tempest of a crumbling empire with great skill. In moments of silence, he would still hear, loftily indignant, Jadika's voice, pride of the village chief, the rustles of textbooks in dim offices of Dakar.

Meli's journey is not luck but a defiance: showing how hunger, when nourished by love and rage, can bend the arc of history. He walked a path strewn with closed doors and clenched fists, but then every scar became a star guiding him home. Through his resilience, Meli became more than a scholar, more than a leader. He became proof that Africa's future could not be stolen, only borrowed-and he meant to reclaim it.

Be it selective or an indefinite event, after Meli had come on the land of Guinea, the land seemed to hum beneath the shuffling shoes, an ancestral whisper greeting him to a destiny thing etched in his bones. His heartbeat towards land was not ambition but devotion; a vow to carve Guinea's name into the consciousness of the world that had turned away. It will no longer linger in the margins, as a phantom state. He would make them *see*: its sovereignty fierce, its spirit unbroken, its soil rich with more than just gold and bauxite but also dignity.

The faded dream of Salim flared anew in Meli's hands. Where others saw futility, he saw kindling. His words were not mellifluous diplomatic comment; rather, the very sound of wildfire crackled through them, the sound bursting with the heat of conviction. Dust rose in shafts of sunlight, the crowds leaned in as if they were drawn by tides, and even the skeptics seemed to feel it: the future unspooling in his cadence. He was a griot of hope; his voice wove tales of Guinea untethered and free from the shackles imposed by foreign whims. A nation really *demanding* and not *begging* respect. Meli defied simplicity with a laughter that stung brightly and disarmed, lifting weary souls like wind carrying seeds. He disarmed with smiles, with wit, and a dance of sorts that made you feel the heat when you got too close-and too far away to be comfortable. Those who mistook his levity as weakness learned fast: joy was his armor, and warmth was his punishable offense, and in the quietest moments his resolve smoldered; a flame he had nurtured in secret, impervious to being pushed away.

He moved through rooms like a current, electrifying air and intention. To meet him was to be *known*; his gaze stripped pretense, his hand on your shoulder a silent pact: *We rise together*. And in that alchemy, doubters were turned to believers. Meli understood what tyrants and cynics forgot: true strength whispers before it thunders. It lives in the ember that outlasts the storm, in the roots that split stone. Time had come for Guinea. And Meli? He was both spark and sickle, harvesting a new dawn from the dark.

He wore no masks. His power was hidden deep within, a molten core-quietly crept into a resolve, that bent but never broke, even when colonial powers brazenly scoffed at the very notion of a free Guinea. And when on December 12, 1958, the United Nations admitted Guinea to membership, it was much beyond just recognition; it was an earthquake.

The earth tilted, calibrated afresh. To Salim, victory tasted of iron and honey: simplest of proof that a will of a people could outlast empires. France was smug in its assurance of dominance; it choked on the silence. How curious it is to think of how the Chinese could block everything pertaining to Taiwan in the UN, while the French could not do as much for Guinea, sharing the same set of permanent veto powers. An ironic twist indeed! Neighbors, who'd dismissed Guinea as a mere speck on the map, now looked uneasily upon it as it wedged its entry into history. No longer a nation pleading for a seat at the very table that excluded it, Guinea was busy *erecting* its own table, with a resonant and unapologetic voice.

Well, New York awaited Meli like a blank page as he was the first Guinean envoy to the UN, then later became the ambassador to the US, he moved through marble halls with the ease of a man who knew his worth. Such was the weight of one's title in the living world. But indeed, such things were of little meaning to him. He was always to be found behind closed doors, handshaking with noisy whispers across grand negotiation surfaces, while a larger dream simmered within. Africa, jagged and torn by borders drawn in foreign ink, whispers to him about oneness: he dreamed for a quilt, braided of Ghana's defiance, of Ethiopia's ancient pride, and of Guinea's audacity, all into something unbreakable. With Nkrumah's fervor and Selassie's regal pragmatism, Meli became the quiet architect of solidarity. No grand manifestoes, no chest-thumping. His strength lay in the tilt of a listening head, the question that unraveled discord, the laugh that dissolved tension.

Meanwhile, Salim, the classical case of *"you can't shame the shameless."* wielded power with a clenched fist at home while clasping hands abroad. Critics called him contradictory; Meli knew better. The man understood that sovereignty was duel, fierce within borders, diplomatic beyond them.

Together, they became a paradox: the firebrand and the bridge-builder. Meli's genius was in making both roles sacred.

And so, in dimly lit chambers during the glare of the outside world's scrutiny, he sewed a revolution of collective might. "A continent's strength," he'd murmur, "is not in one man's roar, but in the chorus of millions." Africa, a generally dismissed continent as a mere pawn in others' games, is now beginning to stir: a lion shaking off sleep.

Meli's flame, once a spark in Guinea's soil, now licked the edges of empires. Through him, a continent learned to speak not in fragments, but in a language of its own making. The world would not hear it as an echo, but as a hymn. And in that choir of voices, Meli's truth prevailed: *The future belongs not to those who scream, but to those who burn.*

Having been broken by colonial borders, and torn apart by conflicting ideologies, the dream of Africa being united was beginning to find shape. After a decade of burning debates and fragile compromises between moderates and revolutionaries, those who urged for patience and those adamant about immediate federation: the Organization of African Unity (OAU) was founded.

It is in the Highlands of Ethiopia, a country never colonized, that the founding fathers pledged to chart a future untethered by foreign influence. No external finance. No imitative ideologies. Only African hands and African minds. The rules were clear; it would have a Secretary-General accountable to Africa, not to any one African state, or to powers beyond the continent.

However, envy cast a shadow upon him from which Salim could never be freed. Even before the names like Meli began to resound through the portals of OAU, whispered with awe by foreign dignitaries and local papers alike, Salim brewed from an acrid envy of respect. That was a man who stood aloof from the compromises that were innate to power, whose reputation was without stain, and whose transparency was doubted by none. Meli's rise with meteoric swiftness and his diplomacy was one that could slice through the gristle of international politics, and this was the main reason why Salim resented needing him.

The choice had been gnawing at him for weeks. His intuition told him to choose Lansia Dane, a loyal man whose obedience could be relied upon like the sun rising. No spectacular consequences would occur; nothing would turn in the end against Salim himself. Planting an unqualified sycophant into the corridors of OAU would have been just a comfort for him but, the world had its eyes on it. The United Nations had already started snorting at the blunders of Salim's regime; one more error, and they would be lost. Salim's pride coagulated into reluctant pragmatism; once congealed, it was irreversible.

His signature fell upon the Meli appointment decree, with a hand heavy as stone. *Necessity,* he told himself, the words bitter in the mouth. Not admiration, never that.

But in the quiet hours, Salim knew a quieter, sharper truth: Meli's ascent was, in fact, a mirror, showing his own corroding legacy. The president who once vowed he would crown Guinea in glory now schemed to keep it from crumbling, and the man who might save it was the same one who made Salim feel small. This made him discover that pride was a poor alternative for progress. Still, it was all he had left.

July 6th, the gathering of heads of state for the first great summit of the OAU gave the opportunity for a strong wind of urgency to blow. Here at Cairo, 39 years of age, a visionary bursting with idealism was to be revealed to the world as General Secretary of the organization. The choice was in fact celebrated and scrutinized. When diplomats highly praised him, some whispered of his naivete. Meli's voice, unflinching and impassioned, pleaded for the release of Nelson Mandela and scorched those arbitrary borders traced by the Berlin Conference. He mediated territorial disputes between Togo, the Gold Coast, and Upper Volta, with words harsh yet softened by a genuine belief in unity. For some, his association with radicals like Salim was rather reckless; for others, he was their only promise of hope: at last, time for the African children to speak for themselves.

The new Africa was assertively coming into being proud of its progress, and self-reliance. Nations expropriated industries, redistributed land, and poured resources into schools and hospitals. Although, colonial shadows still hung over it. Pan-Africanists Kwame Nkrumah and Julius Nyerere preached, and Meli's engagement resonated with their vision: *"Unity is our shield; solidarity our sword."* But even under this fervor, cracks showed: as old masters continued pulling the strings, not all his pairs embraced Meli's audacity. They feared consequences, yes, a slip that could unravel that young fragile sovereignty.

Meli stood at the precipice of history. His praises sang by all around Africa were more illusions of idealism that revealed vulnerabilities. He was a man whose words carried power and revealed policies in a world cloaked by threats but to the whole world clocking his symbol of Africa's diplomatic awakening. Whispers, however, grew around the power corridors: *could such a principled man hold his own in such a ruthless game?* Like Meli himself, the OAU had its trial by fire. Born out of defiance, now it had to prove that a continent divided once could rise united.

During a press conference at the OAU, Meli shared a concern. His message was one from the African leaders to the world. It was one of those moments when a gathering room seemed to dwindle, the podium shone with chandeliers and focused on the non-blinking gaze of Meli. *"Let me be perfectly clear,"* he began, voice steady; "The OAU *rejects* partnership with the UN. Not out of pride but principle. We did not forge this organization to let foreign hands steer our destiny." A ripple of stark alertness ran through the assembly as diplomats, then, stiffened at their seats. The Secretary-General's expression darkened, but he pressed on, words sharp as a blade. "Our purpose is simple, the total liberation of this continent. Every nation still shackled by colonial influence will breathe free. And we will not stand idle while others presume to do *our* work, in *our* house."

Silence pooled like spilled ink. Even the clatter of translators' headsets ceased. It was more than defiance, it was a throwing of gauntlets, a declaration that Africa's future would be written by African hands. Some saw recklessness in his tone; others, the unyielding resolve of a continent finally rising to claim its voice.

However, during his time as the chief of the organization, Meli was faced with extreme challenges. Dealing with newly freed countries that are occupied by power hungry leaders was difficult, and sometimes finding ways to compromise with people, each of whom that had divergent views of topics was exasperating. Social and political change paved the way for some African countries to entertain authoritarianism, where leaders forged their way into power and stifled every opposing voice. Now common were one-party rules and restrictions placed on political freedoms, as the leaders sought to maintain stability and control in the face of mounting economic and social pressure. Nonetheless, opposition movements and civil society organizations flourished in their campaign against the authoritarian regimes, advocating for human rights, democracy, and accountable governance. And if help was needed, Meli was just one door away, and never tired to spread words of wisdom.

He was a darling of the people, yet a glimmer of fear persisted about Salim's potential influence through him. Ghoren, a socialist luminary, sat astride negritude theory and was heavily immersed in French intellectual traditions; his ideologies were polished within European academic halls. But it was this very man who, betraying Salim in his anti-colonial fight, favored rather the assimilation of Africa into the French Empire. He viewed slavery as that grim but necessary steppingstone, if you may, to oppression, and he was deeply troubled by the concept of tiny, fragmented nations that would forever be subjected to greater ones within Africa. Integration, in his mind, was a way for the continent to evolve under the umbrella of the empire, a position Salim all but rejected. Such ideological dissonance set Salim apart and made him an outcast-a contagion to be avoided by the powers that be. Representing everything that the West detested, he was, in subtle ways, an irritant to their interests, being considered a rebel who befriended their foes and whose voice thundered against apartheid, a significant contribution in giving shelter to South African revolutionaries, including Rolihlahla himself, whose resolve was forged at least in part in Guinea, his very first brush with resistance on its soil.

Salim's resistance went further, and efforts on his part to shield figures such as Emery Lumumba from the imperial retribution with the assistance of the enigmatic Sese Seko were doomed to failure. Emery was neither wise enough nor prepared to weather the storm he had brought on himself. Wild and impetuously idealistic to the terrible end, Salim was even rejected by his immediate allies, finally branded an outcast in a world that yearned for conformity. Whereas Ghoren sought middle ground, Salim and Emery cast theirs aside for rebellion, their legacy, therefore, became juxtaposed: between partnership and resistance, between the pragmatism of the mind and the audacity of the heart.

Aware of how his survival would have probably sparked a seismic shift around the world, a potential end to empires and rewriting the destiny of a continent, Emery, when it came to it, chose his wife and children rather than his nation's children. As J.R.R. Martins' adage in Game of Thrones, *"Love is the death of Duty,"* echoed as a requiem in the atmosphere. Emery lived the truth thereof, trading his chimeric mantle of revolution for his fragile venture of family. He was captured and sent to the slaughter by *his own Frankenstein,* Sese Seko. Had he looked beyond the abyss, awaiting fate of his people, the hollowing of his dreams, his resolve might have broken, but once love is surrendered to, there are no last-minute revisions.

His end was a horrifying scene arranged to wipe away not just the man, but all memory. His days of torture ended with his body cleaved by axes and then dropped into a vat bubbling with sulfuric acid, dissolving flesh and bone into a viscous emptiness. They sought more than his death; they desired erasure. No corpse, no trial, no justice, just whispers of a ghost. Yet in their brutality they forged a paradox: Emery, once human, became legend. A martyr not for one cause but for the general soul of the continent. What once was considered outrageous about his acts of defiance now courses through the blood of students, artists, and rebels, a trumpet call for bravery.

Meanwhile, Salim stood alone as Pan-Africanism's sentry, to some revered, to others reviled. He made common cause with any who resisted hegemony, dissidents, exiles, vanishing nations, only to find himself more and more isolated. The powers of the world painted him a rogue, a disruptor of their finely ordered world. Even among friends, unease was born of his inflexibility. Where Ghoren taught assimilation, Salim thundered sovereignty; where others looked to compromise, he demanded revolution. The circle of his associates shrank; yet, they stood resolved, resolute as a diamond grown in the pressure of distance.

In the shadow cast by Emery's gruesome demise, Salim had a bitter revelation: the freedom fight was a labyrinth without any way out, just endless halls of sacrifice. Still, he treaded the maze with a torch held aloft, a torch of the hopes of an entire continent burning down his very hands. Emery's chemical grave had birthed a legion of spirits. The pragmatic yet dreamy Salim would march on, a lone soul amidst a storm of empires, until his very name would be turned to ash, then to anthem.

Chapter 10

The paranoia

The dark days of 1831 set forth that France created what was to become at once a legend and a nightmare: The French Foreign Legion. Upon resolutions of King Louis Philippe, an incorruptible force of soldiers who had been set up, mercenaries, exiles, and wanderers bound by an oath, who came into being through blood and sand. Their motto of *"Honor and Loyalty"* rang like a hollow hymn, for more than honor, they sought dominion. They were the empire's puppeteers, the silent blade in the dark, tasked to perform ruthless deeds for France's colonial ambitions at any cost. Although, the winds of change in Africa placed the Legion of the mid-20th century onward in a transformed role from conquerors to jailers. Former colonies stood trembling at the precipice of freedom; were met not with open hands but clenched fists. Contrived independence was nevertheless offered by France, yes, but an independence laced with venom: Nations like Guinea, Togo, and Mali were and still are offered the Faustian contract: pay crippling annual tributes or watch their economies crumble. What sovereignty came in price for was surrendering to a currency printed in Paris, a noose in disguise of coins.

These are the glories of those who dared too much. Togo, with Sylvanus Olympio at the helm, had negotiated the ridiculous deal of paying France some forty percent of its GDP. Then, he began dreaming of a freedom beyond his new shining chains. 1963 saw him turning away from the colonial currency of France, an act of pride for self-determination. But the Legion's specters haunted even independence. At the break of the cold silence of dawn, Étienne Gnassingbé, a legionnaire with firm loyalty to his old masters, cornered Olympio like a helpless puppy. Three bullets sealed his fate in scarlet warnings: death must follow defiance.

Sometimes you might wonder, do these African leaders ever learn? Because after only five years since his demise, Modibo Keita of Mali, with eyes sharpened from betrayal, perceived the trap for what it was a debt-sinking dressed in the garb of liberty. He pledged to emancipate his people and restore their very soul. Before another shadow could breed masses and soak them with his voice, it happened again: All it took was a legionaried-coupist, and cut short was Keita's promise, documented evidence of a guillotine.

These were not merely political upheavals: these were the killing of dreams by a dying nation straining hard to sustain its wasting hegemony. The Legion, forever faithful to the end, kept alive the old order. What an affair of honor and fidelity.

With rather more stirring echoes, lingering now in the whispered narrative of those who dared too much, the Legion remained a collage of heroism and havoc beneath which lie tales of subjugation. For those who resisted, freedom became nothing but a mirage: glistening just beyond reach, forever polluted with the blood of the bold who couldn't keep their opinions to themselves.

And the CFA, ugh... The CFA franc! Sorry, I can't help it; I just had to bring it up again. I promise it's the last time! Or do I? Anyway, I mention it again and again to have it etched in your brain that it is a gift from above and beyond imperial *generosity*, really. Why should we forget how France *"gently endowed"* Africa with the currency built on the fires of colonial "innovation?" A tender memento, really: *"Here, hold this against your Monopoly money while we loot your cobalt. Think of it as a friendship bracelet, with extra shackles!"* So thoughtful! After all, why let pesky things like "sovereignty" or "economic autonomy" stand in the way of a thoroughly good exploitation scheme?

If it's called *magnanimous,* know that the architects were visionaries, truly. picture it like this: cigar-clutching bureaucrats at Parisian salons, cackling over their fine cognac as they scribbled *"liberté, égalité, fraternité"* on napkins, and in the next moment, drafted a currency to deny all those things to fourteen nations. "Unity through shared poverty!" they chirped, as they funneled African resources into the watery-clogged treasury of France. This currency, of course, was too *pure* for French soil like a vampire recoiling from garlic. It couldn't bear to touch the streets of Paris. Instead, why not let it haunt Africa with much greater superlative: reverse gold mines into IOUs and democracies into vassal states.

So much *altruistic deed!* As if to say, France allowed these nations to trade oil, uranium, or posh dignity for crisp stacks of... *checks notes...* paper backed by the *full faith and credit of their own subjugation.* What else could it be called? French politicians, weeping tears of joy into silk handkerchiefs, while watching their debts disappear quicker than the catch of a

Senegalese fisherman. *"Look at us,"* they'd sniff, *"building bridges of dependency across the Mediterranean! When is the Nobel going to come?"*

Now let's not forget la pièce de résistance: the audacity of selling this whole racket as *"economic salvation."* Imagine selling a leash as a *"necklace for freedom"* and having the pooch believe it is haute couture. The real brilliance of the CFA is that it made exploitation *dull.* Just spreadsheets and paternalistic jargon and a central bank in friggin' Paris, no muskets or warships needed. *"Worry not my dear; it's really your money! We're just... holding it. For safekeeping, you know. Forever."*

And when anyone dared squint at the farce, the colonial gaslighting starts: *Mais dis donc!* You'd hear: *"You're not trapped, you're special! Why, without us, you'd all be... shudders... independent!"* The nerves of these backward nations! Thinking they should have a say in their own direction! Haven't they heard France's manifest destiny is to *civilize* them and their balance sheets?

The world would not have the faintest idea as to what might look villainous without such bureaucratic genius. Bravo, France! Your legacy is not just in the Louvre; it is in the hollow-eyed resignation of a continent forever told to say *merci* while you pick its pockets.

After the *"Congratulations, you're free!"* France chirped in 1960 to the rest of its colonies, while quietly slipping the keys to the *real* kingdom, the economy, into its own pocket. What followed was a carnival of coups: 67 across 26 nations, because nothing says "liberty" like a revolving door of dictators, half of whom owed their thrones to Parisian backroom deals. *"Whoopsie-daisy!"* clucked France, as yet another "unstable" regime toppled. How *convenient* that chaos kept their former colonies too busy to notice the vaults being emptied.

Let's not forget the *secret pact that takes the cake*! Talk about putting lipstick on a pig. A VIP membership where these 14 nations "voluntarily" funneled 85% of their foreign reserves into France's coffers. *"Think of it as a joint savings account!"* crooned French officials, sipping Bordeaux paid for by Malian gold. The math was *elegant*: Africa's reserves propped up the franc, France's economy guzzled billions in revenue, and African leaders got to play "government" with Monopoly money. *C'est magnifique!* Why let colonialism die when you could just rebrand it as "fiscal responsibility?"

And then there is Guinea, the rebellious teen of the family who did dare to refuse the *generous* offer of economic Stockholm syndrome that France was so willing to bestow on her. How rude! Guinea was rewarded with... abject poverty for its insolence. *"See what happens when you leave the nest?"* tutted France as Guinea's economy was subjected to a series of "mysterious" trade embargoes. Really a cautionary tale: resist, and you starve; comply, and you starve *slightly slower*. In either case, France wins!

How could this be? The truth is that colonialism is a roach motel: You may check out anytime you like, but your resources never leave. So, Guinea's plight was not a mystery, it was a *demonstration*, a wink from Paris to every would-be upstart: *"Go ahead, try sovereignty. We'll make sure your people eat hope for dinner."* Meanwhile, French economists would later be free to lament Africa's "governance issues," as if they hadn't *written the damn script*. So here we are a continent under the confetti of independence, dancing slave-like to France's drum. *Vive l'exploitation!*

The weight of these events pressed upon Salim's shoulders like a shroud. It is kind of worrisome to see these leaders being eliminated by their close friends or bodyguards, but he wore it not as a burden, no, it became his armor. He stood, a solitary oak in a tempest, roots clawing deep into the soil of his ancestors, unyielding against the gales of coercion. They came for him, of course, the veiled threats slipped under doors, the poison smiles of diplomats, the midnight murmurs meant to fray his resolve. Yet his voice, rough as desert wind, only grew louder, carving through the silence of complacency. *Let them whisper,* he thought. Fear was a language he refused to speak.

His people gathered, drawn like moths to the flame of his defiance. In town squares choked with dust and desperation, he roared of liberation, of fists unclenched, of a future unshackled from the greasy palms of foreign powers. *"You won't get me,"* he thundered, and the crowd surged, a tidal wave of hope. And in the shadows, his enemies sharpened their tongues. Liam Fatmuray, the ink-stained provocateur, christened him *"The barking Dog"* in venomous editorials. The name stuck; a barbed crown Salim wore with perverse pride. *"Let them mock,"* he sneered. Revolution had never been polite.

Yet fire, once ignited, is hard to contain. His sermons evolved, no longer mere sparks of dissent but infernos of ideology. Marxism, Leninism, Maoism, he wove them into a quilt of rebellion, each thread a promise of equality, of power seized from the gilded few and returned to the calloused hands of the masses. *"The people,"* he declared, *"will be the architects of their destiny!"* But in his zeal, the line between architect and tyrant blurred. Decisions once debated in the open calcified into decrees; dissenters vanished into the humid grip of night.

Paranoia, this disease wrapped around his heart. A tilt of the head seemed to signal a traitor; rustling palm leaves seemed to whisper conspiracies. The man who had once vowed to burn down empires, now hoarded power like a dragon with gold. And his edicts could well have come out of the mouth of the imperialism that he vowed to destroy. The people, once awe-inspired, now started murmuring: *"When was it that our liberator became a jailor?"*

The prophecy whispered by the late wizard under the bone-white moon, could not be outrun: *"Beware the savior who drinks too deeply from the well of power. His light will birth shadows."*

Salim, gaunt and haunted, stood before his fractured ambition. Had the thirst for justice curdled into greed? Or had the world, with its vipers and compromises, forced his hand? His name started becoming a riddle, a cautionary hymn. Hero? Tyrant? History, ever a fickle scribe, would write him as both, because this was just the beginning.

Chapter 11

The witch hunt

Kept captive in the negativity of one's own mind, one confuses reality and illusion and is compelled by this boundless paranoia to act irrationally. Our minds are hardwired to make us dismiss or anticipate undesirable thoughts. Such as our preference of being lied to instead of being told the truth because sometimes being truthful can be hurtful to both the teller and the listener. This squabble opposing Salim to his masters might have started as a conflict where the "virtuous" confronted the malevolent, but the boundaries of the battle remained blurred. And now, people realized that the real conflict, the one concerning morality, played out at home, within the newfound allies.

The year 1954 stepped into mourning for Yaryb. Nayce Loida, his constant ally in the DSG, had fallen, leaving behind a void that turned into some kind of bitterness that seeped into his words, sharpened against the Fula chiefs. Nayce's pragmatism had kept Yaryb's rhetoric in check; with his friend gone, the words crackled with disdain, alienating those who dared oppose him. However, this very ruthlessness caught the attention of The Gardener. Ever the calculative man, The Gardener saw in Yaryb's defiance an instrument to nurture loyalty amongst the Fula, intertwining their hopes with his own ambitions, and to them rally in alliance with Salim, his protégé.

Yaryb wore nobility like armor, a shield against accusations of pretension. When offered a legislative seat alongside Salim, he scoffed, the flame of pride flaring leaping like a match. *Beneath me*, he thought, blind to the sudden tides. Although, his refusal turned into a Pyrrhic victory; because he later took up the banner and successively climbed the ladder from secretary of State to ministerial titles in Salim's Government, redrawing the political battlefield ever since. Plagued by gritted smiles, Yaryb was blind-sighted and never saw the stone of his principles crushed under the iron heel of compromise. Meanwhile, Salim was nourishing his schemes with silent voracity. He came to judge tolerance as currency and poured out lavish sums to buy it from any dissent that sprang up. There was no riotous uproar to yell down the decree when Salim declared his Party the sole legal political party in Guinea; there was just the sound of weary acceptance. Salim had choked the sources of resistance; his throne was erected upon the apathy of those very people who might have opposed him.

Yaryb and Wadu at the heads of BAG and MSA understood too late the cost of their bargain: they had danced in the early years of independence with Salim, believing that their affiliation with the PDG-RDA would shield them from any harm. But the referendum, with its thunderous 94% vote against France, was no rallying cry of unity but a funeral dirge. Their parties stripped of their roots withered away with Salim's machinery in full operation, drawing away their supporters and leaving those parties as hollow figureheads in a government they no longer recognized.

"Unity," Salim proclaimed, his voice honeyed with triumph, "has given Guinea a soul." But the sordid truth remained, earning its due: unity became a hangman's noose. Yaryb's nights, haunted by the ghost of Nayce, with the void of his presence reminding him about an alliance that cost him his voice, his cause, and finally, his home. Wadu, too, wandered the corridors of power like a specter, thinking about how their once vibrant movement now shattered under the heel of a single party. They had bargained with a man who deals in illusions. All that they had to show for it was the silence of a nation learning to speak in one voice, a voice that was never theirs to proclaim.

The minds sat by and witnessed the transformation of an outstanding rescuer into a wrathful despot. He erected a metaphorical invisible wall to alienate himself from the people. As a result of his selfishness blowing on the embers of paranoia tragically tore the thin social layers of the fragile union. Fear was their strongest elixir of dominance. Pulling the strings of the people's emotions, he pandered to their fears and insecurities like a puppeteer. He gave birth to ominous shadows that weighed in on the public psyche. By conjuring boogeymen of doubt, he positioned himself as the keeper of order to shield them from the very terrors he laid at their feet. The uproar of populist rhetoric tore through a disenchanted populace like sirens sights. He styled himself as the champion for the common folk against an illusory elitist class of educated and wealthy people. His words rang through popular disparagement and grievances with promises of radical change to anything other than practicality.

The basis of their argument couldn't withstand scrutiny; in other words, they are castles in the air that rest, so to speak, on an imaginary foundation. His world is full of half-truths, the great guise of deception, never quite out of sight of reality though. He wielded language as a weapon, so skillfully placed in equivocation that even the faintest shadow of doubt could be enough to obscure a misconception. The tightrope walk took him through some very shadowy places somewhere between lies and truths where he exploited these ambiguities for his ends. With negative campaigning as his arsenal, he began launching barrages character assassination and slander on his opponents. Instead of inspiring through his own merits, he rather tarnished others' reputations. The spread of malicious rumors became his ultimate weapon, which were soon followed by distorting records about his rivals and reveling in the chaos he sowed.

By the time the populace knew it, every single vestige of grace and goodwill was completely replaced with an unabated thirst for power. Behind this refined exterior, image builders and spin doctors toiled tirelessly. Every single move carefully choreographed, scripting his every move. In his masterful string-pulling, he crafted the glossy veneer of sincere relatability. Every word uttered, every gesture made, every photo op meticulously designed to evoke trust and admiration, even if they disguised a hollow core. His truth changed gears and wore a veil of deception.

The voters naivete wouldn't allow them to exercise vigilance, peering through the smokescreen of lies and half-truths. They would not demand accountability, challenge the narratives presented, or seek leaders whose actions match their words. People did not believe that in their collective discernment lies the power to dismantle the webs of deceit and restore the integrity of their democratic ideals. Or they just might have lost the will to fight.

Not only that he created his own militia to kidnap and kill anyone opposed to his reign, but he also transformed people working in gathering places into secret agents that would collect data from people by just interacting with them. Among those were nurses, the remaining of the handicap beggars in every corner of the capital, the lady on the corner selling tomatoes to feed her miserable family, before you know it, your favorite coffee shop in town already gave your daily routine to the authorities which in turn send them to the federation. Awkwardness creeped into people's lives, interacting with others became a challenge. Choosing your words wisely became a necessity and befriending someone became a meticulous process. Fear started feeding on people's dignity, to the point of accusing innocent people. It was the birth of psychological warfare. One could be a company CEO or a secretary of State one day, and the next, unjustifiably find himself in a windowless dark hole somewhere via the unfounded claims of the doorman in his building. The country became a place where the more you are close to power the more you are in danger. To eliminate you he would promote you to the post of secretary of State then demote you and open a file against you to incarcerate you. His thoughts on nobody can be trusted led to mass arrests and incarcerations that touched every level of society. Nobody was safe. People learned first-hand the saying,

"It's the snake that you fed that will come back and eat you"

Laysouf had always worn his beliefs like armor. A lifelong warrior against the creeping shadows of authoritarianism, his left-wing ideals burned more fiercely than those of Salim, an old contemporary who, amid increasingly murky policies, had come to stand as a stark equal. Their friendship was made in the fires of youth, bonded by shared rebellion for justice; now that friendship has grown taut under Salim's ill-government. The country, once rich with hope, was now disarrayed, the streets filled with unemployed youth and institutions breeding corruption. An idea gnawed at Laysouf: neo-fascist rhetoric was rising, slithering venomously into Salim's speeches. He had remained silent for far too long. Silence had never been his nature. It was yielding to the complexity of power, to these fragile fringes of friendship. With each succeeding decree, though, even silence was being sliced apart, dreadful laws against dissent, heavy militarized takedowns of protests. Salim had once been the man Laysouf admired; today, he was but a puppet on strings of his burgeoning ego, utterly deaf to the cries of his people.

On a sweltering night, under the flickering fluorescence of the office of the president, Laysouf confronted him. "You are dismantling everything we fought for," he whispered in dark urgency. "These policies are not just inefficient. They are tyrannical. You are becoming what we swore to destroy." With a shifting creak like the tired metaphor within, Salim leaned back in his chair. A well-rehearsed cold smirk parted his lips. "You still see the world in slogans, Laysouf. Governance is not a purity test: It is survival."

"Survival?" Laysouf's eyes opened wide. "You call starvation of children survival? Opponents being silenced? You call that survival? You have traded principles for paranoia."

A flicker of light streaked across the empty eyes of Salim, the ghost of his former idealist-self. Against his will, he agreed to suspend the harshest measures. It was very token fleeting as monsoon rain. Within weeks, the promise was broken again as always. Crackdown recommended, fiercer than before.

Laysouf was deeply saddened yet unsurprised. He had seen the pattern before, the lure of power and desensitization. The few voices that did exist agitating alongside him were drowned out in the echo of Salim's ambition. The country spiraled; a ship steered into the storm by arrogance. There he knew, Salim will never change.

"A log may soak for lifetimes in the river's embrace; it will never sprout the crocodile's teeth."

Nepotism started growing in his entourage. Salim's paranoia occasioned the birth of mistrust among some political leaders, and they needed to react before being the collateral damage of his heedless self-interests. Just the thoughts of being opposed to Salim's ideas and monarchy was a death warrant because their longtime fealty will no longer matter as soon as their thoughts of rejection became a reality and reached his minions. A simple word will shift the relation of friends into foes. Salim resorted to nepotism to help him hold on to power with an iron fist. He could no longer be distinguished from the evil he was fighting. Believing and waiting for his informants only to bring him false accusations was no longer enough. He started orchestrating his own plans to arbitrary arrest and imprison people.

Salim and his regime concocted multiple plots aiming to eliminate those perceived as threats to his government. He firmly held on to the idea that the Guinean intellects, religious leaders, and professionals are an impediment to his goal for the country. These plots, skillfully wrought and pitilessly executed, literally aimed at exterminating the nucleus of the nation's elite.

The first wave of this series of attacks happened in 1960 and would be remembered in history as the "Plot of the Intellectuals." The victims included a fairly known pharmacist, Fode; a bright engineer, Yaya, and

Lamine Kaba, the imam of the Coronthie mosque. Lamine Kaba had gentle sermons about peace and non-violence through which he tried to sow some unity between the dawn of Guinea's independence and the nascent government. This very stand had become his undoing, the message for reconciliation was potentially too dangerous for the new regime.

These men, once considered pillars of society, were brutally executed, sending out a chilling warning from the regime about how far they would go to silence any opposition. Against the backdrop of their brutal murders, a reign of terror was to begin and would rapidly cripple the incubation ground of minds and spirits of the nation.

The second conspiracy plot arrived heavy with the scent of chalk dust and disillusionment. The classrooms still reverberated with the clipped cadence of French verbs; now they were gaping empty pages. The French teachers had assigned their dignity to the void. Their absenteeism gnawed not only at schools but also at the faint pride of a nation striving to stand. Guinean teachers were disillusioned while they had held on to the hope of independence for the future. The government called it progress; they considered it a ruin.

Keita Koumandian, his spectacles perched like a scholar's crown, was the first to voice the heresy: "They've ripped out the spine of our schools." Around him gathered Traoré Mamoudou, whose lectures once made algebra sing; Checik Bayi, a poet of physics; the Baldé brothers, Hassimiou and Mountaga, twin pillars of history; and Camara Enzo, whose voice had ignited a thousand debates. These were not rabble-rousers, but custodians of light. Yet here they stood, ink-stained hands clenched, their defiance a quiet storm.

They'd watched as Salim's government dismissed their fears as nostalgia for colonial chains. But this was not about France, it was about the child in Kankan who might never parse a sentence, the girl in Nzérékoré whose equations would now blur into guesswork. When the state severed ties with French educators, it severed something in them too: the certainty that knowledge could transcend borders.

The president's rhetoric hardened. "Loyalty," he declared, "is the only curriculum." Yet in staff rooms, loyalty curdled into dread. Petitions were drafted, voices raised, not as dissent, but as elegy. They knew the cost. Careers, freedom, perhaps lives. But Keita's resolve was a flint-strike. "We are not plotting," he insisted, "we are *remembering*."

Crackdowns came with an almost instantaneous force. Being allergic to dissent, Salim's regime branded the dissenters as traitors of the revolution. Thus, classrooms turned into courtrooms, and the very curriculum became evidence of subversion. Once, the teachers' names were whispered in reverence, but now the State media spat them out as warnings.

The birth of the independent nation was drenched in hope, while this was the shadow: a nation so intent on denying its past that it would silence those destined to recreate its future. Though the teachers' rebellion was crushed, the stain of doubt was left on the government's manifesto; for how could a nation really stand if its children were taught to fear articulating even the weight of a single question? Well, with these educators, some answers met their own death, swallowed by that silence which follows every storm.

Chapter 12

The Gulag of horror

A paradoxical titan of his era, Dane was a man fashioned by the resilient Mandinka blood and the turbulent postcolonial flows. Among the pioneers of Guinea's independence movement, at critical moments, he appeared like a son of fire: *"The Church and state are chains on the African spirit, they must be shattered."* He once snapped

He was appointed governor of Kankan and Nzérékoré, with the task of uniting the fractured country. But great idealism meant that his path soon became disillusion. In 1960, when commanding the Guinean contingent of the UN in Congo, he saw hope fading when his comrade Salim, overcome with grief at Emery's savage killing dissolved their unit. The UN had left her own unprotected, the bitter thought rankling Dane; thus, the promise of global solidarity had been fouled with shame.

Returning to Guinea, he somehow drifted right into the clutch of Salim's tightening authoritarian regime. In the beginning, while in service as Secretary for Labé, Dane was still somewhat pragmatic; yet, as the dissent grew, so was his hardening. Then, came his prominence as the Minister of the Militia, his true role dawned upon him: as the iron fist of the regime with the task of methodically crushing opposition within its mortal grasp. Power, which was once wielded as an instrument of liberation, was now transformed into something akin to a whip binding him; survival demands the ruthless allegiance of those who will not resist it. The shadows of his militia stretched across the whole nation, a dark monument to those compromises supposedly asked in the name of order. And what are these compromises? Are they at least going to leave souls intact? I doubt it. These minions are as unpredictable as their master.

Our dreams are often believed to be the purest reflections of our deepest desires, a glimpse into what we yearn for, though whether we should be held accountable for them is another question entirely. Are we answerable for the whims of our subconscious? Can we be condemned for a fleeting thought or a vision that has no foundation in action? I think not. Nor should we bear the weight of someone else's dream of us. Yet, the world is not always so understanding. Not everyone shares the same leniency when it comes to the strange power dreams hold over us.

Having undergone a long, restless night, I had a dream that was indeed sweet yet prohibited, one of those forbidden dreams that under Salim's rule, a child of the nation was never even allowed to entertain by thought. The biography of Salim recounts that he utterly imposed upon his people, especially upon the youth, following his ascendancy to power. His reign was of fear: any child's innocuous aspiration was considered a dangerous act and hence punishable. There is a story, a very sad story that still haunts me to this day, one that played out in the city of Daybreak, a city where every corner bore the heavy mark of Salim's cruelty.

I remember clearly; that memory still stays with me, bearing upon my soul: the gruesome description of a scene that struck me so deeply that the tears just would not stop flowing down my cheeks. The people of

Daybreak remained frozen in place in horror at the graphic moment that was playing before their eyes. It was not that they were unmoved by anything; it was in fact their dread of being drawn into the matter or even being seen as accomplices to the dream of a single boy. A dream that should never have been shared.

He was only a child and had one simple dream that many children harbored, the aspiration to one day become a statesman, to stand at the helm of the nation. The dream seemed so innocent, so emotionally evoking; well, not in a country where such dreams could be deemed dangerous. The boy, however, would never have imagined anything dangerous would come from such a dream, not until it was too late. Had he spoken of it to his parents beforehand, maybe things would have unfolded differently. But no, he was just a child who never thought it was more than a passing fancy, an idle thought. So, while on the playground, he mentioned the dream to his little friends, and the sweet dream became a nightmare. The word spread fast and reached Salim who dispatched his minions to hunt the child. From then on, there were no more innocent dreams, all dreams became something to fear, because what followed left a mark on people's memories. The boy had been ripped away from his parents' arms in the dead of night, mercilessly dragged by the authorities to the committee base at Daybreak. From there, the boy was sent to the Federation, then to a place that existed barely in whispers, Camp Boiro. It was there that the tragedy of his life would be boiled over.

All because of a dream. A child's fantasy, one that held no malice, no ill intent. Just a thought, a wish, that slipped unguarded from his lips. But in Salim's world, even dreams could be a crime. The boy had no control over it, no power to dictate the course it would take. His mind, his heart, had traveled somewhere unknown, somewhere he couldn't possibly understand, and for that, he paid the ultimate price. It was only a dream. But in the city of Daybreak, and across Salim's nation, such dreams were not allowed. Not anymore.

When one's peculiar decisions go unnoticed and unchecked, one gets empowered and develop an excessive feeling of mastery and authority in his state of mind. He forgets that he does not have power over them but rather entrusted with people's power, and he knows it, but stubbornness makes him believe that he has the right to impose his will on those beneath him, regardless of how it makes them feel. With an overinflated sense of self-esteem and belief he is impervious to punishment. Thinking too highly of himself and overestimate his abilities and significance.

Society, though, had chosen to avert its gaze and embrace Salim's peculiarities as the eccentricities of a visionary. How else could such a monstrous betrayal have taken place, a betrayal of a child he swore to lift from the shadows of poverty, with vows a life brighter than any under France's cold embrace? He was a master puppeteer, cloaked in a veil of wounded innocence, pouring ugliness and malignity into wickedness, though fiercely righteous. And the people drank his lies like nectar, their hearts swelling with misplaced sympathy, their faith unshaken even as fissures cracked the unity once worn like armor. Brothers and sisters who had stood shoulder to shoulder against imperialist wolves now turned wary eyes on one another, their solidarity poisoned by doubts Salim himself had sown.

By the time the world attained the grasp of the full meaning of his Machiavellian strategy, lies spun with clinical precision, the blade had already fallen. The colonizers he'd raged against were long gone, replaced by new enemies, his own people. The very souls who had crowned him as their savior. The ones who'd scraped together meager coins to fund his rise, their bony fingers trembling as they donated francs earned through backbreaking labor. The ones who'd traded their parents' wisdom and their spouses' love for his empty promises of liberation. They had shattered their own morals, bending reality itself to his will, they believed him a messiah. Instead, he became their executioner.

For power is a fickle, toxic elixir. The man who once vowed to destroy chains created instead a set of heavy and cold chains for himself to bear, much heavier and hated than those of any foreign oppressor. His story is no exception; it is a dirge passed down through the ages, engraved in the blood of nations crushed underneath the weight of betrayal: Benevolent hearts turn to tyranny; idealism becomes a mask for greed. Salim is just another name in this wretched lineage, a ghostly reflection of despots past and a harbinger of those yet to come. And the bitterest truth? Those who loved him most, who built him, breath by breath, were the first to kneel beneath his boot. Their shattered faith lingers like smoke, showing the price of blind devotion.

Every culture had some dimwitted decision makers in history that found reasons to commit atrocities based on beliefs only they know are reasonable. After the war, the allied won, the Americans and the Soviets had no problem leaving Belgium and France when they could have shared these territories, they just left happily and where glad to have helped win the war. You'd think that France would have the same curtesy, but history has a way of stitching its horrors into the same, fraying cloth. The French returned to Africa not as liberators, but as judges and executioners. Tirailleurs who dared to demand the freedom they'd been promised, men who had bled for an empire that spat on their dignity, were lined along riverbanks and left as warnings, their bodies dissolving into the red earth. The Pidjiguiti docks of 1959 mirrored this cruelty: Portuguese rifles barked, cutting down fifty souls whose crime was the audacity to ask for bread instead of stones. Blood pooled between cobblestones, sticky as regret.

And what is a human life to power? The Salem witches, their tongues charred to ash for the sin of existing. The philistine with a bomb strapped to his chest, convinced his god craves the wail of children. The camp guard who files away mothers, scholars, dreamers, *reeducation* or extermination, the result is the same.

But let's talk about the camps history wishes to forget. Even before the world ever came to know *Auschwitz*, Germany had been erecting in African soil its first experiment; the Nama and Herero, their bones ground to desert dust, their skulls boxed away and mailed off to laboratories where men in white coats sought to prove their supremacy. The archives whisper of it, somewhat sanitized and sour, no mention of how Herero women were stripped bare before the camera's eye, their bodies turned into postcards, erotica for the colonial gaze; no ledgers ever in record of the weight of a child's head in a researcher's hands.

Europe builds monuments to its guilt, in polished marble weeping for its own sins. And where are the stones for the Nama? Where is the museum for the Herero girl whose name became a specimen label? Well, as "the North remembered." The desert of Namibia remembers, but its voice is cracked with drought. Nevertheless, it remembers. It is alive with the whispers of those whose stories were buried in colonial files, their truths sifted through the sieve belonging to a liar.

We are asked to mourn tragedies we're never taught. To sympathize with ghosts whose faces were stolen, whose pain was edited into footnotes. The devil, they say, knows when to stop confessing. But the earth does not forget. It hoards the screams in its fissures, the blood in its clay. And somewhere, in the dry wind that sweeps Namibia's plains, there is a sound like a mother keening, for her child, her history, her right to grieve in a world that still refuses to see her.

Salim's reign was not born of chaos, but of cold calculation. He had studied the tyrants' playbook, the French executions, Staline's gulags, the Portuguese massacres, the German camps where science became slaughter, and distilled their cruelty into something meticulous, intimate. To silence dissent, he understood, one must first dismantle hope.

Thus, the *Tropical Gulag* took root. Nestled in Conakry's feverish heat, it began as a Czech blueprint, its walls rising under the gaze of Keita Fodeba, a man whose poetry once hymned African liberation, now twisted into architect of despair. By 1969, it bore a new name: *Camp Boiro*, a macabre homage to a magistrate whose helicopter plunge became state legend. And Salim's half-brother, a boy with a dictator's eyes, presided over a carnival of pain.

Like the smoke, the camp shifted purpose. Initially a cage for "traitors," it began devouring Guinea's brightest scholars who questioned the land reforms, merchants whose wealth outshone the regime's coffers, poets with verses that stung with fact. They would be picked up by midnight trucks, mouths gagged with pieces of cloth, their minds still clinging to the foolish promise that intellect could save them.

Refinements were made to Boiro's methods. Interrogation rooms buzzed with generators, wires kissing human flesh in a sick parody of intimacy. Airless and lightless, cells cradled men until they forgot their very own names. Guards, trained in the art of crushing hope, bellowed the edicts of Salim like psalms: *"A nation cannot bloom with weeds in its garden."*

Yet the soil remembers what the monuments omit. Under Boiro's concrete, the earth kept the whispers of older horrors, the shipping of Nama and Herero skulls to Berlin, the slick of Pidjiguiti docks with laborer's blood. Salim's innovation was no invention, but inheritance. He understood something that all empires know: dehumanization is a language whose grammar is written in scars.

Fodeba, the poet/minister, knew well. Before his aberrance, his own fall from grace, he would walk the camp's periphery at dusk, listening to the muffled cries. Did he remember his verses once burning with Pan-African aspirations? Or did he hear the whimpers in the Herero women posing for postcards, being dissected from dignity into data?

Some survivors spoke of a peculiar madness, prisoners with their fingernails scratching maps of Guinea on the cemented walls with as if to remind themselves that the country existed beyond their cells. But Salim's Guinea had become a funhouse, the sound of his voice tuned to the chorus, and every mirror bent to the shape of his image.

When the world speaks of camps, it conjures Europe's industrial graves. But Boiro, like the German *Konzentrationslager* of Namibia, thrived in the shadows of denial. No plaques mark its ruins; no textbooks dissect its arithmetic of fear. Yet the wind carries its legacy, the rustle of phantom files, the groan of a land forced to swallow its children.

Salim, like the colonizers before him, understood: to erase a people, you must first erase their memory. But memory is a seed. It waits, patient as death, for the moment the soil cracks open.

So, the camp rose on the site of the old Republican Guard camp, an old colonial camp just in front of the central hospital of the country. After completing the construction of the buildings and their individual cells, Fodeba sought an opinion from an expert on the metabolism of the human body, Dr. Roger Accar, Minister of Health.

The camp is surrounded by a tall concrete wall, and the entire compound is cautiously safeguarded by bony armed soldiers. Rundown and in a state of decay, with crumbling walls and a general lack of care. Upon entering Camp Boiro, detainees are stripped of their dignity and all personal things except the garments they came in with. With filthy cells, often housing multiple inmates in close confinement. The cells themselves consist of no mattress or toilet. The walls are deteriorated, and there are no windows, leaving the cells in perpetual darkness.

The camp was not hazardly built. Salim did not improvise in building the camp. He thought of everything, as he always does. With him everything is calculated, from the flash of his shining smile to the way he approaches every matter, and to whom he might bestow his wrath or mercy. This prison he built is not just built as any other building, but a building garnished with heavy human sacrifices through the occultism practiced by the greatest marabouts of the time, the work being so heavy to achieve its aim. By locking men up in Boiro, Salim intended never to have them get out of there, or if they ever do, well, they should be useless to society, and themselves, forever, as well as no longer capable of doing anything against him. It is believed that Boiro's foundations rest upon bodies buried with tons of amulets veiled in special occult works. Salim knew that he would lock there, men powerful, if not more powerful, than he, including marabouts highly skilled in occult sciences who are too fragile to survive in such a sinister place. Countless lives will be broken within its walls, and the ghosts of atrocities will haunt survivors' memories.

At the end of the visit, the dear doctor was shaken but could not help to ask his comrade one question burning inside his brain which might literally burn his lips after being uttered.

"Is this where you are going to put people?" He asked shockingly while his heart skips a beat.

"Yep!" Answered the Minister with no misgivings, no feelings. As if the man carried an iron cast heart behind his lungs or worse, deprived of one.

"It is unbelievable. The cells have neither a window nor a ceiling; with their narrowness, men placed here will lose sight and die like flies." Pleaded the poor doctor, "You shouldn't do this."

"Enough! The visit is over." Snapped Fodeba and extended his hand to show him the exit.

Threats to the unity and dignity of the Salim's children were imminent as the iron fist of the regime crushed any political opponent or dissident, with Camp Boiro becoming an instrument for suppression. Arrests would be made arbitrarily, without justice or due process. Guinea became a place where innocent souls would be snatched from their homes, taken from workplaces, or simply plucked from streets and having their fate sealed by a regime determined to quash any opposition to its power. And once inside camp Boiro, detainees were tortured beyond imagination, both bodily and mental cruelties were meted upon them in full measure. Beating, electroshocks, waterboarding: methods of torture were utter words where they sought to either get confessions or break the spirit of the imprisoned. Under such ambiance, the battered cries of prisoners echoed on the walls as their ears were tortured and set to unbearable degrees of degradation.

The camp carried the stain of blood from many who were never tried. Bodies disappeared into summary executions conducted behind locked doors and away from prying eyes. Audible cries of life were snuffed out without the shadow of legality, never to be heard again. Bodies too disappeared into clandestine funerals, or were tossed into the forbidding, close by sea. A plethora of lifeless bodies from the path toward dictatorship served as a massive chilling warning to those who dared oppose the wrath of authority.

Life in the camp was filled with agony. The cells were too noisy to be called solitary. People were cramped into spaces far too small for the number of inmates, and the place reeked of sorrow, sweat, and fear. There was no sanitation to speak of, which further aggravated the spread of diseases. Malnutrition gnawed at weak bodies of the detainees while medical care was a luxury they could not afford. Death stayed in the shadows around every corner, claiming those left weakened by physical torture and emotional anguish.

However, it was not just a place of torture and extermination; it carpet-bombed the entire paradigm of systematic persecution upheld by the regime. Intellectuals, civil-servants, and other professionals were picked out: the minds and thoughts deemed threats to the regime's ideology. Some ethnic groups, mostly the Fula and the Mandinka, became targets even more than others, accentuating schisms and planting seeds of bitterness across Guinean society.

Salim's sycophants were given the whole autonomy of the camp where they were allowed to operate as it pleased them. Salmany, the half-brother of Salim was the chief prosecutor, often qualified as the idiot brother and his close minion commander of the camp, Kais Retu, a manatee looking guy. He is the devil incarnates who once buried an innocent man alive because he could. Karim Keira, the man of invisible horns, he put out his cigarettes on prisoners' buttocks with no remorse. And there is Emil Cyrus, an illegitimate child of a brief, careless encounter, a stain on society's ideal, yet a mirror of Salim's own reckless origins. Adopted by Salim, the man was not just a son, but a raw embodiment of the dictator's wild, unrepentant past. Cyrus was a living, breathing reminder of the messiness of life, unplanned, unrestrained, and unapologetic. In him, Salim saw himself: a product of impulse and desire, born of a fleeting night and destined to leave an indelible mark. Emil Cyrus was the most loyal spy of Salim in the region of Labe. A region predominantly Fulani, a man who had no qualms of feeding the insatiable Camp Boiro of innocent people. He was a pest, even the governor was petrified of him; let alone the little girls he would do what was done to his mother by his Lebanese father.

These three people were devoid of empathy and self-respect. Salmany's viciousness would have make der Fuhrer's right hand; well… look like an angel. He was fiendishly rapacious. Being boastful of his killings, of whom and when he wanted to kill, was his pastime. Given his brother's bestowal on him of power, it gave Salmany an opportunity to torture, and the more innocent the person, the more jouissance it gave Salmany. The effects of his torture could have given nightmares even to the devil. The torture inflicted was catastrophic in terms of psychological impact. The people constantly lived with fear, having seen so many horrendous atrocities, and having been traumatized themselves. Families were torn apart, and the suffering caused by losing loved ones was all-consuming. Most of the captives either perished or degenerated day by day, both physically and mentally, while a handful managed to cling to their momentum and opted to fight against all odds for survival.

The crimes in the camp provide an eerie reminder of the depths of human depravity and hence the need to strive for a just, compassionate, and respectful world.

It is believed that knowledge is power, and wealth, a crucial component of any government trying to reach its ends. The merger of the two enables a government to win wars, to have control. Unfortunately, Salim had none. His judgment was constantly clouded by mistrust bred out of paranoia, which his entourage only furthered. He would rather choose to be blind with the hatred of a community than compromise to push himself into the world stage of influence. Supposedly his IQ is very impressive. Surely no one could contradict such a fact; considering the etymological origins of the word, that would be an irrefutable fact. However, there lies skepticism behind the people's opinion pertaining to his intelligence because he does not use it for good. His perception and intellect are more adept at seeing evil than good, and he uses this to his advantage.

And it worked; because his bloodthirsty manes do wonders to keep him entertained with his array of rosary, like beads, he says, and the power of apprehension he possesses is so vile that when in one of those beads it happens to "snap" a good into existence, it mutates instantly into an evil one. Nothing but evil exists for him anywhere and anywhere else. A smile or a chuckle from him is reason enough to run for dear life. That charming, disarming visage and demeanor is his bait, not only to lure women but also put his victims to sleep. His heartlessness, if ever it had a manual to follow, is ripped aside from that of a Nazi general. More courteous than polite, he welcomes you to his residence well before execution of your death sentence. You'll have a meal, you'll chat about this and that, and joke around while playing checkers, talk about women as though you were old chums reminiscing about the good days, share a meal, well, *your last supper* if you will. Then you glance at the watch and think it is time to go home. He also glances at his watch, casually thinking it is time for you to die. As you take the first steps toward the exit, you are stood in wait by his revolutionary guard or rather, his militias. *"You are under arrest in the name of the Revolution,"* they tell you, and sadly there is never anything you can do about it.

Chapter 13

Friends or foes

When a man's ambition knows no boundaries, the world itself carves a path to glory or destruction by which he must make his way. A self-made architecture of success had built an empire with the utmost devotion, shaping towering structures and commanding the most elite chambers of influence. Yet with every wealth amassed grows his unquenchable thirst for more, for more power, more control, and for yet another chance to shape the land that has nurtured his spirit. The next stage awaits his grace, and eagle-eyed for the ultimate prize, he lusts for the throne of authority. Leading millions had become a sweet melody with countless possibilities, the very symphony that from its first note the master musician dreams of. But in going for an impossible pinnacle, he ignores an inescapable truth as hard as gravity itself: The kingdom he wishes to rule is neither land of freedom nor competition; it is where an invisible hand plays a string, and any ambition that dares to rise beyond its grasp is not merely unwelcome but blasphemy!

Always ready to be the center of attention, he extravagantly reveals his ambitions, and his very belief in his own impunity drives him toward a fatal miscalculation. With power flexibilized from only one source, there is, in fact, no second chance for those who cross the invisible, untried line. His dreams of grandeur wallop in cold steel on an unyielding regime that is intolerant of rivals, challenges, or even any voice other than its own. In scoring that longed for crown, he will learn that the price for ambition under those laws exacts much more than he ever imagined, and his rose-covered paragons of ambition may demand his whole house and then some.

Meet Petit Toure: the next one caught in Salim's nation's following plot. The third FIGURE-Plot was all about a guy who somehow felt like the wrong man for some political intrigue: *Petit Touré*. A successful and wealthy businessman from Kankan who built his fortune as a trader, but his ambitions stretched beyond mere commerce. Power and influence in the political sphere called out to him. During these times, Keita Fodeba was the Minister of Interior, whose government influence could determine the course of a political career.

Seeing an opportunity, he approached Fodeba with a request. He asked the Minister to approve the creation of his political party as the final step in entering the political arena. Fodeba, knowing well the firm grip Salim exercised overpower, nevertheless approved it. When Fodeba sought advice from his superior, Salim resisted. He had already said in so many words: there must never be a new political party; it would be against his own interests to see any new one come into being.

Yet Fodeba remained firm, saying to Salim, *"I cannot do that, it is not against the law for people to create their own political party."* His words were an outright insult to the absolute power of the president. Salim was left staring at him blankly with his mind, for a small few seconds, unable to grasp the defiant nature of the answer he was given. Smiling wryly, instead of immediately turning around to retaliate, Salim had a different response: *"Oh, really?"* he spoke, mixing disbelief with amusement.

"Yes," Fodeba said resolutely. *"If we don't allow people to form political parties, what are we? A dictatorship? Don't you think we should allow some freedom in this country?"* It must have been Fodeba's well-targeted arguments that caught Salim off guard, for after a slight pause and a softening of his expression, Salim said in rare agreement, "You know what? You're right. Let him do it." He stood up and walked away to his chambers, and Fodeba left.

In retrospect, this was the biggest mistake ever made by either Petit Touré or Keita Fodeba. By allowing the creation of Petit Touré's political party, Fodeba unknowingly opened Pandora's box of potentially dangerous precedents. For Salim, the plan was simple: By allowing parties to form and maintain an air of political openness, Fodeba had undermined Salim's iron-fisted rule. It was a critical error, one precipitating the arrest of both Fodeba and Petit Touré and their consignment to the horrors of Camp Boiro, where death awaited. While Fodeba was of some use and was spared from arrest, Petit Touré was ruined before he knew it. Death had come at dawn, soldiers dragged Petit Touré from his bed, wailing of his family tearing through the morning air. Brothers, sisters, cousins, all swallowed by Camp Boiro's maw. Their sin? A businessman with the impudence to believe power could be legitimately won without blood. Fodeba looked on, spared by the cold pragmatism that saved his life, watching as his soul withered with each rumble of the trucks toward the camp. He had wagered on principle and in doing so, he lost everything but his life. The political maneuver that seemed to offer hope instead set him on a path to destruction, a tragic irony in the world of power and betrayal. Some did not see it coming.

Just like that, Touré's entire family was wiped off the face of the earth. His crime! Ambition.

Machiavellian that he was, Salim sat perched atop his fearful pyramid and knew the truth. The nights stretched long in the presidential quarters. He would gaze into the darkness, listen to the murmur of the city, and feel the earth move. To him, the support from the populace was never a strong chain but a single thread; one tug or even a little spark, and the whole myth of his invincibility would crumble. They had risen before, with united voices and raised fists. They could rise yet again, as it has transpired right outside his doorsteps.

The Ghanaian military had staged a coup, toppling Kwame Nkrumah not long ago with shockwaves travelling across West Africa. A similar fate befell Mali's leader, Modibo Keita. For Salim, these events had starkly illustrated how fleeting power could be, he knew that he could never be too careful. Determined not to let his nation fall prey to the same fate, Salim swore to protect Guinea from any such threat, or rather to protect himself and his *precious* as Gollum would say. He knew that he needed to neutralize all threats and potential plots against his regime.

This led to Colonel Kaman Diaby becoming a major player in his schemes. Diaby was an eminent man of the military elite and the first fighter pilot to grace French West Africa. He had struggled his way through promotions, except that his sudden ascent created many enemies as well as a few admirers among Guinea's elite circles. To protect his rule, Salim had planned the Kaman Diaby conspiracy involving several military officers and civilians of influence; among them was Keita Fodeba, a gambler at the table of fate, putting his bets once again in a bold coup to dethrone his beloved king. But this time the dice went against him, and fortune frowned upon him. Then there was the ill-reputed one, Wadu, a shadow barely gliding through every crack, ever lurking the corners of every plot. And of course, Dr. Maréga, the intellectual, quiet observer, whose mind worked like a clock, carefully ticking through every potential outcome, never really revealing its face.

Before unraveling the meticulously calculated plot called the Labe plot, Salim reshuffled his cabinet, and reassigned Fodeba from a largely symbolic ministerial post, to one that stripped him of any real influence. This move was nothing less than a prelude to Fodeba's downfall. Then, in 1969, Diaby along with his fellow alleged conspirators, was caught and sent to: you guessed it! Camp Boiro. Wadu was narrow-mindedly snared by his detractors due to his opposing opinions about the regime. Salim never liked Wadu, his nomination as state secretary was to keep him closer until the time of his demise along with all his colleagues. His capture and detainment were a piece of a complicated technique that empowered the public authority to free itself of politically inconvenient people at that point. Wadu was only one of many of the denounced, who included different secretaries and committee individuals, senior government employees, and military officials, all assertedly accomplices in the plot not to mention its connection to France. A total of eighty-seven people were apprehended and imprisoned. Mouctar Diallo and Namory Keita died of starvation and dehydration just days after being arrested. Fodeba Keita, the man who designed Camp Boiro, the irony of finding himself in a cell he designed, a cell he was begged by our dear doctor not to put people in. Despite believing that it is sacrilegious to rejoice in someone's demise, his victims believed that anyone who does in the case of Fodeba Keita will be forgiven. Well, I mean, isn't this the perfect definition of "what goes around comes around?" He knew that it was bound to come for he knew that his titanium cast heart belonged there more than anyone! Fodeba loved putting people to death and yet loved life more than anything. He was clinging to life as if his life depended on it. I know, I know… this does not make any sense, just go with it. His resilience was so off the charts that he survived the black diet. The poor fella would not die, which was so unusual that he had to be scheduled for execution by a firing squad.

Cell number 72 was at the far end of the twin blocks that had been ominously barred by iron gates that seemed to herald all things death. Positioned a mere two meters from the toilets, where prisoners emptied their chamber pots under the looming threat of bayonets, the day began as early as 4 o'clock in the morning. It was within this very cell that Fodeba Keita, the mastermind behind Camp Boiro, was a guest of. It read like a premonition of someone who knew his time was up. The words were etched on one of the walls of his cell with something sharp, his powerful declaration:

"I have always served an unjust cause and, in doing so, resorted to arbitrariness. My duty was to arrest anyone who opened their mouths to speak of the aspirations of the people. It was only when I, too, was detained that I really understood." Showing sorrow for his deeds, Fodeba was asking for compassion while knowing that there was no such thing as compassion in the slaughterhouse he had created. However, if he had any doubts about what was on the cards for him, he was going to find out soon enough.

It was yet another scheduled day for sacrifice in the camp and Fodeba and his comrades were on the menu. Fodeba had never wielded a hoe, he might have written a sentence about wielding one in elementary school, but he never held one, and unfortunately found himself gripping a pickaxe and shovel, digging his own grave alongside Wadu. Tears kept rolling down as they toiled in the pitch-black night, illuminated only by headlights from trucks that had transported them there. Soviet submachine guns with gleaming bayonets cast an eerie light over the scene, as if fish were moving through water. Amidst their sobbing, faint Quranic verses murmured softly. Dressed in standard blue prisoner overalls, they were barely recognizable in their emaciated state, their faces now adorned with months-old beards.

To the left of Fodeba stood Minister of Mines and Geology Fofana Karim, while at the other end, Kaman was busy digging his own grave under the watchful eyes of soldiers who had once served under him. Since 2 a.m., these condemned men had been working on their last resting place without rest. At 4:15 a.m., the deepest hole barely reached their knees, an ominous witness to their suffering.

"Not over yet, is it?" barked one of the escorting officers into the stillness. Not getting any response, he moved along the condemned, inspecting, and cursing all the way, and then commanding, *"Join your holes together!"*

Fodeba wept silently, glancing at Wadu, who had paused his digging to recite the lengthy *"Yasin"* from the Quran. Fodeba clumsily connected his pit to Wadu's with swings of the pickaxe methodically, then spoke solemnly, *"What's done cannot be undone. You were with the BAG and I with the RDA. It's politics. Now we stand before God, facing death; we must forgive each other for our past mistakes. You, see?"* He pointed down the hole. *"We'll share the same grave. "Let's shake hands. Here, take mine."*

Fodeba, a man who never felt a modicum of empathy and remorse for others extended his hand to Wadu. *"Keep your satanic paws off of me."* Wadu snapped, with bitterness, shoving the hand away. Then gunshots erupted. Each shooter emptied his arms uncontrollably, or at least for pleasure. Most bodies were swung backward outside the hole, and a member from militias came in to inspect, followed by the leader of the expedition. A Salim's loyal peabrain was always there to watch and report it to Salim who would say afterward, *"I was not alone."*

executions were invariably supervised by higher Party or State officials. The loss of these spirits (men) brought to a close a tension fraught and tumultuous period of Guinea's history that demonstrated the fragile balance of forces at work in post-independence Africa. The violent suppression of the plot was, in fact, Salim's message: no threat, no matter how well placed, could be allowed to destabilize his power. These events would haunt Guinea; they snaked with the poison of fear and mistrust within the political setting. So, why and how did these people come to Salim's crosshair?

It begins with a very undramatic seed planted in February 1969, in Labe: During a rather casual gathering of officers and members of Salim's party, one paratrooper from the barracks casually rolled the statement to Cyrus, the spy: "Be careful, my friend, despite the trust you share with Salim, he will strangle you one day." This off-hand remark did not sit well with Cyrus; his eyes widened as he exclaimed, "What did you say?"

The gentleman smiled coldly and said, "I'm just telling you that nasty little fellows like you always get their comeuppance, believe me, it is gonna come sooner or later. And there will be no "Beelzebub" made me do it." Cyrus was dumbfounded, hanging on to his last words as the beginning of a terrible tale. The little bastard who had ever been looking for ways to please his daddy scurried away with his saucerful full of gifts. He went back to Conakry reporting the warning and suggesting that a conspiracy may be in the making.

Salim did not waste a moment. Restless as always, Salim gave orders to Magassouba Moriba, one of his most loyal secretaries based in Labe, to investigate the matter. After a lengthy investigation, he reported having found no evidence of a plot. But Salim remained suspicious and instructed General Lansia Dane, Secretary of Defense, with Commissar Adamo Boiro, to follow up. The general ended up clearing the officers of wrongdoing after further inquiries yet still ordered that the paratroopers be moved to other garrisons simply out of precaution. And as for Cyrus, just like Momo Jo before him will be disposed of after his welcome in the fold wore off. A simple trip to Camp Boiro where he put people in.

Anyway, the unfolding situation took a gripping turn with the three paratrooper officers escorted by commissar Boiro to Conakry with a brief layover at Kankan. During their stop-over the paratroopers sensed danger, fearing that the Revolutionary Committee was taking them to Camp Boiro. Out of desperation, they hijacked the plane, forcing the pilot to divert to Bamako; however, Boiro was thrown out of the plane mid-flight.

Because of the diminished fuel supply, a forced landing was made near Siguiri, in northern Guinea. Gambled away, the officers were grabbed hold of by activists and taken back to Conakry, where they were put at the disposal of the Revolutionary Committee. This new body, set up just for this occasion, consisted of Salim's staunchest supporters, Salmany, his cousins Lansia Dane, and Kais Retu.

After enduring torture in Camp Boiro, the three officers were broken. They suffered enough under duress to toll out the names of those grouped by the Defense in the alleged plot: Colonel Kaman Diaby, a few ex-French officers who had thrown in their lot with Guinea on independence, and several others. Included in the accused were Fodeba Keïta, dubbed *"the brain of the plot,"* Ba Adamo, *"the grey eminence,"* Karim Fofana, *"the ideologue,"* Baïdi Gueye, *"the financier,"* and Wadu, *"the accomplice."* Torridly named in anguish and fear, these names would soon cast another wave of turbulence upon Guinea's political atmosphere.

Like a dark, ominous storm building on the horizon, this plot was signaling a change, a metamorphosis of the chilling instruments of power that would soon come to define the regime. It was the moment where cruelty and control became something systemic, a hideous dance of oppression. Unlike the earlier, more chaotic plots choked under the weight of improvised and bungled violence, this one was different: a torturous blueprint; the lesson in cruelty that would be perfected and repeated in the years that followed.

Until this moment, the state machinery was clumsy and faltering. The Revolutionary regime and minions had not yet found their fangs; their camp at Camayenne was just a hollow shell of what it would become. Torture had not yet been tuned into fine workmanship; confessions were extracted out on threats, yes, but there were no organized avenues of betrayal, no artful form of corruption of the mind, no systematic erosion of the soul. The first "conspirators," Petit Touré and companions, were eliminated in quick, brutal deaths. Their last breaths were taken away even before they could utter a single word to incriminate more people. No confession was heard; no uttering of remorse or treason occurred, quite simply because the regime had not yet set itself the task of making them say what it wanted to hear.

But something changed with this fourth plot. The State had learned. The aim was no longer merely to kill the bodies of those who threatened it. Physical torture was there, all right; but this time the goal was moral degradation, erosion of trust, poison of accusing one another that made this new system so much more dreadful to bear. Silencing the enemy was no longer the sole thing to be done. These enemies were now to be stripped bare to their minds cracked open, to reveal the fears and dark secrets that they tried to bury. They were made to confess and accuse each other, even those whom once they had dearly loved or never known. Confessions were no longer simple matter of words, but tools of destruction, tools used on the individuals and upon the society they were a part of. It was the demise of all hope for a unitary country. What ensued was an unending crescendo of domination, where loyalty had no abode, and suspicion grew to be its sole law.

The method reminded one eerily of those tactics that Stalin had used in the infamous Moscow Trials, trials that had become theatre of the absurd in which on scraps of genuine fact fabricated plots were dragged into the limelight, with confessions wrung forth from unwilling victims to crimes they never committed. These were the sickening antics that imposed control and terror masquerading as justice; they were trials not of facts but of fear. This macabre parody would, however, nevertheless take root in Guinea, as was horrifically illustrated by a report from *Horoya-Hebdo* on the February 1969 military plot. The plot, conceived in a haze of half-truths and guesses, was finally brought forth to frighten citizens by way of an alleged conspiracy to overthrow the Head of State; a plot spun on nothing more than whispers and innuendo, a house of cards resting on accusations that finally crumbled under their own weight.

Diaby's case, however, was emblematic of the horror of this affair. Diaby had almost been inextricably near to Salim. Their bond had been forged in the rural heart of Faranah, reinforced by family ties, a kind of friendship that transcended politics. Salim embraced Diaby as a younger brother, a symbol of trust and faith, one of those fragile links holding together their shared yet nearly extinguished history. The two had bound themselves together in the traditional way, with one placing a hand into the other's and the exchange of kola nuts as a token of loyalty. It should have been sacred-level loyalty, but in Salim's world, loyalty was a currency that could be devalued, traded off, or just outright discarded whenever it stopped serving him.

From Salim's point of view, Diaby had become a menace. Not for ambition or thirst for power, but for something Diaby stood for, which Salim could never control: the bindings of a solid fraternity of men who shared a lot more than merely politics. A cooperative farm was built by hard work and unity and had blossomed under the foster-care of Diaby and his companions, something like a special bond between soldiers. But to Salim, that farm was everything that stood in the way of his regime: collaboration outside his sphere of influence, unity unfettered by fear, prosperity not gained through his leverage on people. While the farm thrived, Salim's distraction drove the country downhill. The country languished; its once vibrant agriculture being rusted away day by day under Salim's policies.

Diaby's crime lay not in his deeds but rather in those unnatural links, those relationships, and his ability to realize something when the state itself was dying by the day. These bonds that he himself had forged, together with the very friendship and loyalty that once meant everything, had become his chains. Kaman Diaby was just the perfect scapegoat in a bitter irony of fate: as if he was the sacrificial lamb led away to keep the illusion of absolute control intact.

A flimsy sequence of lies and the grossly absurd lies accompanying this setup would provide the setting for the purges that would come later. It was set in stone as the mold in which all subsequent betrayals and executions would be cast: an ugly precedent, full of anger, with no one safe and no bond too sacred to be trashed, no friendship too strong to go down. There will be no trust in Salim's nation; loyalty, instead, would be the kiss of betrayal.

Anyway, the only so-called evidence brought forward against Diaby was a hodgepodge of seemingly useless scraps, each insignificant in itself but cunningly stitched together to fabricate the appearance of guilt. A model of a military uniform from France, the simplest of all samples for a potential purchase, now made out to be a lot more sinister. A pen, very plain in design except for a little etched silhouette of General Charles, the mere existence of it was somehow cited as evidence of covert allegiance. And a letter, dated October 31, 1958, an official communication from a French Officer; an acceptance for Diaby to be allowed to enter into service in Guinea, a request to keep Guinea in the French Community, so harmless sounding in sort of a tone that was even cordial was made out to be the most incriminating evidence. At precisely the same time Salim was desperately asking General Charles to allow Guinea to enter the French Community, a decision which, if taken, was going to be life or death for the nation. That timing made it look more like a betrayal than a mere bureaucratic formality. Oddly enough, also presented as evidence was a letter which came from Dakar to someone called "Nabi Youla" in Paris. Its contents remained unknown, yet it was intercepted and sent back to Guinea, and the report hinted at something suspicious.

Adding weight to their accusation, the documents hinted toward disagreements among the conspirators that Kaman Diaby had wanted to restore order once in power. He wanted the military back to barracks and a semblance to normalcy. The conclusion was that the real perpetrators were politicians and not soldiers and this was drawn without proof and slapped flat without a shade of nuance. There was Fodeba Keïta, Wadu, and Karim Fofana. Each of them was slated for assignment in the new imagined government. Karim Fofana himself was almost a figure of mockery in the context of this plot. He was a "schoolmate" of Salmany, and anywhere that could be understood as an irony between thinking of him as an ideologue or a mastermind of any conspiracy was too laughable for anyone who knew him. He was a man of the utmost pragmatism; really an engineer of great renown who worked among real-world solutions rather than lofty schemes. His only crime, if one can call it that, was his ability to act as a trigger for resentment. He once disparagingly referred to Salmany Retu as little engineer, from a vague or rather unknown school of meteorology, while he, Karim Fofana, had graduated from the distinguished School of Mines in Nancy. This wasn't a rivalry of innocent origins. Fofana's knack of getting under people skin was God given.

The guy had once dared to step up before the political elite, including President Ghoren and the revolutionary Che Guevara, to deliver technical and economic presentations that should have been the spotlight for Salim who could not bear to be whipped so badly in his own ego. In Salim's eyes, Fofana was not just a threat to his power but also to the carefully constructed image of superiority. A great opportunity for Salmany to get rid of this "disrespectful" human being; after all, he was not about to allow anyone to call him a little engineer let alone question his meteorological/economic degree. The real offense committed by

Karim was his refusal to go by their rules. But then there was Fodeba Keïta, purportedly the main culprit in the whole affair, his name was uttered as if behind something much greater. A receiver, used for espionage, in his hands would be enough for the enemies to condemn him. What can one expect from a man who had once been Defense and Security minister? Yet, the deeper truth was insufficiently intertwined with espionage.

Fodeba's real crime, so to speak, consisted of ambition, of imagining a Guinea beyond the petty politics of Salim. He was a man whose intellect and activities far surpassed many; hence he was marked for disposal. The conspiracy against him was never actually about the receiver. It was about silencing a rival who dared challenge the course Salim had laid out for the nation. And then there was Wadu, poor man-gone-in-an-instant. His Islamic faith was bad enough; it got turned into a conspiracy theory faster than one could say "absurd overreach." Accused of using religion for propaganda? Please. Salim's reasoning was the political equivalent of blaming a goldfish for causing a tsunami. What was the real sin of Wadu? Leading an opposition party that dared to exist. For Salim, it was treason just to breathe an air other than the PDG's. Disagreeing with him or his cronies, warranted a one-way ticket to Camp Boiro. Hence, Wadu's fate was determined, not by his own acts, but because of his association with the past. Salim is the pettiest grudge-holder in history, a man who nursed a political vendetta like it were a fine wine, aging it to perfection for decades. Because of such pathological jealousy, the results of an election that took place in 1954 lived rent-free in his head and is always reminded of it at the sight of Wadu. The occupying thoughts forever in one's head make one do unimaginable things.

Did Wadu win the parliamentary seat? "RIGGED!" screamed Salim, clutching his pearls and his ego like a toddler denied candy. Never mind that independence had not been *breathed* for guinea yet, so wounded was Salim's pride that he would make everybody else an issue of it. The loss was one Salim would never forget, never forgive. Fast forward years later, and poor Wadu's true crime wasn't ambition; it was being a living reminder that Salim couldn't win at everything. The man held grudges like it was an Olympic sport.

The great irony: that the conspiracy was eventually exposed by...let me check...one of Salim's other associates. Oh, the uncanny betrayal within the inner circle of a dictator! Turns out the dictator's inner circle was about as loyal as a pack of hyenas eyeing the same carcass. Who would have thought that ruling through fear and tantrums would create such a menace of betrayal? Everyone. Everyone thought. Almost pale in comparison to the political cruelty was the survival of Tounkara Jean Faragué, the man arrested in the third plot who broke under pressure to betray Fodeba Keïta to an irrevocable end. It was in this game of backstabbing and manipulations that survival was of utmost importance killing any other consideration. The plot was never really about evidence. It was about power; it was about fear; it was about those oppressing powers who could strike down anyone challenging their narrative. The real conspirators were not the accused but the power-wielding few who determined what was true and then manufactured the story of their liking. The plot was permanent, as Salim put it, a shadow cast over Guinea for as long as there was power to be contested.

Carrying within it the very heart of a city battered by upheaval, an ominous political weather was brewing on the horizon. Silence crept along, amidst the thunder of Salim's words. Each of his speeches could be likened to a hammer blow on the anvil of revolution. His voice, forceful and convincing, cut through the clamor of the crowds, gathering attention as he laid the framework of a new reality. The target was clear: General Charles, whose very shadow stretched mightily in the future of the nation.

On the evening of March 21, militant fervor descended upon the streets of Conakry. The march that had stitched them together with intent appeared as the spontaneous outburst of loyalty to the revolutionary cause. Even with all the window dressing in the world, it was undeniably brilliant how it was orchestrated. It ended at the *Palais du Peuple*, where the "beloved leader" slid down from the atmosphere, calm before the anxious and enraged people. With indignation in his voice, he praised the almost immortal memory of Adamo Boiro, the martyr of the Revolution. Boiro was not just a fellow to the people, but an emblem, the icon of selfless service to the Motherland, a beacon towards which everyone who regards self-sacrifice can steer. *But was he though!* the poor fellow died while sending innocent people to the slaughterhouse. Oops!

Then, in an atmosphere heavy with tension, Salim revealed the bitter and harsh truth. The conspirators who had dared to plot against the Revolution were named and shamed before the gathered crowd. With harsh and unrelenting words, he set the course for what came next. The Revolutionary Committee then took charge, with the heavy task of arresting those traitors and bringing them to trial. And justice, in the form of retribution, would follow.

The conspirators were categorized with harsh precision. Death was decreed for the Main Actors who were the true offenders behind the plot. Thirteen men had their fates sealed at one stroke, and two more were sentenced in absentia, though the fact that they had fled and were beyond reach did not make them any less culpable.

Active Accomplices comprised those who had conspired alongside the leaders to a lesser degree yet with just as destructive effects. They were sentenced to life forced labor; their futures reduced to the hard labor of exile.

The More or Less Active Accomplices, most of them junior officers and corporals, were sentenced to decades of forced labor. Their role was debated behind closed doors. Had they been manipulated, promised glory and riches by the powers above them? Or had they chosen to act for themselves, out of loyalty more personal than political? The relationships binding these men to the Chief of Staff, to the ministers, the very bonds of trust and secrecy, proved elusive, yet undeniably perilous.

Among the Civil Accomplices, who had supported the conspirators from the sidelines, sentences ran the gamut. Some were convicted to life imprisonment; others served sentences of 10 or 20 years in jail. Dr. Bokar Maréga was among them, the son of Salim's former schoolteacher. A bitter personal history between them cast a shadow over Maréga's fate, Salim could never forgive the man for refusing to let him enter into the revered Conakry Higher School. The heavy mantle of that old grievance fell upon Maréga, a reminder that the faintest slight might very well alter the path of history.

And then there were those people who considered Doubtful Elements: those murky shadows whose implication in the plot was suspected but never proven. Military personnel dismissed from the army;

civilians stripped of their positions of power were left to languish in uncertainty. Their formerly secured lives inside the machinery of the State now lay ruined. Under heavy surveillance, and with every movement watched, they soon became mere shadows of their former selves.

Those freed people were persons onto degradation and humiliation, never to be. And Kindo Touré, who bore witness to their suffering, said that reintegration would have crushed him. To return to the community was not to be welcomed but rather to be put to some test, a journey through misery and struggle without end. Their ghosts of the past clung to them; lives thus forever mired in the stain of betrayal. The betrayal of a man who promised to make their lives better. A betrayal that might have unexpected consequences.

Later in the same year, Salim and Kenneth Kaunda of Zambia traveled together between the airport and *Palais du Peuple* on another gloomy day. The sun was dipping, casting long shadows across the road, oblivious of a storm about to burst. Suddenly, almost as if in a desperate sprint, a young man by the name of Tidiane Keïta, kept his eyes wild, piercing through the moving crowd like a starved tiger, and he appeared unwillingly drawn toward Salim's car. Gripping the president by force, he pulled him away from his entourage's protection.

It was over in a flash. For a fleeting moment came the unforgettable vision of a man tremulous and desperate, standing before the might of a nation. Keita's hands were empty, yet inside he must have had one painful conviction; there was no weapon to be seen if there was, no tangible reasons for his act. A solitary madness, borne perhaps of unseen betrayals or whispers of revolution! But before his action could take hold, he was struck down and exiled from life by the rapid precision of Salim's guards.

The world around him became dead silent. His body lay on the street bitterly cold, indicating the last word of his defiance. The investigation, self-willed and fast, was closed almost before it could start. But the truth of Keïta's existence did not fade away with his death. He had spent time in Côte d'Ivoire wayed in its own secrets, and later was linked with the "Kaman Diaby plot," an attempt at wresting some power from the iron grasp of Salim's regime. His brief moment, however tragic, told of something deeper unrest, an existence consumed in the fiery conflagration that it could not quench and a nation struggling in the wrenching throes of its own.

Chapter 14

The coup

Salim's heart seized with a fire that could no longer be contained within the borders of Guinea. The cries of a continent held in shackles by colonial chains resonated in the inner soul, mutating each of his ambitions into a much greater one, a vehement and unyielding solidarity with Africa's collective agony. He arose, like a storm, as the unshakeable pillar on which movements for liberation held all over the land. To the gasping-for-breath-from-freedom nations, he was no mere commander: he was a brother in arms, a trusted strategist, whose name was uttered with reverence from the Sahel all the way to the coast. His vision cut across maps and borders; he saw not split states but a people, joined together from blood, sweat, and through sheer willpower to reclaim their destiny.

There was a bitter irony in his ascent. Guinea, still trembling from its own hard-won independence, now cradled a man whose influence rippled across oceans. Salim's resolve crystallized into a once in a lifetime moment that would alter history. When Amílcar Cabral, the angry father of the Guinea-Bissau rebellion, arrived in Conakry, it was far from a mere handshake of diplomacy. It was the collision of destinies. The air crackled with electricity between two revolutionaries, their hands clasped not as strangers but as brethren. The never-sated PAIGC of Cabral grew strong from Guinea's victory, and at that meeting, a spark set aflame. The embers of the war for independence in Guinea-Bissau burned brighter from Salim's defiance.

For him, that was not a cold calculation of power. It was sacred. With every resource shared, with every risk taken, there pulsed the memory of the suffering of his own people. Guinea became more than a country; it became the sanctuary, the very heart sustaining the body of liberation. And Salim? He wore his rank not as a crown but as a scar, an emblem of battles fought and those yet to come.

But shadows gathered. By 1970, Lisbon ran out of patience. The Portuguese, with their empire now acridly crumbling at the seams, bristled at this audacious thorn in their sides. Marcelo Caetano, back in his distant palaces, had by then grown tired of being taunted by Salim, on how he harbored guerrillas, how he spat in the face of colonial grandeur, and how he turned Guinea into a stronghold of rebellion. So, they set to scheme. The unleashing of Operation Green Sea was like the uncoiling of a poisonous serpent: propaganda to poison minds, cash notes for traitors, and poisonous whispers turning brother against brother, but then came the real poison, its fangs lay in the audacity of violence, a midnight invasion of Conakry indeed, warships slipping through pitch-black waves to physically strangle revolution in its infancy.

On that night of November 21, 1970, beneath the cover of darkness, four ships steamed toward the Guinean coast. A tank landing ship and another vessel carrying over 200 Guineans disguised as members of the Guinean Armed Forces, accompanied by 220 Portuguese and African

Portuguese soldiers, were among the godsend agents of invasion called forth for one target: to break the Salim regime and cripple the operations of the PAIGC.

Screams of metal and fire rent the air as Portuguese warships unleashed fury against Conakry shores. The harbor, once full of promise, was laid to rest a funeral pyre, another five PAIGC supply boats burned to death, their skeletal remains hissing into the black water. Smoke billowed with claws clawing at the skies, a hideous curtain over the city. Death, meanwhile, had walked in steel boots: Commandos entered Salim palace, spilling gasoline from fury, their bullets scorching shroud, skin, and memories alike. But the Palace was nothing more than a trophy. Salim, eluding, ghost-like was not there. "Is he sequestered away in some so-called Royal residence," whispers of rumors hissed. "Or had the very earth swallowed him." A phantom laughing at their impotence.

Chaos rippling through streets. Doors had been kicked open at PAIGC headquarters, guns were barking... but there was no trace of Cabral's shadow. Was it a cruel joke? Divine intervention? Or maybe Lisbon's spies, drunk on overconfidence, had chosen to disregard whispers warning their prey. The invaders burned with fierceness, that only turned their rage sour. Yet onward they marched, the blades catching sunrays as they tore apart political prisons. Twenty-six Portuguese captives, stumbling into the carnage, squinting at freedom like moles dragged into the light. But the triumph of their liberators screamed desperation, a consolation prize grabbed while the true quarry slipped away.

The Guinean militias fought with the ferocity like cornered lions, their rusty rifles coughing defiance to the shower of steel from behind. The bravery was bleeding from the alleys. At the power plant, commandos flipped the switches, turning Conakry into darkness. But that was when their arrogance showed: The radio station, that relic they had dreamed of seizing was dead, laughing its empty halls at their outdated maps and fraying intelligence.

Dawn arrived, pale and pitiless. The Portuguese withdrew, boots heavy with the ash of half-victories. Twenty-six souls freed, yes, but Salim's ghost still haunted them. Cabral's laughter would ring in their nightmares. Just like Operation Persil, Operation Green Sea had drowned in its ambition: it could neither overthrow Salim nor eliminate Cabral. For Portugal, it was a bleeding wound with salt in it: they had scorched earth but had failed in shattering the spirit festering beneath. For Guinea, the scars would probably linger for a time, with its palaces burned, docks shattered, and the stench of betrayal. But in the graveyards of scorched palaces would arise a significant defiance showing that the assault did not destroy the revolution; it just baptized it in blood.

And as the sun climbed, Conakry's people emerged, their faces smudged with soot but eyes blazing. They gathered the shards of their city, each broken brick a testament. Salim, wherever he was, would rise again louder than ever. Cabral's war would rage on. Lisbon had gambled everything on fear, but fear had long since fled these streets. All that remained was unshackled people, their rage now a song, their resistance an unquenchable flame.

The Portuguese retreat was a ragged symphony of hubris unraveling. As their ships swallowed the freed prisoners and slithered back toward open sea, a brittle hope lingered among the ranks: a skeletal force of 150 men, left crouching in Conakry's ruins like jackals waiting for a feast. They'd been promised revolt, a people risen in rage against Salim's iron grip, eager to tear down his regime with their bare hands. But the streets stayed silent. No chants, no torches, just the hollow wail of wind through bullet-riddled buildings.

The invaders were pacing like caged beasts. *Where was the fury?* The desperation? They had mapped every prison, every palace, but not the heartbeat of the people. Their arrogance from above had blinded them from something seemingly insignificant, a radio station, that dusty relic humming in the outskirts. Its crackling voice still spilled across the night and wove a nation's resolve. *"Salim lives,"* it hisses. *"Resist."* A lie? Perhaps a truth? It mattered not. A steady drumbeat drowning the static of the Portuguese promises.

There was, meanwhile, a scattering of the top brass, feeling that their best chance of survival lay in the play dead mode. They decided to pull a Houdini act and disappear from sight. Kais Retu appeared among them and his cousin Salmany Retu, who was either as legendary or as infamous as he was.

The desperate Portuguese remnants gnawed. No uprising came. No crowds clamoring for liberation, another voice was just watching from shattered windows, silent and sharp as knives. And the radio kept chanting. Salim's voice, real or imagined, wound itself through the city like smoke. At dawn, the resolve of the invaders began crumbling. Their mission, well, already a corpse had begun rotting.

Though Kais, a master of all things *not getting caught*, really did pull a stunt worthy of a spy movie. One might say he inspired the creation of *007*. During the operation, now infamous for all the chaos and miscalculations, he thought the best way to evade capture was by going to a full-fledged hotel lounge lizard. Military strategy and tactics could be thrown out the window; leaving his destiny in the hands of fate, Kais stowed away in the Camayenne Hotel like an ill-conceived cockroach in a luxury suite, dodging any semblance of responsibility while the whole city descended into pandemonium. The fellow was practically begging to be spotted, and yet the very chaos pulled him through. Truly a professional at dodging life's most awkward realities.

Meanwhile, the poor defense secretary, Lansia, who probably expected to lead the charge like a hero, was captured by the invading forces. The man had no idea he was about to be the star of an impromptu "hostage situation" reality show. But, never to lose face, Lansia went on to escape in thrilling fashion from the grasp of his captors and strolled up to the Algerian Embassy as if he had just returned from an afternoon jog. As if the embassy were a five-star emergency evacuation lounge. Classic Lansia, always keeping the drama alive. Operation Green Sea probably remains one of the most spectacular bungles in Guinean history, but hey, at least Kais and Lansia retained their pride because there were only a few who knew that they soiled their panties during their escape, that is, while the country was left to figure out how to patch things up after their great escape.

The plan to oust Salim, filled with schemes, double-crosses, smoke-filled meetings, somehow melted away like overcooked chicken. Guinea was the impenetrable fortress of PAIGC. Salim's government grew stronger in its grip on power and kept tossing its liberating movements across the Portuguese colonies like a bartender giving away free drinks to the rowdy crowd. It was surely a party for the freedom fighters. While the whats and whys added spice to the behind-the-scenes events, imagine family-feud-meets soap-opera... Salim somehow held it all together like an over-caffeinated juggler in a circus.

The internal tensions that brewed were nothing compared to the outer chaos that the plotters had hoped would unfold. Guinea did not crack, and Salim's hold on the government was unshakable. But later, emerges another really important point because this plot was only a chapter in the huge mess that was decolonization and Cold War politics around Africa. Indeed, the stakes were extremely high, with the Soviet Union backing Guinea in one corner and now showering pats on the freedom fighters, while Portugal had its own list of allies, including the motley crew of South Africa and Rhodesia. South Africa was not just there to watch from the sidelines, of course they were themselves dealing with their "own pests", as they liked to call the liberation movements across southern Africa, fighting what they viewed as an infestation of, well, anything that was not them. A little regional housekeeping, if you will.

Salim, still in power, his hands firmly on the reins. But here's the kicker, while he may not have lost this round, the plot served as a sort of trump card for future power play. Tensions increased, and heavier chips came into the middle to the great advantage of Salim, who kept more aces under his sleeves if ever another witting attack be brought down on him. The coup, not really reaching the heights its perpetrators wanted, nevertheless reminded Salim that he was not untouchable. The game was for now in his hands, but certainly far from over.

Chapter 15

The purge

After the hilariously botched coup attempt (because even rebellions couldn't take him seriously), Guinea's Supreme Leader, Salim scrambled to salvage his bruised ego. First, he cranked up the drama: tearful pleas for African Union, frantic letters to the UN about colonial boogeymen, and fiery speeches that somehow always circled back to… himself. But when Félix Houphouët, with actual charm and cash, dared to offer help via a delegation, Salim slammed the door. Why? Oh, just a little betrayal: that sly fox Houphouët had apparently "stolen" Salim's concubine (*gasp!*) some kind of Cain and Abel stuff, you know. Even worse! He refused to bankroll Salim's anti-France referendum tantrum. Cue Salim's inner monologue: *"How dare he defy me, the self-appointed martyr of independence?!"*

Putting the petty spat into the dramatic celestial spotlight, Salim enshrined Portugal's colonial sins at Nations with Oscar-worthy pathos, rallying African leaders to clap together like trained seals. Bravo, Salim! The man intolerant of a rival delegation was now the continental "unifier." Meanwhile, an elite group of Guineans was suffering apocalyptic devastation under the boots of Salim's militias. Their districts had become ghost towns from fear. But who cared? Salim had a *narrative* to sell.

As Portuguese troops "liberated" Camp Boiro (pissed about not finding Salim), they whispered to the prisoners, "Salim's dead! You're free!" The detainees, wiser than the UN, looked upon this offer with great suspicion. *"Is this another one of Salim's sick games?"* one muttered, eyeing the exits. A desperate few ran for it, but most stayed on, haunted by the memories of Salim's cruelty. Free? From a tyrant who just made fun of his own death? Hard pass.

And then, the climax! Fresh off hiding in a bunker during the actual fighting, Salim emerged… on a *magazine cover*. Behold the "Heroic Liberator," posing in a comically oversized military uniform, chest puffed like a rooster who forgot he'd hid during the fox attack. The caption? "I single-handedly saved the capital!" The audacity! The man was so insecure, so rattled by Houphouët's mere existence, that he needed a photoshoot to gaslight a nation. Houphouët, eating *Gharba au poisson and some Allocco* in Abidjan, probably smirked. After all, why feud with a man whose greatest enemy was his own reflection? Never mind that his regime was crumbling, or that the people who stood up to him were burying their dead. Salim had a new hat, a fresh lie, and a UN resolution to wave around even though he knew for absolute certainty that his reign was a tragicomedy of errors: a jealous dictator who alienated allies and mentor in the case of Houphouet, over a concubine, hid from battles but cosplayed as a warrior, and plastered his face on magazines to drown out the screams of his people.

Although rather than using this remarkable leverage to benefit his nation with a prosperous future, nah! He just had to be himself at every opportunity. He went on to cook up yet another false narrative, this time of an imaginary "conspiracy" to destroy those whom he considered obstacles. In this story, the supposed "best friend" of Salim would be engaged in a movement to seize control of the country, an accusation so absurd that it could only come from the mind of a man who thrived on division and paranoia.

To Salim, truth and lies were important weapons, and he wielded them without mercy, creating his enemies and bending facts to fit his own will. In his typical chaotic fashion, Salim would manipulate the masses using half-lies and disjointed pieces of information to stir confusion. He, of course, depended upon this: ignorance shall be his accomplice while an ignorant public shall always lose in the perception battle against a handful of the informed. The games he played were akin to a demented version of *Werewolf*: a psychological game where truth was seldom ever clear and trust was the very first victim. The repertoire was actually simple but very effective: keeping people in the dark, making them fear shadows, and presenting himself as the sole protector against the shadows of his own imaginings. With every word, every whisper practically laid down by Salim, there was an edifice of lies being built. He meant it all! He meant it: The Liar was a victim! The Liar was a martyr! He had convinced those who believed in him that his enemies, the ones who were truly hurt, were dangerous traitors who must be eradicated. This turned legitimate, in Salim's eyes, the violence that subsequently took place and the snakes around him working with him on it turned their fear into an able tool of oppression.

His entourage, loyal to the lie as much as to the man, became his enforcers, turning his fabricated story into a self-fulfilling prophecy. It was nothing new for the community of intellectuals, but this time the consequences were devastating. People that once stood for equality were now branded as traitors, enemies of the state in a narrative they had never agreed to and could never escape. The chaos of the coup was nothing compared to the suffering that would follow, as the fictional conspiracy spread like wildfire, and those who had once been free were hunted down and hanged. This was Salim's best work yet. The doors of the camp had opened, but they led not to freedom, but to a nightmare of fear, and bloodshed that would haunt even the relatives of the detainees. Some of the detainees that had escaped would be replaced by their loved ones, uncles, fathers, siblings, and unlucky acquaintances.

A huge number were gathered in Camp Boiro where Kais Retu introduced an easygoing veneer during cross examinations, frequently serving as intermediary between the detainee and their families to spy and threaten them. He was the sole master of the camp, permitting no one to enter or leave without his permission. With his lack of respect for human life, he tormented and executed whomever he wanted. Some of the victims of Salim and comrades took the public in surprise. Conventionally people are fattened up before the slaughter but in Salim's nation hunger was the way to go. People like Raymond Tchidimbo, the Bishop of Conakry, got arrested and was to be hanged as an example to show that there were no limit and no distance that the sticky hands of Salim's regime could not reach. Fortunately for our dear archbishop, Pope Paul VI intervened and prevented the tragedy. In prison, the archbishop was coerced to "confess" his wrongdoings. Have you heard about dignity, like… do not confess for something you did not do. Well, you have not seen the inside of camp Boiro. You will confess to anything. Anything that Salim's minions write on a piece of paper and give you. It was called *"the truth of the secretary of state"* as mentioned by Alpha Abdoulaye.

Let's not forget Alassane Diop, the former Guinea Secretary of Information and a proud Terangan descendant. His life story is something that of a *"Choose Your Own Misadventure"* novel. After being locked up in Guinea's dreaded Camp Boiro for nearly 10 years, freedom finally entered his life, only to have it come to light that his early years had also been tainted with being held in German camp as a prisoner of war under the Third Reich's accommodation until Allied forces liberated him. Imagine what kind of unlucky person, one must be to go from a European Nazi camp to an African one. Talk about being committed to the shoreline existence of the unwanted guest. While most folks collect stamps, Diop chose to collect dictatorships. And as Loyalty program perks? Just a rusty bunk bed and a good dose of existential dread. Life sure knows how to laugh in one's face, doesn't it? Poor Diop.

Anyway, at Camp Boiro, brooding inmates were given at breakfast a dry piece of bread the size of a box of matches and at supper, very little rice partitioned and boiled with dirty water. Apart from when Salim was carrying out a sacrifice, there was never any meat.

In December 1970, under an icy shadow of political unrest, Yaryb, the proud dignitary servant of the state, was torn from his home. He was arrested swiftly, brutally, in silence, like an echo with a tinge of betrayal. Just a few weeks before this terrible event, he had given his unwavering support to Salim after the violent clash with the Portuguese forces. His loyalty, however, was no saving spell against the iron hand of a paranoid and cruel regime.

Yaryb was not only a man of stature but one of deep convictions, a man who had sacrificed much. He had sacrificed his pension, and in fact, his own future for the cause of his country. He stood as the last man between Salim and total authoritarianism. He was the one who understood well the fine line between resistance and survival. At a moment of extreme urgency, he saved the life of Salim by preventing him from boarding a plane destined to a voyage of no return. A plane on which the passengers would be thrown out of the sky mid-flight. Surely, it was that same Yaryb who whispered the warning, this simple act of defiance to the Angel of death would seal his own fate. What if Yaryb had let him get onto that plane? Would his nation have been in a better place then? Would the children of Salim's nation, who are dead, be alive then? I guess these are the questions, Shoulda, woulda, coulda, huh?

The abduction of Yaryb from his home was anything but ordinary. Salim did not perform the usual cruel carnival of false hospitality of inviting a man to his house, feeding him, only for him to be grabbed by Salim's militia an hour later. Rather, it was far more direct; a swift strike, allowing for no hope or hesitation. Given the choice, he would have rather not have gone to the dreaded camp: the suffering was so pronounced it lingered in the air above like fog. There, Yaryb underwent all manner of horrors that would have broken any lesser man. His flesh was bound, while crude talismans on his shackled hands were forced upon him by his captors. Yet, as the tide of pain ebbed and flowed; Yaryb's spirit clung unstintingly to life. His gaze was filled with the pride and dignity of one who had lived a purposeful life.

Starting in January 1971, a Revolutionary Committee led by Salmany, at the time the secretary of economy, questioned the detainees. In certain cases, inmates were put on a black diet. For prisoners, showing bravery meant neither giving in to torture nor begging for food while on the black diet.

Weeks passed, and so things only became darker. The Night of January 25, 1971, was Yaryb's moment of reckoning. The very essence of death by execution had to itself express this unutterable cruelty, an unimaginable spectacle used to frighten into silence all those who raised a voice against the regime. Along with Balde Ousmane, and Keita Kara Soufiana, Magassouba Moriba, Yaryb had been condemned not by any court of justice but by the whim of despots. He was taken to the famous Tombo Bridge where the winds carried a message of death and betrayal.

Arriving finally, the days quietly saluted their exit, as the men whose hands were stained with innocent blood stood cold and detached in orderly view of that last act. Their fate had been cast at a sham trial, but there had been no justice, no truth, and no honor in that verdict. The four cords wound around their necks choking not only blood but a testimony that deserved to be heard in glaring daylight, that testimony of injustice, a symbol of erasure stripping away all their dignity, all recognition, and their very presence from the face of the Earth. Diarra Traoré carried out the execution under the direct orders of Salim, who together with his loyalists, witnessed the slaughter.

As the noose tightened, Yaryb's noble spirit would not, but rather could not, make an accommodation with anything sinister. His body went down, but his spirit remained defiant. In those dying moments of utter stillness and despair, his heartbeat in unison with the countless other hearts that had been stilled in such silent despair. His sacrifice, the only act of resistance observed in front of inhuman cruelty, was a living monument to the price of truth in a world that had long since forgotten what truth ever was. His name would eventually survive only as a whisper in the shadows, but the reverberations of his defiance would far outlast the winds that carried the last breath of him into that dark night. That very night saw the execution of the only woman to be put to death in the country, Loffo Camara, a former Secretary of State for Social Affairs. Her execution was headed by Mamadi Keita, who was half-brother to the wife of President Salim, Andrée. Such a statue granted him easy access all the way up to the very top echelons of government. He would ironically join the Central Committee for Ideological Affairs of the Democratic Party of Guinea: *"An uneducated demon as an ideological affairs representative, really? Give me a break!"* The members of the committee would whisper in meetings.

* * * * *

The year was 1968. The great actor and diplomat, a former voice of Guinea in the United Nations, received a call from his dearest companion, Fodeba Keita, urging him to *return home*. Marof obeyed his friend, his heart heavy, but oblivious to the betrayal lying beneath such words. Marof had little reason to distrust Fodeba, as those two shared a bond that had weathered the intricacies of their respective careers.

The horrible clime of Guinea welcomed its son with a suffocating embrace. Soldiers appeared on the tarmac, shackling him with a sinister glint. No questions were asked. No theatrics were performed. The world which had multiplied applause for him now narrowed with a leaden hand unto the iron bars of Camp Boiro.

The hopes persisted for several years. In 1970, there was a spur of liberating expectation from his dungeon known as Operation Green Sea. However, the violent endeavor collapsed, and along with it, engendered familiarity among the illusions of mercy. Even after this temporary place of liberation, Marof drifted in an atmosphere choked with tyranny, and each shadow resonated with the revengeful discourse of the regime. In the wave of repression that blanketed the country in the wake of a failed coup, Marof, again, found himself among his companions in captivity. And from then, there was no news about him until whispers slithered their ways out of the camp and found the likes of Manera.

This headline came out as a fine and poetic exclamation of wonder! It hit people like a dagger when the truth came crashing down in 1985: Marof had been executed fourteen years prior, on a wintry January morning of 1971 with no witnesses, no grave, just that dreadful silence of the regime. His charismatic return, that solitary stumble born of trust, had spiraled into a long legacy of anguish. The friend's summons, the shackles, the unmarked death, are all fragments of a huge tragedy carved in memory where love and ill-will collided with the machinery of power.

Chapter 16

Paris

While Salim had always imagined a partnership between Guinea and France, he grew increasingly aware of the complexities of nationhood. The optimism of independence grew ill at ease, clashing with the harsh realities of statecraft. In defiance of the rhetoric that had pervaded the referendum campaign and the increasingly charged atmosphere surrounding it, Salim himself had reached out to the French government, hoping to mend broken ties and perhaps propose a partnership worthwhile to both nations.

And yet, his overtures were rejected. Too late, General Charles had become the symbol of France's aloofness and disdain; his denial of any possibility of reconciliation was not only applied during his presidency, but also after his death. They had always reminded Salim that Guinea had chosen independence and now, Guinea must chart her own course. This was a blow that plunged Salim into an identity crisis: on one side, the yearning to work by the side of France and, on the other, the real hardness of national sovereignty.

With Salim, there have been time and again attempts, always to be frustrated. The door to France remained closed until the death of General Charles and the emergence of Meli in the picture, when hopes of reopening communications began to surface. Calm but determined, Meli advised Salim on how to win the French back with delicate diplomacy. As a result, the relationship between Guinea and France was slowly patched up as the channels opened for renewed dialogue. But even with this diplomatic success, the relationship was nowhere near being fully restored. France reopened its embassy in Conakry, but that was it. There was little that could be done with negotiations and dialogue about leaving behind tensions and colonial history that continued to define their interactions as the new ties seemed mostly symbolic. General Charles might have been no more, but all the people he got humiliated with were still alive and deciding foreign policies.

So, France was not ready to offer the partnership Salim desired, but at least now Salim could live in peace without the constant cloud of bitterness. He could go to France and sail across the globe without looking over his shoulders. It wasn't the reconciliation he had envisioned, but well, Beggars can't be choosers, it was nevertheless an uneasy peace that allowed him to govern without the pressure of ongoing isolation. However, it took General Charles's demise, the presidencies of Pompidu, Valery Giscard, and Mitterrand, for Salim to dare venture in the *city of love, croissant and baguettes,* in 1982.

One must have a very good reason to avoid a city of love, and apparently, Salim has the most valid of them all, or maybe it was just a baby steps strategy. You don't want to come on too strongly into a fragile relationship, at the risk of scaring your second half off, like a stray cat you tried to hug on day one. Suddenly it's gone, you're scratched and left wondering where it all went wrong while holding a can of tuna and your dignity.

After months of tergiversation, the doors to Paris are now opened to Salim, where he would meet his counterpart Mitterrand and then hold a press conference to justify his actions against those whom he considered the traitors of the nation.

Agreeing to take a question or two, from a young journalist named Cyril Lafayette, Salim stood up to wave his handkerchief to the loyalists gathered in the room. His broad smile beaming with confidence, he sat down across from Lafayette and tilted back in his chair, waving around a cigarette and exuding great arrogance. He locked his sharp eyes on the young journalist, preparing to deliver his unrelenting speech. The room hung on his every movement.

Lafayette, pale and scrawny with piercing blue eyes, exuded a different brand of confidence, while sitting across the desk, leg crossed, composed, and still somehow overshadowed by Salim's giant presence.

"Mr. president, how are you?" Said Mr. Lafayette calmly while shaking his hand.

"I'm well, thank you for asking." Salim responded with a welcoming gesture.

"Thank you for agreeing to do this interview, first, we are hearing things about you, about your country, are those things true?" Lafayette started with a smile.

"Well, it depends on what you are hearing." He returned the smile.

"That Guinea is not safe, not only for Guineans but also for foreigners."

Salim let out a laughing sound but a mocking one as he began, his eyes scanning the room with intensity.

"Oh, I see! I knew this was coming, so let's get this out of the way. What a wild country! Guinea is accused of hanging its people, leading French workers and farmers to believe that we had picked up people from the streets, whose political opinions, expressed either through the press or speech, were victims of legal actions and condemnations." He paused, his hand raised slightly, emphasizing his next words. "No! We were the ones who were attacked."

A dead silence, they all listen to the man as he leaned in, his voice raised, "For your information, in case neither you nor the French people seem to know about it, the Security Council, in a special session, recognized the fact and invited the aggressors to pay reparations to Guinea."
His expression hardened, and his head rocked from one side to the other. "I said: No, I do not want it; they are the ones who acknowledged having committed a crime! I want them to go and liberate our brothers from the Portuguese colonies. That was my declaration: No reparation, just free our brothers."

He straightened up, at the same time pacing slightly to another point from which he emphasized the next moment. "A special session of the Organization of African Unity was held in Lagos on the 12th of December 1970, and this time, the unanimity of members was present. It was resolved, with a unanimous vote, to condemn this aggression, to stand in solidarity with Guinea, and to ask Guinea to consider putting into force the greatest possible sanctions upon those behind that aggression." His voice grew stronger as eyes stared down in righteous fury.

"It invited all countries to hand over to Guinea those who, having participated in the aggression." He continued then stopped briefly, the shift in posture marking a moment of reflection, his hand on the table. "I know the history of France," he stated, softer yet sure. "It was taught to us, and I have lived part of it." He was now thoughtful, his face recalling some private memories. "I was here in 1946 at the 8th Congress of the CGT (Confédération Générale du travail), and at that time, the CGT was the sole union center for French workers." His eyes glinted with conviction, and he spoke passionately. "I know the history from France itself and that in August-September 1944, it was tens of thousands of traitors whose accounts were paid directly by the French patriots. 17,000 Communards were executed, 1,100 other traitors were executed by the people, and as is explicitly stated in Historia number 36, the streets were littered with corpses. That dreadful spectacle was a great lesson indeed."

He continued, proudly teaching the French the history of their land, "So, a victorious France was proud of its victory over foreign invaders and French traitors. We cannot understand why the French press is hell-bent on dragging the people of Guinea through the mud for having punished those that attacked them on November 22, 1970," he said, pressing his jaws together. "And how did the press manage to portray it that it was the French people who were the victims?"

Taking an ample breath and clenched his fist slightly for emphasis. "I solemnly declare the information to be false and unworthy," he said without any hint of wavering.

"None of them were French: rather, Guineans, it can only mean Guinean officials from their country who had married French women." In an abrupt motion with his hand, he made a piercing gesture in an attempt to underscore his reasoning.

"But if today French women had married Soviet, American, or German officials and their actions were supposed to be accounted for, why then were those Soviets, Americans, Germans, or Englishmen declared illegal by the courts of their own countries? Do you see the logic?" His face grew a little softer, but his expression was resolute. "I am a man from a small country, and an economically poor country: nevertheless, I consider myself, with full dignity of man, a dignity of his people."

Salim's eyes locked with those in front of him as his face held resolve. "I would like to see the France of 1789 defend the just and legitimate cause of its people, who were attacked and have the right to apply to these traitors what their own laws provide."

Taking a deep breath and exhaling slowly, he lowered the tone of his voice a bit and reflected on his actions. "But what I would want you to know about the French is that I acted humanely, and I do not regret it. It was not for them; I did it because of my conscience." He looked all around the room with a gaze loaded with empathy while looking within himself and remembering.

"I even addressed a speech to the people of Guinea to convey that there ought to be pain on the part of these foreigners who trusted and put their faith in Guineans and are now humiliated through the betrayal of their husbands among their own."

His voice became more somber as he paused a moment. Then he continued: "As these husbands are condemned, they no longer possess their rights; rather, they have relinquished them in the very act of opposing the freedom and sovereignty of their nation." Sitting up, his voice again took on a tone of resolution. "I therefore argue that these wives should be fully recognized in all their rights, because Guinean legislation did not allow these French women to return with their children. The parents of the traitorous Guineans had refused to allow the children's return."

He stared at the audience for a while with a calculating look, choosing his next words carefully as though some fire lit within him. "I was forced to hold the meeting and send the circular to all the party committees explaining to public opinion that if it would be unjust so, then a French woman who arrived in trust should be as responsible for her child's upkeep as a Guinean or her husband. And, if the Guinean is able to betray the nation, then the French woman must have the right, the full right at least, to care for the education of her children."

His compassionate face softened briefly, almost absent-mindedly, before continuing the discourse. "That's all of them coming with the children, and all the children at the expense of the Guinean government. They came there, not by sorrow but with joy because Guinea was so kind to them, but then, in the conflict against our regime, they were organized into associations, used as lies, as shields. They themselves are victims, and in fact, I really pity them. That's the truth."

His voice became earnest by the end of his rant. "I would be very glad if any journalist who wishes to have a deeper insight into Guinea would come not to listen to the president or to a government official but to face the realities in Guinea, take time to visit the institutions, and verify if such democracy as propagated here is true or false."

With that, he nodded ever so slightly and continued, "I would even prefer that the first man who does not care for me be the first to come and be confronted by this reality." His gaze darted across the room. "That, ladies and gentlemen of the press, is all. I did not want to keep you that long; I apologize. But I'm sure that most of what I told you tonight was unknown to you." There was a brief pause, then Cyril cleared his throat, and moved on to the next question.

"Two things that intrigue foreign observers, Mr. President; one is an issue, a second thing would be that you rarely ever leave your country... As far as I understand, you have made only one trip outside since 1967. Why is that?"

He lifts his head cautiously. His eyes meet those of Salim for a brief moment and then immediately hurry back to his notebook. Salim listens intently. His face is, as always, a mask of neutrality, but behind those eyes is the faintest glint of challenge, as if he intended to dismantle any assumption that would question his decisions. Salim leans forward, eyes still narrowing.

"I wonder why there is so much concern about this... President Mao, how many times did he leave China? And did that make the Chinese people sick?"

Salim's voice is calm, but there's a distinct power in his tone, a slow build-up that leaves Cyril feeling both diminutive and mesmerized. Cyril hesitated, unsure of how to reply. He gave a quick nod, clutching at composure, but nobody would have been able to sense how much he had been hurt by the question.

"What about President Nixon?" He continued: "How many times since his coming to power has he left the country? And truly, how many times has any president in Europe left their country? The revolution we speak of is in Guinea; it must, therefore, be carried out in Guinea. The center of the struggle is in Guinea. Even if there were foreign forces, with all the imperialistic powers arrayed against Guinea, the Guinean people, if they stay organized and know their responsibilities and choose to defend what they have, no imperialist power will be able to defeat Guinea. This is a historical truth. Should one be surprised not to see me in Guinea, not to catch me, just as some presidents, always in Paris or in London, resting or dancing? I have work to do and cannot waste a single minute. Everything is useful for the development of revolutionary action."

"Traveling abroad does not always mean resting. It is to maintain and open accounts abroad. Don't you think?" Asked Cyril as a gotcha! question

"Why travel? We have visited almost every country in the world. The first three years of independence allowed us to visit almost every country that has good relations with Guinea. What more are we looking for? We are the African country with the most foreign embassies. This well explains the expansion of diplomatic relations Guinea has with the outside world. Even though France constantly speaks of Guinea's isolation, Guinea has more embassies than Senegal, Côte d'Ivoire, or any country cooperating with France. This information is verifiable."

Cyril, trying to regain his footing, asks another question, this time about the so-called "fifth column" in Guinea. He casually but carefully jumps in, "You've often denounced the fifth column operating within Guinea. Do you think it's still active today? Could it be the reason you choose to stay in Guinea?"

"Well, if I were afraid of the fifth column, I wouldn't stay in Guinea, would I?" He retorted with a dismissive tone, almost derisive. Visibly startled, Cyril gives as much as a slight flinch before stopping the act of talking. A pregnant silence ensues. Salim's eyes fix onto his for a piercing stare that must have meant Cyril was already beyond uncomfortable. He trails off, his voice softening, realizing that he's straying upon precarious territory. His eyes flutter nervously, hungry for any sign of reaction.

"No, but you…"

Almost at once, the shadow on Salim's face cuts him off mid-sentence.

"I would have gone to Paris and peacefully taken refuge there."

As if awaiting this exact reply, Cyril immediately comments. "But you might fear that the subversive elements working against you might take advantage of your absence."

As Cyril continues questioning about the possible subversive elements exploiting Salim's absence, Salim lays back in his chair, using big sweeping gestures with one hand, as if elaborately painting the whole world with his words. Salim says each word slowly but distinctly, scarcely a mood in his tone, something to Cyril's discomfort.

"Take advantage how? The Guinean people are armed; Guinea is the only country in the world whose people are armed. Now, have you seen the aggression, the betrayal? Fourteen ministers had betrayed the Guinean people. thirty-two million dollars were distributed. Most of the senior officers, including the Minister of the Army and the Minister of the Interior, betrayed the nation. All the imperialist powers were sure of succeeding against the Guinean revolution, and its demise was even announced on Bonn's television on 22 November 1970, in a broadcast they declared, the world's great dictator: Mr. Salim has passed away."

Salim's words hammered heavily on Cyril; now, he was unsure how to react. The atmosphere in the room felt heavy and intimidating. Cyril lowered his gaze once again and felt the pressure in his chest growing, his mouth completely dry.

"What…" Salim leans forward, eyes narrowing in anticipation of Cyril's next question. The mood has been altered. This incident is no longer an interview; it is a battle of wills. Salim's voice deepens with intensity; his movements become deliberate. He points at Cyril as an emphasis.

"Guinea does not fear imperialism. The fifth column is just an extension of imperialism. It is a class struggle. If we are not afraid of the master, we will certainly not fear the slave who follows him. That is why here, it was crushed, and every time it reappears, it will be destroyed. You can be sure of that! I assert this before the world. No element acting against the Guinean people will long maneuver without being detected, recognized, isolated, and crushed by the Guinean people."

There's a sudden sharpness in his voice; a powerful finality that makes Cyril pause. His fingers tap nervously on the edge of his notebook, the tension in the room palpable.

"You yourself said: fourteen ministers had been indicted, a number of military leaders, provincial governors, senior officials, and Guinean diplomats." As Cyril tries to ask about the betrayal of ministers, Salim cuts him off once more, his tone now completely commanding. Salim interrupting, almost smirking
"So what? This happens everywhere. Traitors are everywhere, but Guinea knows how to deal with them."

The young journalist opens his mouth to speak but stops, unsure whether to continue. Salim's words echo in the quiet room. Cyril feels the weight of history lessons over him, the deep conviction of Salim's views pressing down on him.

"How do you explain that so many people, very close to power alongside you, some of them long-time comrades in arms, betrayal?"

Salim leans back again, arms folded across his chest, his expression unreadable. The atmosphere is now thick with power; there's no escaping it.

"In 1939, how do you explain so many ministers, senior officials, and military officers betraying France and turning over the country to

Germany? One has to understand; a class struggle is on. People do not have the same view on life, and their establishments are equally not the same. Those few who identify themselves with the people in their aspirations to defend their own dignity along with the dignity of the people cannot admit that they, the people, are actually born and will die but remain the only extreme reference for all values. Society is full of traitors who either implicate certain social classes or individuals in the shift: in the opposite direction, often in the name of personal interest against honor, dignity, and collective interest."

Lapidary and piercing were the last words of Salim in the interview. This was the very last moment for Cyril to keep his composure; he was no longer questioning but surviving the verbal onslaughts of Salim. Calm and cool, almost amused. "We are not surprised that there were traitors in Guinea. There are traitors in every country, but the value of the Guineans is that we have been able to discover the traitors and isolate them from the progress of their own revolution while in our African countries, there are traitors even in power to stop the historical development of African nations by adopting neo-colonialism as a mode of existence. The revolution moves forward."

Cyril nodded, dumbstruck for words to respond. Finally giving him one last piercing look, Salim stood up and thereby ended the discussion. Cyril hurriedly stood, bowing slightly to show his respect. "Thank you, Mr. president." Cyril said while extending his hand to Salim, who shakes his. The momentous tension that filled the room allows Cyril to walk out of the podium. Much relieved to get away from Salim's unyielding gaze, but aware that this would be a moment he would never forget.

Chapter 17

Old friends

In the 1950s, the setting sun crimsoned the skyline over Niger's colonial market. A damp concoction of sensory intoxication arose from the odors of spices in the air and the sweat-pouring breeze, beneath which the murmur of life lured on. Meli made his murky way through the crowd, his worn white boubou resembling modern *Bazin Bamako* gently brushing against vendors' stalls, all threads, memories of home. Memories that awoke a clenched fist inside his chest, as if named ashes beneath his feet making whispering an impending sorrow. Then and *there!* A figure slumped against a sun-bleached wall, swallowed halfway by shadows. His breath arrested mid-air, Salmany. The name married through him like a knife.

Time simply collapsed. There lay the man who had once shared laughter and cheap drinks with him in the Hexagone and now was a shadow. Salmany's skeletal frame put on a dance of collapse under the weight of existence itself: scabies and scars, a hideous mosaic of suffering. The eyes, almost pulsing with the mischief of a shared secret, now stared dry, twin lakes of bare resignation. Meli's throat burned. This was not the reunion he had had in mind.

"Salmany!" The name exploded out raw and trembling, a collision of joy and anguish.

Lips again twitched at the appearance of a smile, fragile and broken, as with an unsteady hand he offered a grasp to Meli. He grasped his hand, a smile too wide and too bright, an awful, desperate act to soothe the gulf of memory and reality between them. "Wonderful to see you, Meli! How's your family?" Salmany's voice was rasping, devoid of warmth.

"They're alright. Jadika and the kids are doing alright; little Noch's taller than me now!" Meli's words tumbled out buoyant. Yet his eyes clung to Salmany's face, searching for vestiges of the friend who had once joked under Parisian streetlamps. But Salmany was scratching compulsively into his own forearm, nails digging into inflamed flesh, a silent scream of shame.

"Listen, I'll be here for a day or two. We must catch up," Meli urged, the plea naked in his tone

"I would love that," was the ghost of a reply from Salmany, already fading as he turned away, shoulders hunched as if to flee some invisible storm. Meli remained rooted to the spot while the racket of the market was becoming distant. In that view, he saw, not merely a man, but the carcass of a man he barely recognized. The sun was sinking further, soaking the sky with the color of a gore, and Meli wondered if hope, like daylight, would ever return.

Meli's heart slumped down, down into the pit of his stomach; drops like these feel as if they are never coming back up. He felt an uneasy chill go through him as he saw Salmany hobble forward. It wasn't just his physical weakness that was holding the haggard man down, but there was something more so, like an invisible force of suspicion, mistrust so thick that one could cut it. His shoulders hunched forward, folding almost in on himself, preparing for a world of insults that were surely about to be flung at him, as if in his mind the universe was just sitting idly by, a couple of elves at work trying to come up with another way to make his life feel miserable. His hands were gnarled and twisted like the roots of old trees, the very hands that must have never felt the soft caress of anything but hard work for survival. There were the hands of hard-luck stories, of struggles to go against fate, and definitely of no time for pampering or luxury.

It's a tragedy for Salmany that his thread of misfortunes did not start in the sweltering heat of Niger, for he had indeed had a juicier past in France. Yes, France: country of baguettes and maybe, of lies. It was thus in France that Salmany was caught practically red-handed in a scandal. He had ostentatiously carried a glitzy degree from a prominent French university, the sort of pride that anybody would have admired. That little jewel of intellectual property turned out to be a sort of unicorn galloping on a rainbow, a degree that just didn't exist. A total fantasy. Just like that, his credibility had gone up in the air, or should I say, faster than a cheap croissant in the sunglow. That is when the boiling cauldron of bitterness started to bubble. A bitterness boiling now with the rage of an empty stove on which stew was left simmering, at a world he viewed as having done him wrong. As if the world had conspired so that he would be subjected to being the punchline of a cruel joke, and there he was, not laughing. On the *contraire mon ami*, he was so livid, he went on to be angry with nearly everyone, everywhere.

Those who had no inkling of his agony were paradoxically looked down upon. The hatred he hurled at them hungered for wild beasts' fury reserved only for unforgivable emetics. Every word he spoke dripped with an acid bitterness of accusation, no, the act of suffering itself had become an unbearable need for him to push the crushing weight of his affliction onto others. Somehow, maybe in a way that even he couldn't explain, his mind came to the conclusion that the only way he could try to claw back a shred of control was the semi-conscious process of vengeance through the mistreatment of others for what life had done to him. Salmany was the living, walking embodiment of a tantrum: he could not let go of the inept offenses of the world, even though they were without real grounds apart from his own mind. Beneath all of that anger and wrath, there lay a pained soul who hungered in his search for that very validation which had placed him in this predicament in the first place. The very core beneath it all, died for connection, understanding, acknowledgment, and not to see another side of hatred but to be worthy of pity.

The next day, the sun rose slowly, casting a golden light on the faded walls and creaky wooden floors of the administrative area. Meli arrived early, his mind still echoing with the noise of the marketplace, but his heart was filled with thoughts about Salmany and their last encounter. With colleagues trickling in, Meli walked through all the familiar hustle of the office, each moment making his heart feel heavier. Right as he was about to start on the job he came for, the door creaked open; his breath caught as Salmany walked into the office, clear morning light slicing through dust motes to frame his figure like a scene from a tragic tableau.

The thin, ragged suit clung to his skeletal frame, its fraying edges whispering tales of long decayed ambitions. A gripping sorrow tightened Meli's chest, *this* is the man who had once roguishly graced Parisian salons? Now he appeared as a ghost wandering through the decay of his very existence, his lies dissolving thread by thread.

The chamber was now shrinking, with its colonial walls pressing against its insides, their paint peeling and judging in silence. Salmany's gaze was a flickering bird trapped in a corner before fixing on Meli. A flicker passed between them for a moment: shame, defiance, a plea through pride's impenetrable shield.

"Salmany," Meli began, voice softer than he had intended, as if saying it any louder would shatter the man standing before him.

"Meli," the rasping voice came from Salmany. He straightened his spine with difficulty; it was almost an amusing parody of an insult: "Come to witness the spectacle?" His dry laughter rattled as he plucked at his suit sleeve, a nervous tic or maybe the itching of scabies beneath.

Meli flinched: the words were barbed yet underneath surged an unvoiced pain. He stepped closer, the reek of unwashed skin and desperation striking him hard. "I'm here on a mission," he said softly, "but I'd hoped...we could talk."

Salmany's jaw twitched. "Talk?" He barked a humorless laugh that drew some glances from clerks shuffling papers. "What is there to say? You have seen the masterpiece I have become." He swept his hand down his gaunt frame: theatrical and desperate. "A living warning, is it not?"

The bitterness hung thick and heavy while Meli gazed at his constantly trembling lip, at how his knuckles turned white gripping the back of a chair. There was neither anger nor temper. Instead, it was a scream stifled in self-disgust.

"Sit," Meli ordered pulling out a chair. The wooden chair in its protest screeched against the floor, making Salmany cringe.

The resistance stiffened every muscle in Salmany's body for a second. Then, with an exhalation, filling with shudders, he sank into the chair, the brittle frame folding just like origami. Up close, the ravages were awful: sores dripping at his collar, yellowing teeth biting a lower lip raw with anxious chewing. Meli leaned forward with an earnest expression, "I've been thinking about what you said yesterday. You mentioned that life is complicated. I want to hear more about it."

Salmany's shoulders went up in a shudder to the question. He carried the bitterness as a sort of shield, but Meli's goodwill dulled it ever so slightly. "I don't know if I can explain," he began painfully. "It just... It feels like I've been stumbling through fog, ever since I got here. People don't know what it means to lose everything."

Meli nodded, absorbing each word. "You mentioned France. And I am sorry about what happened there?"

"You have nothing to apologize for; I made my own bed it's only fair that I lie in it." Retorted Salmany sounding angry at himself.

The eyes darkened, and he turned away, staring into the distance, as if the memories were too painful to bear. "I thought I was somebody special. I had my dreams and ambitions. I even went on to convince myself that having a degree from a prestigious university meant I was going to be this great man." His voice cracked slightly, revealing the gaping void of hurt underneath the bravado. "When the truth came out that my degree in economics was made-up everything came in ruins. Friends turned to whispering, and I became an object of ridicule. I could not bear it. It was as if I were suffocating."

Meli listened intently, his heart aching for Salmany. "And coming to Niger didn't change anything?"

"Coming to Guinea was like going back into a ghost, and so I thought I'd come to Niger and work it out." Salmany admitted with bitterness creeping back into his voice. "I was expecting some sort of understanding or sympathy, but all I got was indifference. They've got their own troubles; they don't have time for mine."

"But you're not alone, Salmany," Meli said gently. "You have me. We can work it out together." "Anyway, why are you really here?" Salmany muttered, refusing to look at Meli. His fingers scratched compulsively at his wrist, leaving angry trails. Meli hesitated. The truth clawed at his throat, *Because I see you drowning. Because we are brothers.* Instead, he gestured toward the papers on his desk, colonial stamps bleeding ink at the corners. *"The irrigation reports. You know these villages in Kankan better than any clerk."* A muscle twitched in Salmany's hollow cheek. *"Charity, then?"* he sneered, but his gaze lingered on the documents. Meli recognized the hunger, residue of a man who once longed to matter.
"Rebuilding the nation," corrected Meli softly. He pushed a pen across the table, and the gold glistening in its nib caught sunlight. "Your mind is still sharp, Salmany. Sharper than those puppets who file away their colonial nonsense. Come home."

A moment of silence went by. Salmany looked at the pen as if it were a viper. When at last, he tried to grasp it with trembling hands, the very hands that used to create elegant signatures instinctively on those phantom diplomas.
"They will laugh," Salmany whispered. Meli barely caught what he said. "When they see me... like this."
"Let them laugh. Then watch the smirks disappear when you outthink them all," said Meli, leaning forward as the desk dug into his ribs.

Salmany flung a blank gaze his way as the flickering hope dimmed with reality. "It's not that simple, Meli. I do not know how to rebuild. I have lost what I perceived as being the core of my very being."

"Then start from the basics," Meli said. "Let's talk about what really counts: your strengths. You have survived a lot. You still have the potential for change. What do you want, really?"

Salmany hesitated. Meli's words weighed heavily on his heart. "I want... I want to believe that I can still be somebody. That I don't have to be defined by my failures." Meli felt more swelling in his heart to know that he felt for Salmany. "Well, let's go grab a few steps together. We can try out opportunities, small ones, perhaps. You know a lot; you have had experiences let's make use of that."

Salmany stared at Meli and saw the sincerity in his eyes. "I don't think I deserve help of that kind."

"Indeed, you do, and I am going to tell you we all do," Meli insisted. "We deserve an opportunity for redemption, a chance at being happy, even if those seem a bit vague right now."

One heartbeat… second, then a third heartbeat, and Salmany jumped for the pen, his nails unexplored broken into the wooden surface. He spat witheringly, "You always did believe in fairy tales," but the venom was all gone. He bent over the papers, his back a question mark, and began to scribble marginalia with mad precision. Gratitude painted his bony visage.

Meli watched, heart aching. The suit gaped at Salmany's neck, revealing scarred flesh beneath. *This is how we begin*, he thought. Not with excuses or cures, but with ink-stained fingers and the fragile pretense of purpose. At that moment, the office seemed to dissolve around the two estranged friends; the noise and chaos slipped into the background, and a thin connection formed between them.

Outside, the sun rose higher, while in that dim office, two men hovered in a liminal space between ruin and salvation: one who hangs on hope, and the other to the depleted memory of who he had once dared to become. Meli knew that the road ahead would be tough for Salmany, but thinking of Salmany's resilience sparked a flicker of hope for him that maybe, just maybe, things could get better when Salmany came home.

Chapter 18

The brain and the brute

Having tumultuously made endless journeys, he arrived on crossroads, slipping through his fingers like sand were those very last hopes of securing a third term at the African Union. In his great struggle for the unity and freedom of the continent, every initiative he took was toward decolonization and toward the restoration of dignity to the oppressed. But with the dark clouds of June 1972 hanging over Conakry, Meli stood aground to the bitter perils of having no brave allies or familiar faces to swear for his name. Those who once stood for him, who once shared his dreams, had either passed on or had been deposed by the forces whom he had so arduously labored to oppose, leaving him stranded. Tearing apart, the once hitherto hopeful campaign for the third term lay among the waves of graft and cold-blooded rulers thirsty for power.

Conakry still seemed alive with an electric tension just itching to be discharged. A foreboding feeling bled outwardly into the city atmosphere, as if history was currently weighing down upon him, crushing his spirit. He had served six years as the General Secretary of the Organization of

African Unity, once a period marked by triumph and progress. He had been a man of vision for a free and united continent, and he worked with colleagues to build bonds across borders so that his people might be lifted out of the shackles and chains of the past. He had tasted the bitterness that accompanies success. The euphoria from victory had started to fade, and in its place the growth of a gnawing sense of disillusionment. The dreams that were once today burning so brightly, now seemed distant and unreachable, like stars swallowed by a dark endless sky.

African leaders' offers poured forth, invitations to new positions in international organizations, hushed conversations heralding a possible future at the United Nations. Meli had become a figure admired internationally, a beacon of hope for those still fighting the shadows of imperialism. Yet all these things mattered very little. None of them could fill his aching void. The limelight, the accolades, these things were no longer enough. International acclaim became a poor salve to erase the emptiness that has taken root in the soul. What he most yearned for was something real, something that could not be found in the corridors of power or something that the glare of international attention could not ever give him. He longed for home.

Meli had an aching desire to be home, to the roots he had once known. But what was home now? The whole political stage that Meli had painstakingly built up had now come down. His friends whom he trusted were no more, lost to the abyss of political intrigues. The ideals that once drove him seemed like wounded ghosts floating through the air, barely holding their own.

Meli stood alone staring out into the atmosphere with a reflective mood, while the years of agonies weighed on his shoulders. Things had changed, and he had changed along the way. However, down in his heart, there was this quiet sadness blooming, a longing for that era and place that now appeared so far away and just like a forgotten dream. So many things had been taken along the fight from him; so many that he probably had nothing left to give. The future, which was once so bright with endless possibilities, now presented itself as an alienated pathway, which Meli no longer had the strength to pursue.

Standing behind his office desk facing the dusty window in Addis Ababa, Meli is lost in his thoughts, staring far away into zone; those thoughts went into memories about the first meeting with the enigmatic Moss, a weird-looking, elfish-build Belgian man who had escaped from Bukavu with mercenaries. Whether Moss was among the mercenaries or was caught within their midst, that much was never agreed upon; one thing was certain, however: Moss had been wearing their uniform when the African Unity organization intervened to free him. He had walked out unscathed, slipping quietly into the next part of his life and leaving behind the shadowy past of mercenary terror. Those were good days; he smiled at himself; then, snapped out of it.

Salim, now a shadowy figure of both charisma and menace, and a friend of Meli. With friendship came a growing paranoia and fear that his power was waning. When the news broke of Meli's planned departure and sever his tie from Salim and embark on another adventure, Salim's desperation led him to make unmistakably urgent pleas for Meli to return home. It was an offer under the guise of loyalty; yet threaded with an unspoken tension that neither man could ignore. Meli's heart still held onto a stand for justice and equality, and this led him back to Guinea. Though, Meli had tendencies of being reckless, getting overly passionate about things. It was feared that he would allow himself to forget that he was no longer abroad, amongst people of his own caliber. They feared that he would forget that his dear homeland had morphed into a communist and fascist society. It had become a system by which one man decided the fates of others. Meli used to be a source of pride, but now he was a threat to Salim outside the country. Therefore, Salim blocked Meli's bid for General Secretary of the United Nations, which opened the door for Kurt Waldheim to secure a second mandate. In Salim's political imagination, prestige could not exist apart from the president himself. Meli at the head of the UN would have been harder to manage, too visible, too autonomous, and therefore a rival. Meli was not merely respected; he was independent, and that independence unsettled Africa's authoritarian leaders, not only Salim. They remembered his insistence on institutions over men, on autonomy over loyalty. The UN favored discreet consensus figures, and Meli belonged to no one. Ironically, the very qualities that suited him for global offices made him dangerous at home and across the region. The system, it seemed, was designed to exclude men like him.

Anyway, the trip home was much more than a return; it was a leap into an abyss of doubt. Friends had warned him of the shifting tides, the way leaders had perished by betrayal and blood. Every interaction became a thin veil for paranoia and suspicion. Sometimes men corrupt their minds to believe what they choose to; for Meli, these were but the concerns of cynics. He ignored their warnings, with a naive spirit which was capable of doing so and which was even his strength: In his mind, *he was hope*, a man who could ignite anew in the hearts of his people the revolutionary spirit. Yet, he would enter into a stark different reality, one where the ghosts of colonialism still roamed, albeit in a new kind of master, a master who wore a black skin. He accepted the call once again and returned home in search of justice and happiness for his people. Most people in Guinea have long held the belief that Meli could in no way have resisted the call; for he was lured back to Guinea through occult means by his frenemy best *karamokos*.

Upon alighting from the plane, the thoughts of expectations weighed on his shoulders. The place hummed with a strange concoction of hope and fear. Quickly, Meli donned the mantle of Minister of Justice, a position that wields influence over the very nature of society. He conceived a new Civil Code that would be a reflection of Guinea itself rather than the relics of French oppression. But with power came surveillance. Salim knew that Meli was the only person who could potentially challenge his reign. What a dilemma? Meli was both a threat and a solution, and the answer to this predicament for Salim was to keep him closer and keep an eye on his every move.

So, Salim's secret police, ever wary, began weaving a web around him, tracking his every movement, waiting for him to make a mistake.

The shadows closing in on him could not extinguish Meli's joy at sharing justice with a generation he so passionately believed in. But with every lecture or impassioned conversation came the soul-crushing realization that his words would be twisted and used against him. The fervent idealism that once fueled him sharply collided with the harsh realities of the regime he had returned to serve.

In this Guinea, Meli was both a protector and a target. A man in the crosshairs of loyalty and ambition. Being the closest adviser to Salim truly gave him a rare place as his trusted ally and potential rival, a precarious position demanding all of Meli's intellect and charm to negotiate. Yet, beneath the surface, the tension simmered, hinting at an inevitable clash between the brain that sought justice and the brute force of a regime that would stop at nothing to maintain control. It was one holding the keys to a torture chamber and the other, a key to a nerdy office. Meli's office contained nothing, but bookshelves filled with legal texts, many of which had been used rather well, the passages were underlined, with dog-eared pages, all carrying a faint scent of mildew. His office windows were barred, thus allowing narrow hand-like shadow across the desk that saw many hours of learned concentration on the Civil Code with a dream of reform and revolution stirred faintly through its pages. Outside those bars were the streets of Conakry, throbbing with a different kind of life, a life infused with danger and disillusionment. As he labored on, faint drumbeats echoed at a distance, giving voice to the vendors in the street calling out their wares, stark reminders of a culture brimming with life. This was the Guinea he sought to uplift, the Guinea he had fought for in distant quarters of power. But today, the cries of people seemed smothered, weighed down by Salim's administration, with the omnipresent gaze of the secret police lurking around every corner. Sometimes Meli would catch himself staring through the barred window, deep in thought, wondering if he truly made a comeback for his people or was sold into an intriguing trap set by the same man who welcomed him.

Time slipped by. Days into weeks, from weeks into months and the initial excitement of his return started to fade. Meli found himself in the midst of a treacherous terrain full of political intrigues. Every conversation now seemed to be filled with hidden meanings, every ally possibly a spy. Trust was something he used to take for granted, now a commodity, and Meli's naivete once an inspiration could now be his downfall.

He tried to garner support for his vision of a Guinean Civil Code, talking to community leaders and intellectuals. Their eyes often told a different tale. Some nodded in agreement; others exchanged glances that spoke fear. They had seen what happened to dissenters, the whispers of disappearance ringing in their heads, shutting their lips with fright. Meli kept going with the firm belief in justice, yet he could feel the earth sliding beneath his feet because he had realized that even noble intentions could sometimes be used as weapons to be wielded against him.

While the city basked in the warm hues of sunset, an unexpected visitor appeared. Amina, a young journalist and daughter of a Camp Boiro victim who is known under the veil of anonymity for her biting critiques of the regime, entered his office. She set her eyes ablaze with admiration and wariness as she sat opposite him and silently contemplated him.

"Meli," she began in a voice both low and urgent, "I suggest you be cautious in the game you're playing. You believe you are here to help, but Salim doesn't see it the same way. He sees you as a threat. A rival so strong that he could inspire the very people he holds through fear."

Meli leaned back absorbing the words. "I am not here to usurp anybody. I want to help rebuild our country, our justice system, the things that we have all fought for, so that our people may have something to believe in."

She shook her head. "Those ideals sound wonderful, but they do not correspond with reality here. You are looked at as a beacon of hope, yes, but also as a possible contender of the status quo. You have to watch yourself, or you may find yourself in danger."

The ominous feeling of her warning fell heavily on him, and the faint seed of doubt planted itself in his heart for the very first time. He had believed that his return would be a fresh start and a chance to regain his place among the people. But now there was the looming specter of betrayal, with far stakes than he had bargained for.

In the subsequent days, he found himself increasingly isolated. Once a sanctuary, those corridors of power turned into a labyrinth full of traps. Every time he appeared in public, he would feel the eyes of the secret service, and spies upon him, beholding each one of his moves. Unbeknownst to Meli, the rumors started circulating about his meetings with Amina, spun then into stories of insurrection and conspiracy. Thus, he was forbidden from traveling and seeking psychiatric treatment to Paris, which he had so far done occasionally.

Weeks slipped by, and Meli's enthusiasm began to turn sinful with frustration. The idealistic dreams of a new Guinea he had so tightly held felt more like a burden than a calling. He longed for those simple, vibrant days of youth, where hope still glowed as a pure flame. But as he looked back into the mirror, he saw the weight of responsibility deeply etched into his features, the naivete of a man who believed he could change the world without a cost.

Indeed, with that moment of reflection, Guinea's future was not only a political one but a struggle for his soul. The clash between the brain and the brute was not only taking place in governance but within him as he wrestled with his desire to make a change amidst the harsh reality of his society steeped in fear control. Meli was at a crossroads, and the path he chooses might very well decide the fate of his beloved homeland. Yet, he did not know that it was much closer to him than he would ever have imagined. Pacing back and forth in his office, thoughts about the marvels of the future filled his mind, with Salmany storming into Salim's office on the other side of the building; the tension thick enough to cut with a knife. He immediately dropped into the chair opposite his brother's with a face framed with fury and desperation. "It's him or me," he spat, eyes blazing. "Either we throw him in Camp Boiro or I leave. You decide."

Since his return from abroad, Meli has held a PDG membership, which is Guinea's only ruling party. Salmany can't bear the sight of him doing inspections at the PDG cabinets and going on missions for the party. This grudge turned to jealousy and brought forth this sudden outburst.

Salim leaned back in his chair, arms crossed, a carefully crafted expression of mixed concern and skepticism. The purge must continue; international attention weighed down upon it like a heavy shroud. Who better than his own brother to tighten the grip on power? But the choice had not been easy.

"He humiliated me, brother," Salmany barked, his voice rising, suffused with emotion. "He destroyed my life. You have no idea what I went through in Niger."

"And yet, today you are here because of him," Salim retorted casually but with firm conviction. "Meli brought you back. Of all people, he was the only one who found it necessary to save you when you were nearly at the edge of death."

Salmany's fists clenched, trying hard to subdue his boiling rage. "I was suffering because of him! He put me there!"

"No, he didn't. You put yourself there." Salim leaned forward, the glint in his eye suggesting a hint of mockery. "You were bragging about this diploma you never had. He just exposed the lie." He stops for a moment and then continues: "And I don't think he was the one who said it. I think it was that arrogant Karim with his smug face always showing that he is better than us."

The words were like venom to Salmany, igniting his anger further. "I don't care. I want him to pay! Look at him now roaming these corridors acting as if he owned the place," he shouted, his voice bouncing off the stark walls of the office.

"Ok, ok, fine. We'll put him on the list," Salim finally said, a hint of resignation creeping into his voice. He knew how deeply Salmany was humiliated, but he also saw the convoluted loyalty driving him. In this game of power and revenge, the stakes were higher than either brother anticipated. Salim knew that Meli had nothing to do with the information that leaked out about Salmany's degree, but he desperately needed someone to paint a target on Meli's back. He needed it to be suggested, even if just by a simple peasant.

Salmany moved closer, his breaths gradually becoming caught as he tried to leverage Salim's acquiescence. "You don't understand. It's not just about revenge or anything like that. It's about restoring my honor. Meli humiliated me in front of everybody. I was a laughingstock."

"Honor, Really? That's what you're going with?" Salim asked sneeringly. "Your honor? You lost that the moment you lied about your school back there. And maybe he just exposed the truth."

"He had no right!" Salmany's voice broke into tears and his anger and sorrow spilled over. "He did not simply expose a lie but destroyed my entire life! I was a ghost in Niger, fighting scabies, fighting to stay alive. And he made that happen. He could have helped me instead of dragging my name down."

Salim's expression grew a little softer, but the cold harsh reality of their situation pulled him back. "You really think locking him up will fix that?

You think this will give you back your life? Come on, Salmany. You can do better than this. You survived Niger. You fought your way back. Don't give yourself over to vengeance now."

"But it feels so good to think about it," Salmany said softly, with that dangerous edge lacing his words. "To see him pay for what he did. To realize that now I am not the one at the bottom anymore."

"Revenge will never fill the void, brother." Salim said, a hint of weariness in his voice. "You will only become what you despise."

"Maybe." Was the reply of Salmany, his glare hardening with an intense resolve, "But at least I won't be weak anymore. At least I won't be a victim. I refuse to be his victim ever again."

A weight was dragging upon Salim while sighing. There was an immense feeling within the room now as the air started to resonate with the remembered footsteps of their past, of a childhood glowing with dreams of grandeur since they were small, of roads that diverged when unfulfilled ambition and betrayal took hold.

"Fine," Salim relented, his acceptance bordering on resignation. "But listen to me: once we set foot on this road, we cannot turn back. I cannot have you doubting this or feeling remorse when the time comes."

Salmany nodded, the fire in his eyes undiminished. "I'm all in. one hundred percent." He replied with excitement. Salim leaned over his desk, opened his drawer pulling out a list of names as he sprinted ahead in his mind with the ramifications of their decision. He showed it to Salmany, who immediately spotted Meli's name in the middle of the list. He squinted, "what? Did you have his name already? Were you just pulling my leg all this time?" He smiled, "You old devil." He continued with joy in his face.

"Well, I must protect this power, and this can't be guaranteed as long as Meli's alive, why do you think I brought him back and let him be comfortable?" He stared into the void, trying to think for a little while, then uttered with finality, *"Meli must die."*

Time was ticking, and the walls came in. Meli had to be disposed of, fast. There was no room for weakness in this ruthless game for power; and hence the brothers would need to be changed into the very shadow that disturbs their enemies.

As Salim laid out their plans, a dark shade of resolution washed over Salmany. This was going to be a start to the reclamation of his own life, not just from Meli but from the humiliation that had so nearly crushed him. Dark road, but this one's his. And he would stop at nothing to ensure that his tormentor paid the price.

Chapter 19

The Martyrs

Living souls, in their quiet, human arrogance, have a peculiar tendency to lower their guard when they feel safe. Comfort may wrap around them like a cozy blanket, thus ensuring that their vigilance will be lost. They can drift into a new unrealistic world in their minds that would normally reject realistic thinking with its hard edge-to-edge trueness, converting distrust to trust, and caution to complacency. But in the act of comforting the world, they actually distort it and put danger behind a curtain of pleasant familiarity. Many before him had fallen for this very same trap. Meli had trusted too much, drinking the Kool-Aid without question. His trusting nature, his unwillingness to question, were deeply ingrained flaws, flaws he would come to regret in a way he could never have imagined.

Imagine being lured into the lion's den by your "friend" for a dinner meeting with claims that could change the geopolitical aspect of a whole continent. Once there, you realize that you are the change. Yes, a dreadful change indeed, a change that would alter the continent for the worst. The absurdity of Salim's logic about being good is uncanny. For instance, the definition of being lenient, caring, and sentimental to his "friends" is that

Salim, never fails to bestow privilege upon them with a last supper. Fattens them before sending them to the slaughter where he starves them to death.

It was supposed to be an innocent dinner, a dinner meeting with his comrade. Salim, the ever-charming enigma, had promised to disclose something capable of changing the course of history. Meli, ever the optimist, sat his hopes on his words. He couldn't fathom the price his naïveté would demand. He certainly couldn't see that he was marching into Salim's real world. Even had he been aware, what options did he really have?

He stepped into the dimly lit living room of Salim's residence with the same casual ease he had countless times before. The evening was to be a somewhat carefree dinner among friends, a respite from the relentless pressures weighing upon them in their political lives. Salim, with the somewhat forced smile, the kind that never quite met his eyes, as if a world of sorrows lay just behind them welcomed him. They sat in the leaving room and ate, they talked about all and anything, their children, the country, those few rare moments when both of them would manage to grab a sliver of peace in the immense chaos surrounding them. And of course, they laughed as they used to, a sound that would graciously remain in Meli's memory way far longer than he would ever be able to anticipate.

But then as time dragged on and it became the moment for Meli to leave, something inexplicable occurred. The distance dissolved; Salim leaned into him, invading his personal space, with a grave intensity that at first didn't gel well with Meli. He was staring at Meli, searching for something that he could not find.

"Dear Meli," Salim said softly, his voice steady. "There is one thing you should at the very least know about me… and that is I never let my guard down and get surprised."

Those words fell between them like a heavy mist. There was no humor left in Salim's voice. Gone was the spirit of camaraderie of the past moments. He gave a short laugh, one that was not really from mirth, being torn from the depths of his soul, a sound that echoed more of resignation rather than laughter.

Trying to lighten the mood, Meli gave a weak smile and said, "Who do you think want to surprise you, Mr. President?" However, even he could feel the time concisely slipping away.

The answer was simple, and it dissected Meli's half-hearted attempt to lighten the situation: "Goodbye, Meli." He said. There was no emphasis behind the words, no warmth anywhere in his voice. It was strange: he dismissed him with an almost unnatural finality, as if his equal no longer applied, as if his friend with whom he had shared countless meals and talk in this very room was suddenly snatched away.

The face of Meli froze with the suddenly decided aura draining from his expression. He blinked once and then twice, trying somehow to assimilate the change. The playful banter seemed to be swept away by an ominous presence that Meli felt he could not quite comprehend. His mind was racing to a desperate search for some solid meaning concerning the situation. While Meli still tried to lay his hands on the meaning of Salim's words, the president got up from the sofa and strode off to his office, leaving Meli sitting in the engulfing silence.

Meli stood utterly frozen as thoughts swirled wildly in an instant. What was that? A strange sense of foreboding creeped over him and gave his chest a tight squeeze, very unsettling. He wanted to say something, to ask Salim what the hell was going on, but some strange impotence prevented the voice from coming out. He honestly didn't know what to do now: stay back and wait for Salim to return, or go and risk being called disrespectful, an invited guest that walked out without a proper goodbye. Suddenly, a sickening clarity descended upon him. Amina's words echoed in his ears. Changes, or more precisely, dreadful changes, cannot be written in any history book; instead, they are far more personal and far more dangerous. Meli realized, he was the change. He was the catalyst that set into motion the disaster about to unfold, the tipping piece, unwittingly becoming the very trigger for the greatest shift in the continent's fate.

Salim had his good manners and a winning smile; he had perfected the act of the last supper. A metaphor, perhaps, but they all heard about it, and one has to come back to confirm it. Yet, no one came, and Meli would realize it much too late. Each generous offer, each indulgence, each sweetened promise was one step in the process of undoing Meli. Like a lamb being fattened for slaughter, he had been blinded to the intentions of one who called himself a friend. And as he now stood on the edge of the inevitable, he would come to see for himself how absurd the logic of kindness could be if wielded by a man who thought himself above morality. He would learn that leniency, in the eyes of Salim, never meant mercy but meant the exertion of power. And when the moment came, Meli would learn what happens when trust is given to the wrong person and when innocence is used as the ultimate tool of destruction.

Meli sat on the big sofa in the vast living room alone and waited. Seconds felt like minutes and minutes stretched out to eternity. No one came, not even the servants to empty the ash tray. The silence was deafening in there; it pressed upon his shoulders. His mind was a storm full of thoughts all conflicting, each one pulling him away in a different direction. Finally, with a heavy sigh, Meli stood up and walked toward the door. He found the guard outside, forever at attention. The man offered him a smile that seemed more mechanical than genuine. Meli returned it with a hollow smile and nodded. "Goodnight," he said, an odd layer of sorrow underneath. It began to dawn on him as he walked away from the house. It just hit him on the way home, like a hammer striking his stomach. It was going to be the last time he would see Salim. That friend. That confidante. The one beside whom he stood in every trial. There was that painful clench in his heart. He did not understand what had transpired, but deep inside, he knew something was terribly amiss.

He drove home worried, and once inside, he sat in the living room for a moment, then made his way into the bedroom where Jadika was laying. The worry in her eyes preceded his voice. "I think today is the day." he muttered, his voice trembling, brushing her face with his cold hands as she rose up from the bed.

"What's the matter?" inquired Jadika, her voice thick with suspicion, scrambling out of bed and hitting the floor with soft thuds. Meli looked at her, his eyes swimming with terror and tears of regret. "I think they're coming for me. Listen carefully: Do not antagonize them. Just let me go with them peacefully." Jadika frowned in puzzled incomprehension on hearing that. "What do you mean?" She stepped forward.

"I'm sorry for everything. Look after the children... tell them I love them." Saying these words broke Meli's heart, but he had to, it might be his last chance of saying them.

Jadika stood there, perplexed, when there seemed to be the inexorable clicking of boots-thundering heavy and deliberately in the stillness of the night. Meli's heart almost stopped. It's the militia.

Jadika's breath got stuck in her throat; tears filled her eyes at the realization. Meli stepped closer to hug her, but she pulled away from him, her sobs echoing through the room. The children, wide-eyed from fear, ran into the living room on being awakened by these sounds to find the dreadful dark figures standing there in their home. The guards were there; bony hands gripped Meli's arms, prepared to take him away. Jadika fell on the floor while sorrowful cries filled the house. Meli knelt beside her, pulling her into an embrace, his voice soft and steady as he tried to reassure her.

"I'll be back soon," he said, though even he didn't believe the words.

But the guards were relentless. They dragged him away, through the cold night, under the harsh glare of streetlights. At 3 a.m., on July 18th, 1976, Meli was loaded onto a truck bound for Camp Boiro. Under the order of Salim. As the truck rumbled to life, Meli's eyes scanned the faces of the other men with him. Barry Alpha Oumar, Dramé Alioune, Fode Cissé, former ministers, once powerful figures in the government. They all stand accused of a conspiracy to overthrow the government. This was the *Fula plot* crafted by Moussa Diakite another demon in human form roaming in the corridors of Salim's palace. Diallo Alhassana, Kouyate Laminé, army officers, all now prisoners like him, bent inside a truck and used as footrest for the guards' heavy boots. The realization of it all settled in like a weight on his chest. Once seen as the most brilliant who brought the OUA to life and often regarded as one of the fathers of decolonization in Africa, being trampled by the people he liberated. He had never imagined it would end like this. And yet, as the truck bumped along the road, Meli couldn't shake the feeling that, somewhere in the distance, Salim's final words still echoed in his ears: *"Goodbye, Meli."*

Days passed in vain, and Meli tried to get an explanation for his detention. Days turned into weeks and then came a letter from Salim. The letter opened the opportunity for further exchange of letters between the two. In that damp and shadowed prison of Camp Boiro, Meli's skeletal fingers grasped the stub of a pencil, scratching out the few words allowed on smuggled paper. The absurdity, here was a man condemned for "treason" penning counsel to the very architect of his torment. Salim's letters were promptly delivered, almost routinely: passed along the bars by guards who sniggered at the degrading charade. It would always start with "Mon frère..." the ink was glib and feisty: "Your wisdom remains indispensable. How do we navigate the OAU's accusations? The Soviets grow impatient..."

Meli replied, though not with hope, more by force of habit, a diplomat's muscle memory. His answers were clever, carefully worked out, but his hand shook as he wrote them. The hunger had grown until it was a constant gnawing at his ribs since the onset of that black diet. Yet at those moments, Meli almost managed to pretend the old fellowship lingered once, almost. Then his eyes would drift to the walls glistening with mold, the piercing cries that drifted out of Cell Block 5 came back, and he thought: Salim needed his mind and not his life.

The trucks arrived at dawn. That February morning in 1977, Meli saw through cracked lenses the soldiers dragging Barry Alpha Oumar and Dramé Alioune, who had once been ministers and had toasted independence with glasses of *Ataaya* and homegrown *nana*, inside the yard. Their eyes met his, hollow and glassy. No more speeches now and no more defiance. Just the whimper of men turned ghosts. By the end of the month, five were gone. Salim's next letter praised Meli for his "loyalty."

Loyalty. That word turned sour in his mouth. Nights blurred into feverish dreams: Fodé Cissé scratching at his throat for a few drops of water, but he could not bring himself into doing what Mr Thiankoy did. A year prior, Mr. Thiankoy was a wealthy merchant accused of plotting against the regime. He was sent to the gulag. Parched beyond endurance, Mr. Thiankoy had even resorted to swallowing his own urine just to wet his throat enough to breathe when he heard the distinct sound of someone watering plants barely a meter from his cell. Desperation took over; he pushed a grimy scrap of cloth through a tiny hole in the wall and hissed, "Psst! Psst!" The gardener jumped, spotting him, but immediately hesitated, terrified of being caught by a guard. He knew the man was silently begging for water, yet the fear of punishment, maybe even being thrown in a cell himself, froze him. But the gardener couldn't bring himself to ignore the raw plea. Acting fast and with eyes darting like a hawk, he subtly swung his watering can towards the prisoner's outstretched hand, letting a few precious drops fall onto the cloth. He did this twice more, each time scanning frantically for any sign of trouble. The moment the gardener stopped, the prisoner yanked the damp cloth back inside and sucked it desperately dry, clinging to that tiny bit of moisture for his life. This made the gardener feel good about himself, however, it did not help because poor Thiankoy's body got removed from the cell two days later.

Anyway, Fodé Cissé fought hard, clung to life but alas Azrael does not negotiate; After Fode came the turn of Diallo Alhassana, it felt like the angel of death was on a special mission. Alhassana's body was deposited in a lime pit. Each death inscribing itself anew on Meli's spirit, yet the letters went on. "How fares your health?" Salim wrote in March, as another five died. *The nation prays for you.* Meli laughed, a rasp that turned into a cough and then into a sob.

By the end of February, the pencil had ceased to exist. There was a rainstorm of meals for him, lousy rancid broth, the very sort that thinly mocked, and then the guards glared at him inquisitively: *"Still writing, Professeur?"* But when Bah Adamo arrived, a native of Labé who had dared to return to his homeland, Meli saw that there was terror, something raw in those eyes of his. He remembered they once at a café in Paris, shared cigarettes and worried of a Guinea in which a revolution *ate its children.* Now Bah's screams joined the chorus: eight by August. No more ink to write the story.

The last letter was as wet with rain as he was with tears. *"Your counsel on the border dispute..."* Meli did not finish. From nowhere arose a clarity, cold and brutal. With shaky fingers, he grasped the rusted nail lying around. Drawing it across his palm, blood swelled gloriously against the ironic wall: *Salim dévore les intellectuels, vole l'avenir des enfants.* The words shone with a crimson glaze, an epitaph. Outside the rumble of trucks invoked more souls for the grinder.

He died the way the others had, thin cracked lips, empty hollow bellies, and minds on fire with curses. For his body, an unmarked grave where the message was erased before dawn. But the spirit of that message traveled around the alleyways of Conakry, and Africa, swelling up like smoke, a rumor, a myth, a truth too searing to conceal.

And Salim? He ate his steak haché, enjoying the blissful quiet of emptied cells. This restlessness gnawed at one's spirit. His hand trembled as he reached for the bottle of red. Were these the ghosts of intellects past or the creeping void where a nation's soul used to beat? He would never say. The black diet spared no one.

Salim had always had an answer to justify his deeds. While sitting at the press conference in Paris, he sounded defiant, hard and unyielding, daring the world to contradict him with each strain of a word. When asked about his vendetta against Fulani and Malinke intellectuals, he barked back, eyes narrowed, lips compressed into a thin line: "First of all, I did not say the word Fulani, you did." Jabbing his finger at them. His tone was dripping with disdain, purposeful and malicious. Then he threw a venomous smirk at them: "And we have recordings and witnesses that can attest to that." He waved his hand around and continued, "Secondly, you are talking about asylees. This is how you manipulate the French people."

He leaned forward, shoulders squared, a storm of indignation brewing beneath his calm. "I am at ease, and I'll be at more ease if I could not see a president but a militant at the front of this public place doing a contradictory conference with anyone from any other nationality." Raising his voice unapologetically. "The truth is simple, and easy to understand." With a flourish, he thrust a crumpled French newspaper aloft, shaking it like a weapon. "This is the general commissary's list of names of all asylees in the world. I would like you to find the name of Guinea in this list."

Silence hung thick as he paused, letting the challenge simmer. When he spoke again, it was slower, heavier, each word a hammer strike. "There are no asylees from my country. All this concept is created here in Paris to mislead the French public opinion by people who extend their palms to agencies that nourish for their survival." His jaw clenched, bitterness seeping through. "These people wish not to have a reconciliation between Guinea and France because this will be a threat to their livelihood."

Suddenly, his chest swelled with pride, voice softening almost tenderly. "These people, talking about dictatorship, could they find any other leader from anywhere in the world that could equal the reception I receive in various countries…" He listed them like a mantra, *Teranga, Ivory Coast, Niger, Upper Volta, Mali*, each name a badge of honor. "I had the pride of certifying the unanimity… of Guineans."

Then, his face darkened, shame twisting his features. "The one thing I am mostly ashamed of is when some of my citizens come here and insult Mr. Salim, so they can get a job at the detriment of an honestly working French citizen. The only thing I'll never do is let my citizens disrespect a French president in my country. Never. Me and the French government have our ideological disagreements. Nonetheless, my people would not dare disrespect my guest let alone a French president." He spat the final words, voice trembling with disgust. "It is shameful." He continued defending his position. In the meantime, poor Mr. Bangoura among others is harboring dozens of Guinean refugees in Ivory Coast in a two-bedroom apartment, and life goes on.

Chapter 20

From friends to foes

Laysouf had always been an enigma to the people, untouched by the whirlwind of betrayal that had torn through everyone else in Salim's cercle. His survival to the plague that snuffed everyone had been a mystery to anyone. He had been the one to offer him a hand when Salim was nothing but a shadow, a man without purpose. Laysouf had seen something in him, and for that, Salim had felt an unspoken debt, a debt that had not yet demanded payment. In the long, complicated battle for revolution, Laysouf had remained the one figure Salim trusted, or perhaps, more accurately, the one-man Salim had not yet learned to distrust. It was believed that the bond between these two men was the result of an occult pact, one that had been forged in the early days of their struggle, an agreement whispered in the dead of night, witnessed by none but the wind. The pact was simple, but chilling: anyone who betrayed the other would not simply face death, but a ruin far worse, a punishment that would erode the betrayer's very soul before the body could catch up. They would be cursed, hollowed out, consumed by the consequences of their own treachery, long before it was ever carried out.

The pact had been so staunch during the initial years. Through ever test from other betrayals, Salim and Laysouf had stood side to side in an unshakable bond of loyalty against the price: neither questioned one another, for they knew a pact forces the price of betrayal in much uglier ways than simple murder; it was an assurance that held them together, a thread weaved tightly through the chaos of war.

Then, time, like an agent of rust, began to eat away at their bond. Especially as it was rust borne by the very force of revolution, which had once been here to forge the bond. What was once shared needed a harsh survival furnace to be cruelly mashing all in its path. The battle moved on, eating men and ideals. Salim, adhering yet to the pact, found the shift underway in Laysouf: subtle changes at first, almost going unrecognized, the faintest cracks from his once unshakably certain air, fleeting moments of hesitation too long for a glance, words with a faint edge to them that Salim could not grasp.

A revolution, a standing threat of death, and weighing upon them so many decisions began wearing away at the bond uniting the two. And in the silence, a creeping fear popped into Salim's mind: Could this be the very beginning of something worse? The entity that had built this bond with them had started changing in nature; where it had once been a guardian, it was now something darker. The shadow, once a shield, was now simply observing and awaiting the moment when it could get its dues.

Whispers about Laysouf's secret meetings had started to trickle into Salim's ears, carrying rumors of his hushed conversations in the dark. Was Laysouf planning something, something that had been feared as betrayal? The pact did warn them: A whisper of betrayal would suffice to let the curse sink its roots. But could it really be true? Could Laysouf the man who had been with him through it all actually be the one to tear their bond asunder?

First came that day when the very shadow of betrayal ceased to be a far-off possibility and morphed into a tarrying chill that demanded to be addressed.

Their faces stood apart. A hard set-out, frozen mask of cold determination crossed Laysouf's countenance while suspicion remained etched upon Salim's eyes. It was time to sit down with his boss, spill the truth, and hopefully avoid being promoted to "entrée of the day." Laysouf entered Salim's office and stood there before him, shoulders rigid and eyes never meeting his. It was a pregnant moment of tension unwelcomed by Salim. The pact, once an unbreakable promise, was now hanging between them like a ghost that had cast a shadow upon everything. Before Laysouf could dare to utter a word, Salim was already in his head, his thoughts spinning with all the rumors he had heard, are there secret meetings? Are there whispered alliances? Is there a betrayal on the horizon?

"So, it is true then. You have been behind my back, plotting; You've already made your choice." Salim said, his voice, barely able to express the anguish of a thousand doubts unuttered.

Laysouf's eyes darted in confusion, then glared in harsh pain. "What are you talking about, Mr. President?" he said, with a voice trembling from an emotion Salim could not identify. "There are no plots, Salim. No betrayal."

"You think I don't know?" Salim paused as if to savor the details. "The rumors say you've been meeting in secret, talking to people behind closed doors. Did you forget our pact? Do you really think I wouldn't find out? I have eyes everywhere."

Laysouf stepped back, his expression softening, and raised his hands in a gesture of peace. "Listen to me, Salim. There is no plot. There's no betrayal. I'm not meeting with anyone I shouldn't be meeting with. I've been... seeing a doctor."

Salim blinked; the words slow to register. A confused disbelief scattered on his face; "A doctor? What kind of nonsense is that?"

"I'm not well, my old friend." Laysouf confessed in a low and hesitant voice. "I haven't been for some time now. The pressure of everything, the continuous fight, has been wearing me down. I do not know what is wrong with me, but the pain is becoming worse. I needed someone who'd be discreet about it."

The revelation hit Salim like a blow to the chest, feeling the weight of something that should have been inspiring hope. Beyond all rumors and whispers he had heard, everything had turned out to be a lie, just fabricated lies, and it did not take Salim long to realize that this was the work of his beloved brother Salmany.

Salmany had always felt the bond between his brother and the Gardener threatening, which prompted his sowing the rumors, knowing that in the heat of revolution, trust could become brittle.

"Why didn't you tell me?" Salim was quieter now, weary sadness in place of the rage that had filled the air previously. "Why keep it secret?"

"I didn't want to burden you," Laysouf revealed, now holding Salim in a steady gaze. "I thought... I thought I could handle it myself. But I see now that it was a mistake. I should have come to you, told you from the start. I never intended to make you doubt me, Salim. Never." The weight of his words fell between them, and the tension gradually draining away. Salim himself had an aching conscience, the more he thought about it, the more he realized how easily he had been played for a fool by Salmany's machinations: Salmany had tried to fracture their trust just enough by inserting doubt to a degree that made Salim question everything, including his most loyal companion. The silence between them stretched for a moment, both men standing there, the truth pressing slowly into Salim's heart. "So, what now?" Laysouf asked, softly but firmly.

Salim rose from his seat and leaned forward; his voice set in a tone of reassurance and determination. "We're going to get through this, as always. A simple headache or a tummy ache will not deter us from our goals, Laysouf. We shall remain true to what we have fought for. Together. Our pact may have been shaken but it was not broken and will never be as long as we are together."

Grappling with the tumult in his heart at the thought of being a sellout, Laysouf nodded reluctantly. Salim looked at Laysouf, his comrade, his friend, and found in his eyes not the shine of a traitor but the fortitude of a man that has already fought his own demons as many others before him. Laysouf rose and pushed his chair back, and a wave of melancholy slid down salim's spine. At the door, Laysouf paused and looked back. "Stay alive." Salim said softly.
Laysouf gave a faint, tired smile. "You too."
They clasped hands once, firm, final, then Laysouf turned away without looking back. Salim lingered behind his desk for a moment, then stepped outside, drawn by habit more than thought. As he stood on the balcony and scanned around, he saw Salmany enter the gate. What he saw in Salmany's eyes was the look of one who is lightly playing a deadly game with a match, as though the flames of revolution could be sparked by a single, careless word.

"Salmany," a deep sound came from Salim with great effort, as if thunder were boiling in the distance. He walked towards him. "What are you doing?" asked Salim as he approached Salmany who's pacing with a slight smirk in the dim light of the courtyard. "Here we go again!" muttered Salmany.

He did not try to deny it. "I am doing what must be done, brother. War has already started. As usual, in a revolution, sacrifice is demanded. I should not have to tell you this." His eyes grew sharper, yet an edge of recklessness ran through them.

"You speak of Laysouf," Salim sharpened his tone and became coldly measured. "Why?"

"Why not?" Salmany shrugged, his hands lifting as if the answer were plainly obvious under the sky above them.

Salim stares at him in disbelief. "He's the one who gave you everything, have you forgotten that? You even named your son after him!" He snapped.

"But we stand at a point where everything is put to the test; loyalty is among the tested. Who knows whether he might be involved in some kind of conspiracy? He is an outsider, a foreigner in all but name. You have seen the way he looks at things, at us, he is always calculating. How far do you trust him, Salim?"

"Exactly! Do you think if he was planning something you could know about it? You have no idea who you are dealing with, you are an ant comparing yourself to a titan." Salim snapped and stormed back into his office, shadows curled laden with the iron scent of secrets. Looking back, Salim realized that he had never really considered Laysouf anything other than a benefactor: a man who had pulled him up from the abyss. But now Salmany's words were bitter on his tongue. What if? What if the revolution had blinded him to something darker? Something he could never come back from.

To deepen the roots of his lies, Salmany began to speak of unpredictable changes to feed immense hunger for shifting revolutions. Desperation had gnawed at his chest, forcing him to seek a prisoner who could confirm the rumors, a man caught in one of the many whisperings of plots against the regime. The prisoner, a nameless soul who had heard the tightening of the ropes around his neck, had been given an ultimatum: betray someone and be freed. The single word "Laysouf" had slipped past Salmany's lips as though it held no significance. But it did not slip the prisoner's mind. With a gaunt figure and bitter with those truly hollow eyes, the prisoner looked broken, someone who must have already given away everything to stay alive.

"You know," said Salmany smoothly as oil, "you want to walk free, don't you?"

The prisoner nodded, hands trembling.

"Then you tell me something," Salmany went on. "Tell me Laysouf is part of this plot against us. Tell me he's been working with the enemies of the revolution, and I will make sure you see the light of day again. You owe him nothing, but I... I can help you." He said convincingly.

The prisoner hesitated; his eyes flickered with something: defiance, perhaps, or a memory of dignity now old and gone. Then finally, the man spoke in a hoarse, yet solid voice.

"No." said the man, looking steady. "I will not sell anyone for my freedom. Not him. Not anyone, not even you."

Salmany's smile slowly faltered. "You realize what this means?" he whispered, his voice dropping. "You're condemning yourself for a man who wouldn't do the same for you."

The prisoner didn't respond, and for a moment, Salmany simply stared at him, the silence between them heavy with unsaid things. Then, he turned around and walked away, realizing that he had just made a mistake. He realized that he had crafted two problems that needed to be dealt with, and quickly, before news of this unsanctioned mission reached Salim. With the fate of the poor prisoner already put in motion, Salmany went to see Salim and began to plead his case, arguing with a conviction that seemed to grow by the minute.

"We have to kill him" Salmany said, his voice laced with the bitterness of someone who had been left out of the grand narrative.

"Why is death the solution to every problem of yours? Every time you step foot in here, it is either about hanging someone or plotting a way to torture someone. Why? Who is it, this time? You know what; I don't even care, do whatever you want…"

"I'm sure you'll like this one, it's Robert!" He answered in a titteringly joyful manner and turned to walk away, but Salim suddenly calls him back. "Hey, wait… wait," Salim's eyes widened, he could not believe it. "Robert Lecarnu?" He asked

Salmany nodded with a wide smile from ear to ear. "We have to hang him. Killing a French national is a statement. France will see it, and they will know we are not afraid of them. We are not beholden to them."

Salim's hands clasped behind his back, paced the room slowly. "And what in the world makes you think that's wise?" he asked, his voice colder now, each word measured. "To kill a foreign national, to show them that we are… not afraid? What happened to you brother? I mean, what is wrong with you?" Salim asked with a sense of sympathy for Salmany's idiocy.

Salmany's eyes narrowed, the flicker of frustration obvious in his gaze. "We do not bend to them, Salim. This is a revolution. We can do whatever we want, whenever we want. It is our country, our rules."

But Salim, for all his ferocity and ambition, felt a gnawing sense of doubt in his gut. "There's more danger in that than you know. You might call it a statement, Salmany, but it's a reckless one."

Salmany scoffed, dismissing the notion with a wave of his hand. "They'll never respect us. They already think we're afraid of them, that we cower when they roar."

Salim shook his head slowly. "You forget," he said, his voice steady but grim, "that sometimes a single kill can change everything, and this is the one. Salmany, we're not yet ready to take that risk."

His eyes reddened, and for a moment, it seemed as if he would lash out. Instead, he muttered again: "I told you, Salim... you don't understand. You've always been too cautious."

"Perhaps," Salim said in a half-whisper, several years weighing heavily on his shoulders, "yes perhaps, and I believe it to be the reason we are still standing."

The silence that followed changed the atmosphere and for the first time, Salim began to question whether it was time to cut him loose. Robert Lecarnu's refusal to implicate Laysouf into an alleged conspiracy at the price of losing his own liberty made one thing clear: the allegiance was far more powerful than fear and far more powerful than a so called *"revolution"*. That was the allegiance Salmany had to understand, whether he liked it or not.

Months later, the scent of medicinal herbs filled the faint room with an earthy fragrance as family members knelt beside Laysouf's bed. The once bright revolutionary lay gaunt beneath threadbare blankets, shallow but steady in his breathing. Time had gnawed at him, carving pain on his face, yet his eyes, well, they are still sharp, still *alive,* softened as Salim entered.

"You came," Laysouf whispered, a fragile smile tugging at his lips. His voice, formerly a mighty call used to galvanize thousands of people, was now faint as the rustle of dry autumn leaves.

"Did you think I wouldn't?" Salim replied as he grabbed his friend's hand. The heat of fever radiated through Laysouf's skin, contrasting harshly with the chill of the room. He cleared out the lump in his throat. "We stand together. Always."

An intense yet tender silence surged over the place. Outside, down in the distance, the hum of the city, merged, unaware, steadfast, as if the world was unwilling to grant a moment of pause for this occasion. Laysouf's eyes strayed toward the window, where dusk set in and the sky shimmered with an amalgam of amber and violet. "Do you remember...the night we lit bonfires in the square?" he murmured. "How the flames leapt higher than the soldiers' rifles?"

Salim chuckled, wiping a sting from his eyes. "You shouted yourself hoarse. Then you snatched the commander's hat and paraded it like a trophy in front of the nation to show that we had won."

"And you," Laysouf wheezed as laughter for a brief moment sparked in his chest, "you fell flat on your slogans." The memory flickered between them, warm and bright, before it faded again into the grim reality of the sickbed. His smile dimmed. "I'm sorry, Salim. For the secrets. For letting Salmany's lies fester."

"Don't." Salim squeezed his hand, fierce and forgiving. "I should have known. Should have seen through the rumors… seen you, you know!"

Laysouf shook his head weakly. "You're here now, and that's enough for me." His breath caught in his throat by which time for a split second, Salim felt that death had come. Softly, he added, "The fight… it doesn't die with me. Promise me you'll keep it alive. Promise you won't let bitterness poison your heart."

Salim's eyes grew stubbornly blurred. "I promise. But *you*… you can't leave yet. We still need you; we need your wisdom." The words cracked out of him, stark, almost childlike, and he hated himself for having uttered them.

Laysouf's thumb brushed Salim's knuckles, an ephemeral comfort. "You don't need a dying man. You need the fire we ignited." He paused, drawing a rattling breath "And… you need to forgive Salmany."

"What?"

"Not for him. For you." Laysouf fixed a stare onto salim's that was ardent yet calm. "Hate is a heavier burden than pain."

Salim opened his mouth to protest, but the words died as Laysouf's body sagged deeper into the mattress, exhaustion claiming him. The room stilled, saved for the uneven rhythm of his breathing.

The hours waned away. Salim remained, recounting stories of victories and protests that shook the capital in the early 1950s, of underground presses they had smuggled in, and of out-of-tune songs they'd bellowed off-key in safehouses. With each tale, Laysouf's smile returned, faint but unbroken.

When the end came, it was quiet with a sigh and a final squeeze of fingers.

"Rest, brother," Salim murmured, pressing his forehead into Laysouf's. "You've earned it."

And as the daylight faded into dusk, the expression on Laysouf's face softened with peace, an elusive smile waving farewell. No more pain. No more war. Only the stillness of a man who had fought so fiercely and loved so passionately now let go and happy.

Salim did not cry. Not yet. He just sat next to Laysouf's lifeless body and lit a candle, the flame burning small but defiant against the dark, and whispered the rallying cry of the past. A vow. A requiem. Outside, the world turned on its axis, but in that room lay an unbreakable pact.

Chapter 21

The hospital room

Few shoulders could bear the very heavy burden of grief-cum-leadership. But Salim stood hard; his heart could breathe pain anew. The very dying of his friend and comrade was an extremely personal loss beyond the realm of politics. Acting as friend and brother-in-arms, Laysouf was no simply a colleague. That mend was perhaps a pillar or a strong arm in the treacherous road of nation-building. His death had created a vacuum that no title or office could fill. Still, Salim chose to proceed in an honorable way through this thin veil of solemn commitment. He had his mourning inside; behind the folds of his presidential cloak, his sorrowfulness was enshrouded.

The months that followed saw Salim at work with a fevered pitch, which could well have appeared superhuman. He held meetings, addressed the nation, and pursued his vision for Guinea with a vehemence that concealed the agony of his loss. The speeches of his were fiery, very impassioned, yet after the Crisis, they had acquired this very subtle, almost air of melancholy, a quiet acceptance of the fact that this very man who had once stood by his side was no more. But he would not stop, for duty called him, and he was a man who had for many years given over his life to the "service" of his people. But even the strongest of leaders are not immune to the frailty of the human body. Though, to overcome his grief, Salim shifted his attention to a community that neither colonial bureaucrats, nor fiery sons of Futa's elite dared to venture into.

In the shadowed valleys of Futa horizon, a foreboding storm brewed. Salim, as tempestuous as the winds whirling amidst the mountain heights, had once again cast a vast shadow of fear over the land. And this time the prey is the elders of Futa. His militia, heads bent like a gathering tempest in its wrath, marched toward the helpless villages, their dark purpose obscured by clouds amassing on the horizon: to seize these Sheikhs, spiritual anchors whose luminous faith he considered anathema. These men were no simple clerics; they were the conscience of the people, keepers of an ancient wisdom, their voices meshed with the land and the air. The news that the arrest of these men was imminent seeped into the villages, and panic erupted like wildfire. Mothers clutching their children, elders trembling in silent prayer, the air itself seemed to thicken with the scent of unmitigated anguish. For all who knew in Futa that Salim's wrath was that of a capricious beast: a few could be hunted down in the beginning to devastating consequences for whole communities: homes razed, lives uprooted, futures swallowed by dust.

The night fell, uncertain and suffocating as villagers huddled under a dim oil lamp with faces drawn in terror. They stood around the Sheikhs, these men who seemed calm amid growing chaos. They knew that the militia would be there by down. They were petrified. An elder with eyes deep as starlit rivers stood among the trembling crowd. His presence was soothing, and his stillness contested the fear heavily gripping their throats. When he spoke, it was only a low rumble, steady as the roots of ageless *Teli* trees (poisonous trees). *"Do not fear,"* he uttered, the words slicing into the thick tension as sharply as a blade through smoke. *"Those who dare tear down what God has ordained, without His consent, will themselves be torn down."* The promise, standing luminous and unyielding, was a lifeline thrown into the galloping sea of their dread.

The night crawled by, each moment taut with torment. On the day of arrival, as the sun climbed the horizon, a hard, crunching thud followed. Boots grinding gravel into dust in a steady, merciless rhythm, metal rattling from the jeeps ahead, the sound loud enough to swallow breath and leave silence feeling afraid. Then, seven kilometers away from their destination, inexplicably, the impossible happened. The militia were a sinewy column of menace snaking its way to the villages, and now they had stopped. As if summoned by an inscrutable force, they turned to retreat toward the capital, like shadows retreating from the dawn on **March 27, 1984.** No unholy boots stepped on the soil. No chains clinked and clogged the air. The Sheikhs remained, with their wisdom unfettered and their people unscathed. Relief disgorged across tearful embraces and yawns of laughter as the villages now trembled not in fear but with raw trembling joy. The prophecy of the old man had come to pass, clear evidence to the powers no despot could ever lay claim to.

Afterward, the realization dawned on men who knelt with open hands accepting *Amin* from the Sheikh's *Duas* as their whispered prayers were carried away by the wind. They rejoiced with the Sheikh in his foresight and with the Divine that had saved them, showing that even in their darkest hour, their faith could outshine tyranny. With faces bathed in the rays of the rising sun, the villagers knew that true power does not rest in the fist that strikes, but in the spirit that hangs unflinching under the watchful eyes of eternity.

In the waning days of March 1984, Guinea held its breath, a nation suspended between the weight of its past and the tremors of an uncertain future. A storm of whispers loomed over the restless city, while an unyielding silence wound through the labyrinthine streets where billboards of Salim, the invincible "Elephant of Africa" still hung like vestiges of a faraway revolution. For 26 years, an iron hand had sculpted Guinea's persona with a blend of fervent nationalism, socialist zeal, and the scars of political purges that even the loyalist found themselves looking over their shoulders. Across an ocean, however, the man who had defied colonial empires and forged the destiny of a young country lay vulnerable inside the sterile confines of a Cleveland clinic; his heart running thin beneath the glare of foreign machines.

Rumors of his collapse in Saudi Arabia spread from one center of influence to the other, to the ears of those sycophants and survivors alike who murmured under their breath. In the land that he had ruled almost like a secular deity felt unmoored. The dereliction of his towering statue suddenly instanced a truer reality beneath the feet of millions who had known no other leader. In little villages where his name equaled both a prayer and a curse, the elders would gather under the shade of a baobab with faces wrought with the ill omen, whereas the young, in sheer dread, dare not nurture a tiny bit of hope within. Guinea, a country fatigued by decades of isolation and ideological fervor, found itself on the far edge, its soul twanged with the silent asking: What happens when the sun sets on a man who had claimed to *be* the sun?

The ticking of the clock in his hospital room became a funeral drum. Each tick penetrated deeper into Salim's brain, scornfully echoing the irregular thumping of his own beating heart. The clinic air was sterile, reeking of ammonia, a discomforting contrast to the scent of iron-rich that blood gave off in interrogation chambers, which souls would have inhaled with delight. His body was less a fortress of intimidation; a memory now having sunk into the mattress; IV lines spread all over his arms like parasitic vines. Machines hissed and blinked, indifferent to the collapse of a man who once made others collapse with ease. But real agony lived in the shadows.

First came the murmurs, voices crisscrossing with the ventilator's sighs. Then came shapes: a woman with a neck scorched by the noose, a child holding a bullet-riddled doll. His eyes were never those of an accusing fiery gaze as he thought; they were *hungry* voids sucking the light away from the room. The clearest was the boy from Daybreak, with his face mended in a hundred pieces. *"You promised we would build Guinea together,"* he said through lisping broken teeth, blood oozing from his palms as though offering. Salim's throat constricted tightly in that very instant. The name of that boy returned to him now, scribbled in a file marked "subversive." Bakary. A 10-year-old poet, not a rebel.

Power is sacrifice; Salim had told himself that day as he had watched Bakary being dumped into the pit. The lie curdled in his stomach now.

Pain stabbed in a white-hot blade through his chest. Nurses were adjusting his oxygen mask, sleek gloved hands under the harsh light of fluorescents. They, however, did not see Bakary's specter sitting at the foot of the bed, his ghostly fingers tracing upon the ECG. "Watch," the boy whispered as the spike rose. Salim's vision broke into splinters, and suddenly there he was, not on his death bed but on the sunbaked courtyard with his younger self barking orders, as the soldiers dragged a writhing woman toward a firing wall. The toddler squeezed the woman's skirt, wailing. Salim lit up his Marlboro and turned away. *Necessary,* he thought.

The memory dissolved, leaving him gasping and choking. The toddler's wails now harmonized with that of the heart monitor's alarm. Guilt was not a wave; it had the power of a riptide that dragged him under. His hands clawed at his sheets, nails splitting. *"I am sorry,"* he rasped, but the words disappeared. In response, Bakary laughed a wet gurgling laughter. *"Sorry feeds no one. Sorry raises no dead. You believed you were a demi-god, why are you sorry?"*

Coldness spread from his core. The room darkened, not too black, but to a sickly greenish hue, as if the walls themselves were rotting. The other ghosts pressed closer. A man missing his hands laid stumps on Salim's chest. *"Feel it?"* he hissed. *"This is the weight of my daughter's hunger. She ate dirt before the soldiers came for her."* Salim's breath shallowed. He wanted to scream, to beg, but his tongue felt leaden.

A sudden clarity pierced the delirium: this was not a deathbed. It was a tribunal.

The monitors flatlined in a sustained drone. Salim's body arched once, then collapsed. But his consciousness, *trapped,* plummeted into a void teeming with whispers. Bakary's face materialized, inches from his own, decayed lips brushing his ear: *"You don't get to leave. We're your country now."*

March 26, 1984, In the clinic, a nurse closed his eyelids. Peaceful, she thought. The next morning in Futa, boots stumped on rocks in a hurry to get back to Conakry.

She didn't see the shadows congealing beneath the bed, pooling like tar, nor hear the chorus of voices swelling as they dragged him deeper, not into nothingness, but into a kaleidoscope of his own horrors, eternal and echoing. *It was all for nothing, but when has human nature ever changed? We cannot, and Salim knows it as he cashes in his one-way ticket.*

The alleys of Dixinn and Kaloum city clung to Salmany like a funeral shroud, the air thick with the iron stench of fear and the rot of a decaying regime. He slunk through the shadows like a scavenger, his footsteps a restless skitter, mirroring the rats fleeing through the gutters. Above him, the moon hung like a cataract eye, bleached and unblinking. His brother's ghost haunted these streets, not in shadows, but in the way the cobblestones seemed to whisper *Salim* beneath boot soles, in the way the humid wind carried the timbre of his laughter. Salmany had spent a lifetime orbiting that man's malignant star, craving its heat, its annihilation. Now, with Salim's body barely cold, the vacuum of power yawned before him. *Mine*, he thought, sweat pooling at his collar. *Finally, mine.*

But power, he would learn, was a shapeshifter, especially when it involves people like colonel Malakai Entoc.

The sixth-grade level clung to Malakai like burrs before giving up and joining the military. He bore the weight of his fractured French and political ignorance as scars from a life of survival and not scholarship. Midnight-soil burnished; his face bore the grit of a colonel who wore survival as his armor. The sun carved lines into his broad nose; his lips, dry from command, and his eyes smoldered like embers in dust-rimmed sockets. So much were the Marabouts' fetishes clawing at him to unmask him as Salim's heir that duty shielded him tighter than any spell. The news of Salim death came as he inhaled a big blow, crushing his cigarette, with the ash drifting like a phantom shroud as the jeeps tore toward Conakry under a bruised sky. Behind him, gunfire swallowed an ending to the plantation's song.

The road thrummed with the weight of what lay ahead. Malakai's mind racing as fast as the jeeps, the wind carrying whispers of the old songs, *those same hymns peasants sang when dabas cracked the soil for fonio seed to rest.* Conakry's lights flickered like dying stars. By dawn, shadows swallowed ministries, their corridors echoing with the clatter of boots and the metallic tang of fear. The coup had ripened like a rotten fruit; its bitter pulp smeared across radios and bulletins. The generals named it *revolution*; a word that the people have heard before, when they gathered, they called it nothing at all. They just marched towards the airport, crowding the streets to see if the rumors had teeth, if the plane carrying *you know who* had arrived, and if *you know who, had really kicked the bucket.*

There was nothing yet. Only tire marks on the tarmac, the blood of a "traitor to the nation" baked into the ground for over a week now, and soldiers in their youth with hollow eyes, petrified with the knowledge of what they had unmade. Malakai stood apart, his shadow stretching in the rising sun. Some did recognize him, the colonel who'd once saved a child from a mother's tough love, the colonel who'd bartered bullets for bread. They murmured as he kept his gaze fixed elsewhere. The curses from the marabouts still lingered in the air, with their fetishes now turned to ash. Nature let them scry and rage. Not etched by prophecy his face remained a cipher, carved by the land itself, a map of scars even the night couldn't swallow. He was the hidden face that even Salmany could not trace to have sent to Camp Boiro.

What became of Salmany and his gang, anyway? Well, his conspirators flanked him, hollow-cheeked jackals with eyes skittering like fireflies. Staying just about an inch from one another, they muttered in coded language about armories and midnight broadcasts. Only their hands betrayed them as they trembled together along lines of the map. They flinched at the bark of a dog in the distance. Salmany loathed their weakness. And from all their twitches, he saw himself mirrored. Marionettes, all of them, further tangled in strings that the dead still held.

The soldiers did not thunder. They *seeped*, benign as poison put in a cup of wine. Just a moment before, the alley was a throbbing vein of possibilities, and now the dark was blooming rifle barrels, metallic orchids. There was tightening in Salmany's throat; he knew that stench all too well cordite and rancid fury, the same great perfume of Salim's purges.

"Traitors," hissed a voice. They tried to skedaddle but there was nowhere to go. Soldiers are standing at every exit. "Where do you think you're going?" shouted the voice one more time. A young lieutenant in the Guinean army and son of Bakary Daff one of the first in French Guinea army. Mandiu Daff stepped forward; his uniform frayed at the cuffs. Salmany recognized him: the baker's son from Kindia. Two years ago, he'd stood barefoot in the rain, begging for his mother's remains as Salim's men collected her shredded body parts from the square. Now, the boy's finger curled around the trigger, his hatred a living thing. Remembering stories told to him by his father about the honorable Wadu. Remembering Wadu lecturing his father about patriotism when they came to his doorstep asking him to betray his country. Remembering how many good men Salmany and his brother took from the nation. Tears start streaming down his cheeks.

"My father did not do anything to deserve what you did to him, Wadu wanted what was best for this country, Kaman was a loyal soldier, Meli was the light, and you extinguished it. *Why?*" He cried.

"It wasn't us!" Salmany's voice cracked like a dam breaking. "It was Salim, he forced us! We wept for you, for your families!" Lies slithered from his tongue, viscous and familiar. How many times had he rehearsed this plea in gilded mirrors? But the soldier's face remained a mask.

Behind him, an older man emerged, his posture bent as if carrying the weight of mass graves. "You wept?" he rasped. "I watched you sip champagne at State House while they hosed my daughter's brains off the pavement." His gaze flicked to the baker's son. "Remember the radio broadcast? His voice, *"The people must sacrifice for progress."* He frowned, then looked at Salmany, "So, no. You do not get to pass the buck today, you evil spawn. You are dying today."

A flinch. Salmany's own words boomeranged, grotesque in this context. He'd penned those speeches himself, savoring their sonorous lies. Now they lingered, putrid.

The soldiers debated methods, a truck dragging, a firing squad, their voices sharpening like knives. Salmany's bladder released, warmth spreading down his thighs. One conspirator retched, bile splattering his polished shoes he had stolen from a camp Boiro's victim. The humiliation should have seared him, but all he felt was the icy clarity of a hunted animal. *This is how the boy from Daybreak felt*, he realized. *This is how they all felt.*

Colonel Malakai Entoc raised his hand. "Enough." The word cleaved the night. "They are demon seeds, yes, but we don't parade corpses. That's *their* theater."

Salmany's breath hitched. "Mercy?" He thought, but the man's eyes held none, only weariness that mirrored the soil itself, the kind that outlives tyrants.

"Kneel."

The cobblestones bit into Salmany's knees. He thought of Salim's deathbed, the ghosts swarming his brother's final moments. *Were they here now?* not with gunpowder, but with the rotting stench of the mass grave outside Kindia. A child's laughter rippled, disembodied. Salmany and his friends were so broken and defeated that they dropped down on their knees in trembling anticipation of their certain death. Their eyes pleaded one last time, but it was clear that their destiny stood sealed. They were nothing more than cowards, miserable human beings who had caused untold suffering, and now, the moment had arrived for them to pay for their sins.

Click. Rifles cocked.

With the silence closing the volume between heartbeats, Salmany understood that this was not a coup's end but rather a confession. Each speech, every single time an execution order was signed, every little look he had ever thrown aside, now somehow pooled in the consciences of those soldiers and in the steady aim of the baker's son. His brother's legacy was not power. It was this. Some of them lost control, their fear ringing out over them. One by one, they wet themselves; the urine trickled down their legs, flooding the air with the foul stench of fear and panic. Others did not have the fortune of dry land in their trousers. As if trying to hold back the humiliation, soiled liquid ran down their legs. The soldiers watched, some with dismay, some with quiet pleasure. They had witnessed enough of misery these men had put on the people. It was now their turn to pay the price.

The executioners, calm and steady, approached with their rifles in hand. Salmany and his sadistic companions such as Kais Retu, Karim Keira, Diarra Traore, Lansia Dane and others begged for mercy, their voices cracking in desperation, but it was too late. The soldiers could no longer hear their cries. They had no pity left to give.

The soldiers raised their rifles, and in unison, a single shot rang out.

bam.

The shot tore through myth. Their lifeless bodies crumpled; their heads shattered by the bullets that had ended their miserable existence. Their blood weaving into the same stones that had drunk Salim's victims. The silence that followed was absolute. Birds took flight from the trees, scattering into the sky, as if fleeing from violence. And at that moment, for the first time in many years, there was peace. It was the peace of a nation freed from the tyranny of a cruel regime; the peace of a people finally able to breathe without fear. Above, vultures wheeled, patient as history.

The soldiers melted into the dark, their silence louder than triumph. Dawn crept in, timid, testing the waters. In *Poredaka,* a widow whose husband responded to the call of Salim against the colonial empire peeled a cassava root, her knife scraping rhythmically. A toddler wailed, unpunished. And the city, for the first time in decades, did not answer with gunfire.

All the misery, all the skimming, all these atrocities because of an inferiority complex that poisoned the soul of a man who grew up in a fatherless home.

Salim died as he had lived: hollow and hunted by the ghosts of his betters

The hospital in Cleveland was a mausoleum of beeping machines and foreign whispers, but the true emptiness lived inside him. It gnawed, relentless, as his organs failed, a cancer born not of cells, but of decades spent clawing at a legacy that slithered through his fingers like smoke. He had dreamed of joining the pantheon: Lumumba's fire, Nkrumah's vision, Meli's charm, Yaryb's loyalty. Names etched into history with the permanence of diamond. Instead, he would rot unnamed, a footnote smudged by his own venom.

Before his last breath, feverish and gasping, the ghosts of his victims faded away, then came his betters. He saw *them*. Lumumba Sitting all alone in a corner, with glasses cracked; his eyes blazed with that cruel clarity of a man martyred mid-sentence. *"You burned villages to feel tall,"* he hissed. At the foot of the bed stood Nkrumah all draped in Kente cloth, his voice rolling out like thunder: "You confused fear for respect. Remember when you rounded up all your handicaps whom you considered abominations and dumped them in a common hole and buried them alive?" Salim tried to shout against them but out came only a wheeze. Cabral seated beside him reminded him of the betrayal that led to his demise simply because he advised him to stop sending the kids of Guinea to the slaughterhouse. "Pathetic, you've always been pathetic." He steupsed.

The shards of truth were stabbing at his gut under the feeling that he had never been their equal. Never intellectually. Never morally. Wadu, whose commanding eloquence had once silenced an assembly, haunted him. In the beginning of the PDG, Salim had watched Wadu brutally dissect colonial policies with the precision of a poet, the entire room leaning into the speaker like sunflower heads. Salim's hands had been trembling under the table. Years later, he had signed Wadu's arrest order himself, having made up the charges of "ideological impurity." The man died in Camp Boiro; his fingernails were peeled from him for refusing to repel back his brilliance.

Jealousy had been Salim's compass. As a kid in Faranah, he had burned watching faster minds rake in admiration from teachers, cousins, and even his "father's" friends. By 20, he had learned to hide it behind a veil of bluster, his words a fireworks display of borrowed rhetoric. But the brightest among them should have known better: Meli, with his razor wit, had once rendered Salim all stutters during a strategy meeting a week before he disappeared, died a slow agonizing death in Camp Boiro, wrists bound in that same signature red cord appearing in Salim's name.

His power was always a performance. He surrounded himself with sycophants whose loyalty was measured in shared mediocrity. Ministers who flattered his "genius" as the economy crumbled, who applauded when he outlawed dissent as "un-African." Yet their laughter rang tinny in private villas, their eyes darting when his back turned. He knew they mocked him. So, he purged them, again and again, replacing thinkers with thugs. The nation became a hall of mirrors, each reflection uglier than the last.

Eventually, the world had turned away. Nkrumah's face graced posters in London protests; Lumumba's speeches were recited in Havana. Salim? A caricature. A tyrant who'd turned liberation into a cult of paranoia, who'd built not schools but torture chambers. At the OAU summits, other leaders clapped politely, then excused themselves. He heard their aides snicker: *"The Peacock of Conakry,"* they called him, all feathers, no flight.

Eventually, even banishment from the nation by the spirits of the old sheikhs failed him. The son of Meli became a physician of great renown in Toronto, Emery's daughter hosted dignitaries for lunch. Salim's children, you ask! Went to Marrakech seeking asylum, their accents scrubbed clean of his influence. His eldest son, locked up in the US for breaching the minimum wage laws while clinging to the fabled dreams of his father ruling Guinea now long gone. Their dreams and Salim's net worth emptied into the piggy bank of the past. Salim's progeny arrived in a wheelchair in February 2025 with health ailments developed during incarceration. Bytes of the outdated empire fell as he looked to his homeland, where there is no bronze or gold-plated alabaster in his father's memory. No nameplate with his name engraved on it; only a cohort that forewent his name itself. a generation that spat whenever the name Salim was mentioned.

The final hour of Salim mocked his existence; no vision of his ancestors, and drums were not played to call his spirit back home, the only sound was the sterile click of an IV drip in his ears. His mind snapped back to 1958: General Charles's condescending smirk as Salim defiantly declared, *"We prefer poverty in liberty to riches in slavery."* The crowd roared; for one brief second, he felt like Nkrumah. But was it worth it? The proud NON, the infamous quote, was it worth it? because, yes, indeed, the children of Salim's nation did not only live in poverty, but their dignity was also not spared. Guineans believed in the illusion of being "independent" for over six decades and have nothing to show for. They believed in being better than their neighbors for saying no to France yet today they travel to those neighbors for a better life. He asked for independence in the guise of doing something for them. Yet he did not keep his promise and do things for them, instead he did unimaginable things to them. Freedom would have been good if it came with the perks, but *hélas!*

In that bed, he finally realized that liberty was far more than just slogans; it required the grace he had suffocated and the minds he had buried. His lungs cracking, he realized he had been poverty itself. He realized he had been the conflagration that devoured everything on its passage.

The nurse found him at dawn, eyes wide open, mouth permanently frozen in mid-snarl. She sighed, noting the time. No tears, no ceremony: just another corpse of the paupers' wing.

A continent away from his death bed, a student in Conakry scribbled an essay on Nkrumah's Pan-Africanism, another one on de Gaulle's bravery against Germany, and another student talked about Reagan's foreign policies. The papers made no mention of Salim. Maybe the absence of his name on those papers was for the better because some silences are mercy. Yes, they are. The fortress of Salim was unbreachable for more than six decades. Neither the machinations of foreign powers nor the passing years could not prevail over its mighty walls. It outlived the reign of Salim himself, the rule of his predecessor, and was still there in the end as a defender of the principles of a world ruined by compromise.

However, nothing is permanent, for the stalemate held till 2018, and the breach, when it finally came, it was not from the outside; no, a foreign troop did not storm the gates, but a betrayal from within, a Trojan horse lying dormant. A deceitful son infiltrated his lovely, yet troubled land. He came not as the prodigal one but as a pretender, the punisher of dissidents, the sharpened blade for a corrupt government, and thus he positioned himself. He played his role with chilling conviction, earning trust and consolidating power in the darkest corners of the regime he served. Like a lion's patience, he bode his time, waiting for the power structure to show a single, hairline fracture. And as soon as that instant came, he acted with merciless efficiency. The trusted enforcer turned against his master, toppling the very boss he had pledged to serve.

In the ensuing upheaval, a seismic shift occurred. The very first time in more than sixty years, the reins of power were seized not by a native son but a foreign legionnaire. The fortress that had so long resisted external domination had capitulated at last, its spirit of resistance seemingly quenched by the very forces it had once kept at bay. The people who endured the pain of his brutal regime just stood silent. And the fallen leader just said, "I didn't know he was a legionnaire when I allowed him the create a special force unit and be the head of it."

So, yes, silence, because there is silence that soothes, and another that stultifies-milking a mute mercy: The tongue that silences can keep one from horrid truths, while the voice that screams in anger comes down to be stifled by the crushing lies. For Africa's children, silence has become a prison: Their voices are muted not by the foreign chains but from the very subtle murmurs of their own leaders who have taught them to swallow the poison of inferiority, who have taught them to blame the ghosts of colonialism for every stumble, every failure, and every deferred dream. Leaders, cloaked in the tattered robes of liberation, harness the word "neocolonialism" like incantations to release themselves from their greed, rot, and hollow governance. They have held back their people's forward view, forcing them to kneel before historical wounds while the present bleeds unnoticed. The children become numb and resigned no longer asking why the roads crumble and the schools stand empty, confusing oppression as fate and donning their leaders' excuses as shackles. The silence grows thick, a dreadful darkness that feeds on stolen futures, while the architects of ruins grow fat on the lie, they've sown.

We've all heard it; we have heard the refrain so many times. In fact, for decades, the word "neocolonialism" has been bandied about in Africa, a convenient refrain sung by leaders to cover up their avarice in the martyrdom of history. The tears are crocodilian in nature for what the continent has had to bear, as these leaders lay blame on foreign shadows with their own hands more deeply snatching from the happiness of their own people. Independence, which used to glow so brightly with promise, is now just little more than a smoldering relic being trampled upon by those who swore to protect it.

Once "revolutionaries," now tyrants, they have become masters of their own deflection. They spin tales of Western exploitation for the youth, their voices shaking with false rage at the Western world while they erect palaces upon the graves of their people's dreams. How long will they keep selling this lie? How long will they keep blaming faraway powers for the mastication of rot in their own halls of power? They hoard wealth like dragons cradling stolen gold while mothers rummage through garbage for scraps and kids drown in the stagnation of neglected futures.

Take Rwanda for instance, it is a nation that, practically rose from the ashes of genocide, a phoenix hailed as a beacon of progress. Now, in constant conflict with its neighbor DRC, converting once fertile lands into wastelands of lost aspirations. The silence of the African Union is, in itself, a companion in these crimes, as Congo's useless government have no control over its natural resources. Being in Kinshasa, one would find the people drinking *tchoukoutou* or *Munkoyo* and dancing *coupé-décalé* in dim lit maqui bars, their laughter, a fragile defense against bullets outside. People are not naïve; they know that their enemies wear masks that are all too familiar, but they are too unfamiliar with the methods of unmasking them.

And Sudan? Nothing to see there, it's just a nation eating itself from inside like the Necrotizing Fasciitis. What makes it worse is that they are all warlords in uniform, claiming to do what they do for the people of what was once one of the greatest civilizations in the world. Two generals, intoxicated by power and foreign arms, turn the streets into slaughterhouses. Oil stains their uniforms; gold weighs down their pockets as villages burn and a generation is washed away. The world turns a blind eye; yes, and the rest of Africa's own leaders ignore as their coins dangle before their eyes, deafened to agony. As thousands of refugees flee, the chorus of blame rises endlessly: *"It's the West! It's history!"* As if history could absolve those alive today from their sins.

A continent's soil groaning with abundance, there is oil, bauxite, cobalt, diamonds, and yet the people starve in the agony of the unfulfilled. These resources ought to be lifelines, but they have turned into curses being siphoned away by kleptocrats and world markets. But let us set the record straight, the greater stealing is not in Brussels, London, Paris, or Washington; it is in the vaults of African elites who trade their people's dignity for a seat at the table of the powerful.

Enough. The time for excuses is over. Neocolonialism was real, but it is not the monster that scares every little child into bed. It does not explain why roads crumble while ministers drive fleet of SUVs; why bandages do not find their way to hospitals, but down, a leader casually glides in Swiss clinics after glancing to see if his account is still intact in that famous Swiss bank. People can see through all this masquerade. They have gotten tired of being pawns in the game where their leaders act as victims and villains in the very same script.

Africa is never going to be redeemed by laments about the past: those willing to look inward and cut the rot of greed; silence the drums of war; and finally, *finally*, stand up for the ones they swore to liberate. The world has indeed betrayed, but the actual knife that cuts deepest is wielded at home. And the leaders' voices have resonated into the youths' ears because in today's Africa, you'll hear them say, "the Europeans don't like us, the Chinese don't like us, the Americans don't like us, they're only here for their own interest." Instead of holding their own leaders accountable, their blames are externalized. Blaming foreigners for Africa's problems is a mistake no rational person can defend. Foreigners do not elect African leaders, control domestic policy, or manage local resources, Africans do. Corruption, failing schools, weak healthcare, and poor infrastructure are direct results of the choices made by those in power and the citizens who empower them. Foreign actors pursue their own interests, yes, but they cannot force governments to mismanage or neglect their people. To claim "they don't like us" is to confuse perception with causation, and it only perpetuates passivity and victimhood. Real change comes from holding local leaders accountable, responsibility for a nation's success or failure rests squarely at home, not abroad. But hey, who am I kidding.

Let this be a requiem for the age of blame. Africa… no wait, actually the world deserves more than martyrs in gilded cages. It deserves leaders who shall arise not from the ashes of excuses but from the fiery bellow of accountability.

END

9 798999 466940 2